COLLECTIVE ACTION AND POLITICAL TRANSFORMATIONS

COLLECTIVE ACTION AND POLITICAL TRANSFORMATIONS

THE ENTANGLED EXPERIENCES IN BRAZIL, SOUTH AFRICA AND EUROPE

Aurea Mota and Peter Wagner

EDINBURGH
University Press

Edinburgh University Press is one of the leading university presses in the UK. We publish academic books and journals in our selected subject areas across the humanities and social sciences, combining cutting-edge scholarship with high editorial and production values to produce academic works of lasting importance. For more information visit our website: edinburghuniversitypress.com

First published in hardback by Edinburgh University Press 2019

Edinburgh University Press Ltd
The Tun – Holyrood Road
12(2f) Jackson's Entry
Edinburgh EH8 8PJ

Typeset in 11/13 Palatino LT Std by
IDSUK (DataConnection) Ltd

A CIP record for this book is available from the British Library
ISBN 978 1 4744 4296 1 (hardback)
ISBN 978 1 4744 4297 8 (paperback)
ISBN 978 1 4744 4298 5 (webready PDF)
ISBN 978 1 4744 4299 2 (epub)

CONTENTS

Part IV   Rethinking the Possibilities of Political Agency

ABOUT THE AUTHORS

Aurea Mota is an interdisciplinarily oriented sociologist whose main research interests lie in social theory and comparative historical sociology. Her PhD is from the Institute for the Study of Society and Politics (IESP, formerly IUPERJ) in Rio de Janeiro (2012). She is a member of the Political Philosophy Group of the Latin American Council of Social Sciences (CLACSO), and an associate researcher of the 'Participatory Democracy Project' (PRODEP) at the Federal University of Minas Gerais (UFMG) and at the Center for the Study of Culture, Politics, and Society (CECUPS) at the University of Barcelona. She worked as a post-doctoral researcher at the University of Barcelona in the Project Trajectories of Modernity (TRAMOD). Her publications are about Latin America, social thought and political participation in contemporary Brazil.

Peter Wagner is Research Professor of Social Sciences at the Catalan Institute for Research and Advanced Studies (ICREA) and at the University of Barcelona, as well as project director at Ural Federal University, Ekaterinburg. His work aims to combine concerns of social and political philosophy with investigations in historical-comparative sociology to provide a critical diagnosis of the present time. Currently, he is involved in the research project 'The debt: historicizing Europe's relations with the "South"', funded by the consortium Humanities in the European Research Area (HERA, 2016–19), and directs the research project 'Varieties of modernity in the current global constellation: the role of the BRICS countries and the Global South', funded by the Russian Science Foundation (RSF, 2018–20).

FOREWORD AND ACKNOWLEDGEMENTS

In this book, we explore the question of whether and how collective action can bring about political transformation. We pose this question out of a sense of urgency. Humanity faces problems reaching from persistent poverty, high social inequality and increasingly diffuse violence to the very destruction of the conditions for human life on earth due to environmental degradation, rampant resource extraction and climate change. Change is sorely needed. Furthermore, we pose the question out of a sense of paradox. Given current levels of education and wealth, available technology and infrastructure and degrees of freedom and political participation, arguably, humanity has never had more and better means at its disposal to deal with the problems it faces and often has itself created. While some of those means are indeed employed in addressing urgent problems, others are left idle or their use even creates new problems or exacerbates existing ones, sometimes unintentionally and sometimes in pursuit of partial interests.

There has been no lack of general ideas about how humanity may overcome obstacles and solve its problems. The most familiar ones are rooted either in Enlightenment-based liberalism or in varieties of historical materialism. But as general ideas they lack credibility today, and to us it appears that one of the main reasons why they lack credibility is indeed because they generalise in an erroneous way. They make assumptions on the basis of too limited experience and too narrowly cast interpretations of such experience. Thus, one of the main contributions of this book – as well as a major challenge in writing it – is, we hope, the bringing together of different experiences with recent sociopolitical transformations and their impacts in three world-regions. More precisely, the writing here is based on the authors' personal experiences of growing up in a working-class neighbourhood of Belo Horizonte; in

Katlehong, a township east of Johannesburg; and in Lütjenburg, a rural town near the Baltic Sea coast in what was then West Germany, respectively. To this was added the intellectual experience of university education in Belo Horizonte and Rio de Janeiro; in Johannesburg, Brighton and New Haven; and in Hamburg, London and Berlin.

The specificity of experience is related to time as much as space. We witnessed, at different stages of our lives, the end of military dictatorship in Brazil, the end of apartheid in South Africa, and the fall of the Berlin Wall and the end of Soviet-style socialism in Europe. Even though it is rarely put in this way, the combined effect of these events was to radically alter the conditions for collective action bringing about political transformation. This leads us to the particular way in which we pose our question: we are interested in whether and how collective action can bring about political change *today*, with due regard for the specific conditions in different places.

Fortunate circumstances allowed us to get together for a few years in Barcelona and to exchange our interpretations of those experiences while working together on understanding the trajectories of modernity in 'our' three world-regions. As we moved to writing up our research findings and conversations, our third co-author, Jacob Dlamini, had to take up other commitments at his university and could not accompany us in the last step. Thus, contrary to our original plans, this book is written only by the two of us, even though Jacob's voice is present throughout.

The fortunate circumstances alluded to above were provided by the generous funding of the European Research Council (ERC) for the project 'Trajectories of modernity: comparing non-European and European varieties' (TRAMOD), based at the University of Barcelona as ERC Advanced Grant no. 249438, on which most of the research presented in this book draws. We would like to thank the ERC for making our extended conversations possible and all members of the TRAMOD research group for intense discussions on the possibilities for political change under contemporary global conditions. In many respects, this book is the concluding point of our long-term endeavours within this project. We would also like to thank the numerous people – resource persons rather than interviewees – with whom we have spoken in Brazil, South Africa and Europe during our research. Without their help and generosity we would not have been able to write this book.

Peter Wagner would also like to acknowledge support from the consortium Humanities in the European Research Area (HERA) for the project 'The debt: historicizing Europe's relations to the "South"' (HERA Joint Research Programme 'Uses of the Past') and, during the final phase of writing-up, from the Russian Science Foundation (RSF) for the project 'Varieties of modernity in the current global constellation: the role of the BRICS countries and the Global South' (grant no. 18-18-00236), based at Ural Federal University in Ekaterinburg.

Last but not least, we would like to thank Samuel Sadian, once again, for careful editing of our manuscript.

Barcelona, August 2018

COLLECTIVE ACTION AND POLITICAL TRANSFORMATIONS: AN INTRODUCTION

Not too long ago, the perception was widespread that only little space was left for the pursuit of plural political options. 'There is no alternative' – the expression used by former British Prime Minister Margaret Thatcher – came to symbolise a whole new political condition. While that conclusion was widely diffused, the attitudes towards it were marked by stark contrasts. On the one hand, the new situation was hailed: finally, the ideas of free and self-regulating markets and liberal democracy had been accepted and were about to be implemented almost worldwide. They were supposed to have contributed to the regime changes in Brazil, South Africa, Eastern Europe and elsewhere. In more sociological terms, the notion of globalisation was used to underline the increasing connectedness and interdependence between societies, which made deviations from the common course unviable. But, on the other hand, there were also those who saw these developments as highly problematic and protested against them, underlining that globalisation meant nothing other than a globalised form of capitalism that, freed from the constraints that earlier political action had imposed on it, would lead to greater poverty and social inequality, political disempowerment and environmental destruction. This alter-globalisation movement, as it was often referred to, though, was more focused on contestation and, where possible, on resistance than on elaborating and building alternative forms of socio-political organisation on anything larger than a local scale.

The reasoning that we develop in this book is necessarily set in this context. Critically addressing the unfruitfully dichotomised view of the political consequences of so-called globalisation, we look at three world-regions – two in the South, one in the North – to identify conditions for collective action that can bring about positive political

1

change even in the current context. We started out from the assumption that conditions for political action still vary and that the spaces for bringing about change are not as limited as the prevailing 'Northern' view assumed. And we also had reason to assume that those spaces may indeed be larger in the 'South' than in the 'North', and equally so the willingness and determination to use them. But as we proceeded, we became more and more aware of changing circumstances that we needed to take explicitly into account.

Some of the presumed effects of globalisation have indeed happened over the past few decades. As regards economic matters, most societies now show a higher degree of integration into the world economy than, say, twenty years ago. This is indicated by, for instance, share of foreign trade in overall trade or share of foreign direct investment in overall investment. As regards politics, the accountability of governments to the resident population has also increased in many polities, even though the term 'democratisation', preferred by political scientists, is decidedly inadequate. Both of these trends had been highlighted as consequences of free markets and the widening commitment to human rights and democracy by those who had praised the lack of alternatives. But these trends, while widely identifiable, are far from unproblematic. As a consequence of increasing world market integration, employment in manufacture has decreased in many 'old' industrialised societies, including not only Europe, both East and West, and North America, but also large parts of Latin America and South Africa. Given that this employment constituted a major share of the 'good jobs' with decent salaries and regulated working conditions, the overall working and living conditions of workers deteriorated. In terms of politics, this and other negative effects of 'globalisation' increased the pressure on governments to counteract them. For some time, the response was that indeed 'there is no alternative', and the temporary reaction of citizens then was disaffection with politics. But this situation has proven unstable, and this is exactly what characterises the new circumstances.

In the supposed core of 'Northern' democracies, the British and the US electorate have recently been attracted by proposals to regain national control over economy and society, as exemplified by the referendum vote for the United Kingdom to leave the European Union and by the election of Donald Trump as president of the US. A similar attitude is adopted by the president of the Russian Federation, Vladimir Putin, with the annexation of Crimea, and the president of the Republic of Turkey, Recep Tayyip Erdoğan, with his national project of combining moderate Islamism with capitalism. With much less global significance but interesting particularities, the recent attempt at turning Catalonia into a state by breaking with the provisions of both the Spanish and Catalan constitutions falls into the same category.

All these events show – or at least are intended by their protagonists to show – that there are alternatives; that collective action to bring about political change is possible, in contrast to those widespread expectations mentioned before. They are all brought about by governments, often preceded by election campaigns, and thus through established political institutions. But they are also supported by some supposedly direct expression of popular will that is created as the aggregate of the expression of individual preferences, often through referenda. Furthermore, they usually have a basis in 'civil society' organisations that mobilise for particular causes. In terms of content, they aim at establishing control over the territory to which they refer, often phrased as re-establishing a control that was lost due to some preceding events (which can be as different in form and as distanced in time as the end of the Soviet Union, membership of the European Union or the War of the Spanish Succession). To re-establish control, things as different as restricting immigration, limiting the plurality of expression or re-regulating foreign trade are proposed.

In light of these events, one might even have concluded, by the time of finishing this book, that our project had become unnecessary. The belief that there are no alternatives is no longer dominant. Rather, alternatives are created, often in the most unexpected ways in different parts of the globe. Thus, what we intended to show through detailed comparative analysis had, one might have argued, already been shown in actual politics. To some extent this is indeed so. If, however, we had agreed entirely with this conclusion we would not have continued working on the book. But it is true that this recent shift in global politics has made our task more complicated. Let us make two observations that will help to explain these complications.

First, from our point of view, the emerging alternatives are of a very problematic nature. While they have popular support, they are brought about through the mobilisation by political elites of parts of society, often directly against other parts. To achieve its objectives, such mobilisation polarises public debate and thus makes open-minded, problem-oriented communication more difficult. In terms of content, the overall aim of regaining control leads to policies of segregation and exclusion, be this by limiting cross-border exchange or by creating living conditions within domestic society that are highly unequal between supporters (and beneficiaries) of the project and its opponents (and those disadvantaged by it).

To put it simply, we do not like those alternatives. Nevertheless they are alternatives to this free-market/liberal democracy situation, purportedly without alternatives, that we aimed to address. Their existence, therefore, forces us to be much more specific with regard to the alternatives that we have in mind.

Here we come to the second observation. The rise of these alternatives went in parallel with the decline of political projects that had indeed been the focus of our attention. We had been intent on looking at broad social movements that aim at intensifying political deliberation, extending social and political inclusion, and embracing plurality and diversity. And we had – and, we think, still have – reason to believe that this is not just wishful thinking or an utter distortion of any reality that one might encounter. We were looking at some Latin American situations, in particular at Brazil after the military dictatorship, from where also the alter-globalisation movement received a strong impetus, and at the case of early post-apartheid South Africa, in which a remarkable rebuilding of society after the dismantling of one of the most despicable, oppressive regimes in recent history was under way. Furthermore, we aimed at comparing these 'Southern' alternatives with a Europe whose West had in many respects been a model during the early post-Second World War period, but which had become tired and strongly marked by citizen disaffection and the abandonment of any political project capable of challenging the political and economic *status quo*. Still, European integration could to some extent be seen as a political response to the adversities of globalisation, and democratising social movements were rising, in particular in the south of Europe.[1]

That had been the idea. But at the time of concluding this book, the link between social movements and political projects has considerably weakened both in Brazil, as indeed in many parts of Latin America, and in South Africa. The second president of Brazil to come from the Workers' Party, Dilma Rousseff, was ousted from power. (The manuscript was finished before the election of Jair Bolsonaro as President of Brazil.) The main organised force of anti-apartheid struggle in South Africa, the African National Congress, remains in institutional power, but it has been losing support, due to both corruption and lack of sustained transformative policies. In Europe, the European Union had not yet recovered from the consequences of the financial crisis of 2008 when reactions to war- and poverty-induced immigration created new divides. The social movements, in turn, could not sustain high levels of mobilisation and their encounter with political institutions has overall been sobering.

But rather than accepting that our project had become either superfluous or pointless, we concluded that it was even more needed in the current context. The problem we had started out from, the seeming lack of alternatives, remains. The space for transformative political action is very different today from what it has been in earlier historical periods. But as we are witnessing, it has not disappeared. We no longer have to ask whether there are alternatives; we have to ask much more precisely what they are.

This question has at least two key analytical dimensions: on the one hand, we have to look at the constellation of actors that is involved. This concerns both the time-honoured question about the relation between the multitude (citizens or subjects), elites, and rulers, already addressed by Aristotle, and the question that arose with the 'entrance of the masses' into politics in the twentieth century, first explicitly thematised by Antonio Gramsci and Leon Trotsky, namely, the relation between movements and institutions. On the other hand, we have to be concerned with what is at stake, the substance of political change, the direction in which collective action wants to move society.

With regard to both of these dimensions, we want to be able to make a distinction between desirable and undesirable alternatives. This requires us to further introduce a normative understanding. We will elaborate core elements of such an understanding based on the key notions of equality and freedom. This grounding has several – we think, useful – consequences: it is an understanding that is widely, though not unanimously, shared today. As such, it informs many current political debates and struggles. Furthermore, some commitment towards freedom and equality has characterised many historical struggles for emancipation and liberation. Thus, this reference is useful for understanding historical transformations of political institutions. At the same time, this commitment does not determine the shape of political institutions, because it contains ambiguities and tensions that make it open to a wide range of interpretations. Therefore, while giving normative guidance, it does not unduly limit the space for the elaboration of political alternatives.

These three aspects – the constellations of actors, the substance of political change and the normative horizon – frame our analysis of the potential for positive political change today. They require us to review two large debates in the social sciences for our purposes. First, we need to place our investigations in the context of the debate about 'modernity', a term frequently used over the past few decades to signal both the commitment of human societies to freedom and rational organisation and the actual trajectories of historical transformations supposedly started in Europe at the end of the eighteenth century. This debate has given rise to a bifurcation between those who observe a single trend towards modernisation with only minor variations and those who argue that there are persistently multiple trajectories of modernity. If the former claim is sustained, then there will be only limited space for alternatives, whereas in the case of the latter, such space is much wider.

Second, we will need to distil an understanding of 'politics' for our purposes from the multi-faceted and often fragmented debates within political philosophy, empirical political science and public policy analysis. Each of these fields provides elements for grasping potentials for positive political change, but none of them on its own is sufficient for our purposes. Towards our objective, we needed to link analytical and normative elements of those debates to elaborate a comprehensive understanding of politics that is founded on the combination of: (1) collective autonomy; (2) problem-oriented reflexivity; and (3) a capacity for transformation-oriented intervention.

In brief, anticipating the more detailed elaboration in Chapter 1, our understanding of politics entails (1) that collectively binding decisions in the contemporary world must be arrived at in the absence of external sources of determination. In other words, collectively binding decisions must be taken under conditions of *autonomy*. Such autonomy can be fully justified only when all those affected by binding decisions can participate in their making. We might say that all political action takes place within the horizon of *democracy*, knowing that the horizon may in fact be far away at times. This approach enables us to understand processes of democratisation, such as the end of the military dictatorship in Brazil in 1984–8 and the end of apartheid in South Africa in 1990–4, as well as critical discussions of political practices, such as that concerning the 'democratic deficit' in the European Union. But our approach goes beyond the formal understanding of 'democratisation' and 'legitimation' of political institutions found in mainstream political science.

We argue in particular that democracy in a fuller sense requires that the collectivity that exercises its autonomy mobilises (2) problem-oriented reflexivity, and (3) is capable of acting upon itself in a consciously self-altering way. In short, one might say that the former issue used to be addressed as the question of the *public sphere* and the latter as the one of the *state*. But those concepts have lost much of their force with the rise to hegemony of an individualist-liberal understanding of democracy.

(2) The contemporary hegemonic understanding of democracy is *individualist*. It looks at the collectivity mainly as an aggregate of individuals and considers public opinion the sum of individual opinions. This understanding is institutionally expressed in the 'one person, one vote' principle. Historically, however, that principle has never prevented the formation of collectivities defined by class, religion, status, tradition/ways of life or otherwise. The rise of opinion polling in recent decades has exacerbated aggregative individualism through the pretence that it can measure public opinion on a continuous basis through surveys or, now, big-data analysis. Historically, in turn, public opinion was supposed to emerge through communicative exchanges among citizens about problems at hand. This is what we mean by problem-oriented reflexivity, which is absent in any merely aggregative understanding of political will-formation.

(3) Furthermore, the contemporary hegemonic understanding of democracy is *liberal*, often excessively so. It assumes that almost any expression of individual autonomy is self-justifying by definition while any collectively binding rule needs strong justification because it might interfere with individual liberty. Debates about the limits of state interference were of course a central topic of nineteenth-century liberalism. Subsequently, state capacity has grown in most settings through much of the twentieth century – though not always in the context of democratic states. However, as mentioned above, if the contemporary world has abandoned reflexive debate about collective problems in favour of the arithmetic aggregation of opinions, this abandonment has entailed the weakening of justifications for collective transformative intervention *tout court*.

Both aspects must be seen in the context of increasing *interdependence* between political collectivities in general. The basic model of democratic political action assumes that all members of a collectivity discuss their problems and possible solutions and then endow themselves with the capacity to address these problems effectively. Individualist-liberal thinking weakens the quality of reflection in common and the capacity to generate effective action. In addition, the boundaries of any given collectivity are arguably more open today towards 'others' than at any time in history. This has created greater interdependence, leading to situations in which collective problems are no longer simply 'ours' but are shared with others. This means that action that would have been effective within closed boundaries before – like the election of a government or head of state – is no longer self-contained because of this greater interdependence.

THE REASONING IN OVERVIEW

We embark on this work of retrieval on modernity and politics in Chapter 1. While illustrating our reasoning with observations from the three world-regions that we study, the main purpose of this chapter is conceptual elaboration. It provides the framework for the historical-comparative and politico-sociological analysis that follows in the remainder of the book. Readers who are to some extent familiar with the debates about modernity and politics will find the chapter useful for situating our approach within those wider discussions. In turn, readers whose foremost interest is in knowing more about the three world-regions and the historical trajectories and current potential for political transformation may well wish to start with Chapter 2 and turn to Chapter 1 at the end of their reading.

We are interested in current possibilities for political change, but we also hold that those possibilities are conditioned by past political action. Conditioned, but not determined – human beings 'make their own history, but they do not make it as they please; they do not make it under self-selected circumstances, but under circumstances existing already, given and transmitted from the past', as Karl Marx (1852) put it in his reflections on the political transformations in mid-nineteenth-century France. Therefore, we trace key elements of the historical trajectories of Brazil, South Africa and Europe from the early nineteenth century to the present, with particular interest in the perception of key problems and the constitution of political agency (Part I, comprising Chapters 2–4).[2] Importantly, we do not see these trajectories as running in parallel, but as highly interconnected and 'entangled', to use Shalini Randeria's

(1999, 2006) felicitous term. Such entanglements start with the ideologies and interests that entered into the foundation of polities in the three world-regions and continued with the asymmetric exchanges of people and goods between them; in brief, with Brazil and South Africa importing people and Europe importing agricultural and mining products. It is in this light that we sketch the three trajectories up to the early twentieth century (Chapter 2). As we will show as we go on, many of the key constraints and possibilities for political transformation, up to the present day, result precisely from those interconnections.

With the main features of the socio-political orders constituted by that moment, the three regions underwent two similar transformations, but each with specific characteristics, during the twentieth century. First, they experienced the 'entrance of the masses' into society. In each case, the existing elites could not prevent this from happening, but they devised measures to contain its wider impact on structures of influence and power. As a result, characteristic interpretations of modernity crystallised in each of the three regions (Chapter 3). Second, from the 1960s onwards, these interpretations of modernity became increasingly subject to contestation and to pressures for political transformations 'from below'. Given their differences, the nature of these pressures was highly distinct, as were their outcomes in terms of actual transformations. At the same time, this is the period, roughly from the 1960s to the 1980s, when our present socio-political constellations were brought about. Thus, the different conditions for political change in these three regions emerged in the course of these contestations and their outcomes (Chapter 4).

Subsequently, we explore these conditions in more detail and along the dimensions that, in a first step, have emerged as constitutive for the specific interpretations of modernity in our preceding analysis (Part II, comprising Chapters 5–7) and, in a second step, have risen to prominence in more recent years (Part III, comprising Chapters 8 and 9). In both cases, current tensions and problems are seen as giving rise to a need for reinterpreting modernity for our times against the background of the experiences with the consolidated forms of modernity in the respective regions. Our reflections identify moments of crisis in existing interpretations of modernity in some settings and for some issues, and moments of transformation in and for others.

Chapter 5 starts out from the broad commitment to democracy that today characterises all three regions, but remains in tension with the simultaneous commitment to integrate regional economies into a capitalist world economy. This is the occasion to review the tensions between democracy and capitalism in general, and to grasp with more comparative precision the specific constellations of democracy and capitalism in Brazil, South Africa and Europe. In particular, we show how what one might want to call 'metropolitan capitalism' could be transformed into a 'mass production, mass consumption' capitalism that was compatible with formal democracy, whereas 'dependent capitalism', based on exportation to the metropoles, furthered the emergence of an elite that showed little commitment to its own society. Against this background, Chapter 6 explores how the current inclusive understanding of democracy was shaped by the patterns of inclusion and exclusion, both within given societies and with regard to their outside, that have historically been dominant in the three regions. That those historical patterns are far from being a matter of the past will be shown in Chapter 7, which addresses structures of social inequality that persist despite the fact that political equality has been achieved, at least in formal terms, in all three regions. Political action to overcome social inequality, when it occurred, has not been ineffective, but it has encountered obstacles that reveal the persistence of historically sedimented socio-political structures.

The issues discussed in Part II are the staple of the political sociology of supposedly 'modern societies', but we argue that our historical and comparative perspective throws new light on them. In turn, the two chapters of Part III address relatively novel concerns, namely ecology and personal security, in which the contrast between 'Southern' and 'Northern' societies is even more striking, but of a different nature.

Everyone is today aware of the damage human action has done to nature since the beginning of industrialisation. But it is often assumed that awareness of this issue arose in the North from the 1960s onwards and that effective action has been taken there. In turn, Southern societies are considered to be less inclined to protect nature and, when they do, less effective, while at the same time being responsible for essential natural assets such as the Amazon rainforest or the rhinoceros and other animal species threatened by extinction. Our analysis shows that neither the one nor the other is exactly true, with Northern societies externalising negative impacts and shifting responsibilities and Southern societies remaining largely unable to deviate from the growth path historically established in the North (Chapter 8).

Chapter 9 addresses a theme that was central at the very outset of what we now call modern political theory, namely domestic peace and personal security. Thomas Hobbes's main concern was that human beings should not behave as wolves to each other. During the early post-Second World War decades, Brazil, South Africa and Europe fared relatively well on this account, at least compared to other historical periods and world-regions. While personal security was high in Europe for everyone and this was achieved by moderate police and legal measures, it was largely limited to the elites and middle classes in Brazil and South Africa and achieved by exclusion and oppression. Today, security has returned to become a key concern in Europe and for the upper classes in Brazil and South Africa. In the latter cases, a prevailing impression among those groups is that moves, as limited as they in fact were, to a more inclusive society have eroded the mechanisms providing everyday security. In Europe, the threat is increasingly portrayed as coming from the outside, through immigration of culturally diverse people. As a matter of fact, however, the people who die daily as a consequence of criminal or police action or by drowning in the attempt at reaching Europe are not members of the established sectors of society.

With these analyses, the basis will have been provided to return, in Part IV (comprising chapters 10 and 11), to the question of the current conditions for effective collective action, framed by two further observations. First, the hegemony of the individualist-aggregative understanding of politics described above is ambivalent. On the one hand, it is dominant in those societies that used to dominate the global situation, in short, the 'Northern' societies. In fact, this global domination – to some extent a fact of the past – is strong enough still to have a global impact. On the other hand, one can point to present political experiences that defy this hegemony through the exercise of a collective autonomy that combines problem-oriented reflexivity and the development and use of a capacity for transformative political action. Brazil and South Africa have been examples of such experiences.

Against this background, Chapter 10 takes up the search for the sources of collective action, as mentioned above. Shaped by the European historical experience with the workers' movement, the main such source has long been seen in social movements challenging states that were, in turn, considered to be bastions of elite power. From the 1960s onwards (as discussed in Chapter 4), this view seemed to be confirmed by the rise of 'new social movements' in the North and the anti-apartheid and anti-authoritarian movements in South Africa and Brazil (or indeed the anti-colonial and anti-oppressive movements in general). One often assumed that social movements were always agents of democratisation and pressured for the widening of normative horizons. The picture, however, has become more complicated in the present time, in which the political energy of those movements often appears to be fading, whereas movements arise that defend partial interests and are often opposed to the normative achievements made or claimed by the former movements.

Over the past quarter of a century, Brazil and South Africa have been exemplary cases for collective action achieving a partially successful transformation of society. Key components of such success, as limited as it is, have been the emergence of key persons coming to symbolise the call for change and the ability to arrive at positions of institutional power. Chapter 10 also addresses the role of charismatic personalities with the examples of Lula and Mandela, past presidents of Brazil and South Africa respectively, and reflects on the absence of comparable figures in recent European politics.

Chapter 11, in turn, moves to consider the link between collective action and political institutions as a requirement for bringing about effective political change. Despite the combined impact of individualist-liberal thinking and increasing global interdependence, existing states remain the most significant embodiments of political action in the comprehensive sense outlined above. If democratically constituted, in whatever qualified ways, states are the sedimented expression of collective autonomy. They are the focus of societal debate on common problems. By receiving and acting on the outcomes of societal debates, states (and state-like polities like the European Union) serve as potential agents of binding collective action aimed at transforming society. Our analysis of states does not entail any assumed primacy of politico-administrative action. Rather, we aim to show that the criteria for democracy and reflexivity are often best satisfied when state institutions are challenged by social movements and, possibly, when political debate is driven forward by charismatic persons.

As noted at the outset, reflections about the global possibilities for bringing about positive political change through collective action have been marked by a pronounced scepticism. If one looks more closely, these doubts were based on a double observation. During the early post-Second World War decades, on the one hand, (West and North) European societies were considered to have achieved the most acceptable form of social organisation in human history, based on equal inclusion and democratic freedom, with whatever limitations that had remained. This European experience had served as a model in many parts of the globe. But, clearly, this supposed model is struggling to survive and is marked by regress in terms of social inequality and a weakening of democratic participation. On the other hand, 'Southern' societies had then been regarded, in particular by disenchanted Europeans, as having the political energy to bring about significant change. But they are not fulfilling these expectations to the hoped-for extent, and today the focus has returned to those entrenched politico-institutional and socio-economic features that make profound political change difficult in the 'South'. If anything has changed, then there is a tendency today to identify the key features of the current global socio-political constellation from a 'Southern' rather than a 'Northern' perspective.

We agree with the shift away from what some call 'Northern' epistemologies, but we furthermore suggest that any perspective that ties knowledge gains too tightly to socio-political space is problematic (Mota 2017). Both the possibilities of, and limits to, political change are conditioned by the entanglements between world-regions rather than by a position in socio-political space. Significantly, those entanglements often allow elites in all regions to displace conflicts and avoid any solution to them that would challenge their dominance. The outcome often is the deterioration of a situation – be it in terms of environmental destruction, social inequality, weakened democratic capacity or other harmful outcomes. As a consequence, collective action for political change today, more than ever, needs both to be based in the specific situated conflicts that it addresses and the institutions available to resolve them, on the one hand, and on the other, to identify and connect to related issues in other regions and aim at co-ordination with distant actors. This is difficult but not impossible. If it can be achieved, positive political change remains possible.

Chapter 1

POLITICS AND MODERNITY UNDER CONTEMPORARY CONDITIONS

Collective action can still bring positive political change about; this is our starting hypothesis. To develop criteria with which we can identify whether this hypothesis can be confirmed or not, we need to develop a concept of the political that is sufficiently comprehensive to capture significant aspects of political action and that contains an adequate normative component that permits us to say whether a change is positive or not. We will outline such a concept in the second part of this chapter, to be substantively enriched as our analysis proceeds. But we also maintain that answers to the questions of what kind of change is possible and how it can be brought about vary widely with the social context within which collective action takes place. This is why we adopt a historical and comparative perspective in our investigation into the possibilities of political change through collective action today. More specifically, we ask the question against the background of its particular historical trajectory over the past two centuries and across what one can call the 'Atlantic world'. The first part of this chapter is devoted to substantiating this choice of perspective.

HISTORICITY AND INTERCONNECTEDNESS

The decades around 1800 are often referred to as the beginning of 'modernity'. The standard account emphasises the combined effects of a triple revolution that supposedly brought 'modern society' about, namely: the cultural–intellectual transformation through the scientific revolution and the Enlightenment; the economic transformation through the industrial revolution and the emphasis on the alleged capacity of markets for self-regulation; and the political transformation due to the new emphasis on (very selectively granted) individual rights and (the rather vague promise of) collective self-determination. Recent works in global history have confirmed the significance of this period, but they are much more open and ambivalent as regards the key characteristics of the arising 'modern world' (Bayly 2004). Furthermore, rather than locating the site of novelty in Europe, as was formerly the case, they emphasise the highly increased degree of global interconnectedness (Osterhammel 2009), which some might want to call a first period of globalisation. The density of political, economic and cultural relations increased in particular in the triangular exchanges between Africa, America and (Western) Europe (Mota 2015; Wagner 2015), thus giving us good reason for focusing our exploration on three regions within this 'Atlantic modernity'.

In this new light, the revolutions of the late eighteenth century and their aftermath remain a key point of reference, but they need to be placed within a perspective that takes in more than these familiar landmarks. They altered the political situation in some European, African and American societies, even though less so than initially expected. The Vienna Congress of 1815 and the Panama Congress of 1826 both represent a new perception of how internal and external conflicts could be dealt with. By that time, the revolutions had created the context in which the American movements for, and declarations of, independence could be interpreted as a form of emancipatory political practice.[1] Similarly, the shift from Dutch to British domination in the Cape region of southern Africa, and the wars and resistance activities that arose there during this period, can be considered in the framework of the rise of modernity, bearing in mind the characteristically different manifestations that would over time lead to distinctions such as the current one between a Global North and a Global South.

Viewed in this light, furthermore, the significance of this period may be seen as lying less in the actual institutional changes that came about – without denying their relevance – and more in the fact that the revolutions opened up a wide horizon for future improvements of society. At the same time, they largely failed to bring these expectations to fruition. This discrepancy had a double effect. On the one hand, a political imaginary emerged that would orient much future action, based on the principles of freedom, equality and solidarity. On the other hand, the subsequent nineteenth-century political reality drastically diverged from that imaginary, however interpreted. The most significant calls for political change during this period addressed this discrepancy. They found their voice in the workers' movement, in the women's movement, in the movements for independence from Spain and Portugal, in indigenous, slave and republican revolts in Imperial Brazil as well as in the Cape Colony, which had multi-racial suffrage for some time, and in the republics set up by descendants of the Dutch settlers in southern Africa. Several native societies in South Africa were not subjected to colonial rule and combatted colonisation; and in the large interior areas of Brazil many indigenous societies remained without contact with the settlers and their descendants.

These latter remarks lead over to the comparative aspects. As underlined above, the globe around 1800 was already marked by a high degree of interconnectedness. The temporal proximity and mutual impact of the revolutions in Philadelphia, Paris and Saint-Domingue are testimony to this fact. But the relations between world-regions were highly asymmetrical. In North and South America and in South Africa, the European settlers came to dominate over the native populations, even though this domination was preceded by more open encounters as well as by military resistance, which was of a particularly long-lasting nature in South Africa. When the so-called 'settler societies' reached independence, in South America in the early nineteenth century, in South Africa in the form of a self-governed dominion in the early twentieth century, then this 'independence' had two significant specific characteristics: first, it did not mean that 'societies' had become independent; it meant that the descendants of the European settlers became free to impose their rule on the previous colonial territories and on native populations (in different forms, as we shall see). The issue of possession, dispossession and concentration of the land of those colonial areas in southern Africa and South America is a key aspect of this process of emancipation through imposition of European settlers' rules in the settler societies. And second, while the new states were formally independent, they remained dependent on Europe in economic terms, increasingly with regard to Britain, which came to dominate world trade. The combination of these two features marked the onset of lastingly unequal relations.

As mentioned before, one of the questions that we want to answer is whether the conditions for collective action towards political change vary between the 'South' and the 'North' (see Comaroff and Comaroff 2012 for a position on this question; for our own discussion of such concepts, see Wagner 2017). But the preceding observations on the historical co-creation of Northern and Southern societies and the persistence of asymmetric forms of connectedness rule out a comparison of 'Brazil', 'South Africa' and 'Europe' as separate and mutually isolated units, in the way in which standard comparative sociology conceives of comparison. Rather, we follow the historical trajectories of these societies through their interrelations, and we will keep asking what the specific state of dependency of some societies on others is and how it impacts on the conditions for generating political change (Randeria 1999 coined the term 'entangled modernities' to capture socio-historical connectedness under conditions of modernity; see also Randeria 2006).

MODERNITY AND AUTONOMY

Having said this, we have already taken distance from the common view that 'modernity' emerged in Western Europe and spread slowly but inevitably from there across the globe. In as far as the period around 1800 indeed witnessed the birth of the modern world, this was a global condition, even though one with great regional variation. We are confident that our sketch of the historical trajectories of Brazil, South Africa and Europe in Chapters 2, 3 and 4 will convince our readers that this is the appropriate view. However, we still need to position ourselves with regard to another great divide in the understanding of modernity.

On the one hand, sociologists and historians have often considered 'modern societies' to be characterised by powerful, linear and largely steady tendencies such as rationalisation, individualisation, secularisation, commodification and democratisation. After the Second World War, the term 'modernisation' came into use as a comprehensive concept for the sum of these tendencies, thus assuming a particular logic of societal development over time. On the other hand, social and political philosophers have tended to assume that the historical novelty of modernity was its commitment to freedom and self-determination. One could say, as an approximation, that the former stressed the scientific and industrial revolution as events that inaugurated modernity, whereas the latter placed the emphasis on the Enlightenment commitment to freedom and on the political revolutions of Philadelphia, Paris and Saint-Domingue as expressions of collective self-determination.

If considered as foundational, these two views of modernity stand in striking contrast with each other, the one postulating long-term trends of history and the other focusing on the will and intention of human beings, able to bring about change and create history. This contrast, however, has not always been at the centre of attention. Rather, it has often been considered of minor significance in actual practice. In as far as the tendencies set in motion generated greater material affluence, longer life expectancy, higher levels of education, enhanced political participation and greater spaces for self-realisation, they were providing what reasonable human beings actually wanted. In that sense, there was no contrast between freedom and modernisation trends. The one fed harmoniously into the other, even though it remained rather unclear how this convergence came about.

This view of 'modern society' was prominent in the sociology of modernisation and development during the 1960s and 1970s. It has been widely criticised since, but it remains alive, not least because it appeals to the self-understanding of 'Western' societies as being superior to others in both functional and normative terms (Knöbl 2003; Wagner 2019). That is also one reason why we need to recall it here. The other reason is that this conflation of two distinct views of modernity allows us to raise three related oppositions with regard to which we needed to position ourselves during our research.

First, the view of an unfolding process of modernisation conceals the difference between a view of social phenomena as being based on the meaning human beings give to their situations and their lives, on the one hand, and on the other, as emerging unintentionally, though following some logic, from the interactions between human beings. The latter view has shaped much of the sociological tradition: let us just recall that Adam Smith spoke of the 'invisible hand'; Karl Marx of phenomena emerging 'behind the backs' of the human actors; and Max Weber argued that the spirit that motivates human action had 'escaped from the cage' into which human life-conduct had been imprisoned in modern capitalism. Clearly, these authors have provided fundamental insights about organised social life. But the ways in which they have been read has also often obscured the fact that human meaning and intention stand at the outset of all interaction and that no interaction or institution will ever entirely be dissociated from meaning and intention. It is precisely this foundation of human interaction that permits an understanding of such phenomena as critique and resistance, defying the prevailing, institutionally sedimented interpretation of society (Boltanski 2009), and social creativity, bringing about new social forms by offering new reinterpretations of the given situation (Sewell 2005).

Second, insisting on this human capacity is certainly not to deny that human action always takes place within a given setting and is conditioned by it. And it is exactly for this reason that we develop a historical-comparative perspective, namely to grasp that which specifically limits the possibilities for political change in each of the three regions we look at. Recent social science debate has proposed the concept of path-dependency for analyses of the course of socio-political processes over time. Human social action is seen as taking place on a temporal path which earlier steps have laid out. Past steps have determined the place at which one stands in the present, and thus limit the places one can reach through future steps. Elements of our analysis fit well with such a perspective. But, in contrast to some path-dependency theorists, we insist on the fact – permitted by the metaphor – that there are always different directions in which one can go from the present. The past cannot be altered, but it can be reinterpreted to allow for a variety of future options.

Finally, we need to say something more about the term 'interpretation' that we already have used very often. We agree with those scholars who see human beings as 'self-interpreting animals' (Charles Taylor). Furthermore, we also hold that there is often an enormous variety of ways in which human beings give meaning to their situation by interpreting it. Language, in this sense, is more than a means of purposeful communication; it allows for the expression of a way of being-in-the-world. This, exactly, is the basis for assuming that there can be varieties of 'modern' socio-political organisation. When relating this perspective – of social ontology, if one wants to use such terms – to others, we maintain that it is not in opposition to individualist-instrumental or functional views of social organisation but is broader than those and thus capable of including them. In other words, we do agree that human societies have to address and solve social problems, and we also recognise that in some aspects this is done by individuals pursuing their preferences. But social problems first need to be identified and given meaning; and 'individuals' always live in social relations and do not formulate their 'preferences' in isolation from other human beings with whom they maintain meaningful communication.

Thus, when we say that we work with an understanding of modernity as the commitment to autonomy, this has to be understood in the conceptual context sketched above. It does not mean that we embrace an understanding of modernity as being based on isolated individuals deploying their rationality, an understanding that certainly emerged in Europe during the Enlightenment period, but never became dominant in such reduced form. Commitment to autonomy rather means, first of

all, the insight that human beings have to give themselves their own
laws for living together, or vice versa, that there is no external source
that can be relied upon to provide these laws. This commitment, however, can be triumphantly embraced as a normative breakthrough, as
some Enlightenment philosophers and some revolutionaries did. Or it
can be met with resigned scepticism as the only maxim that is available
for human action after other legitimations have been found wanting or
can no longer be agreed upon. In as far as the period around 1800 can
be seen as the onset of modernity, it was clearly more marked by the
insight into the absence of external justifications of power than by the
actual commitment to freedom and equality that might have followed
from that insight.

MODERNITY AND POLITICS

Thus, the harmony between personal and collective freedom, on the
one hand, and larger societal processes, on the other, supposed by the
sociology of 'modern societies', is a far-fetched assumption from our
point of view. Furthermore, it is an assumption that is undermined by
socio-historical investigation. At this point, it may suffice to give just
one illustration of a tension that will be of central concern throughout our reasoning, showing the variety of expressions of a societal self-
understanding. The question is: if, as was the case, the issue of free and
equal collective self-determination was clearly on the political agenda
at the end of the eighteenth century, why was inclusive liberal democracy, today often seen as the epitome of political modernity, not the
institutional outcome of the revolutionary transformations? A standard
answer to this question has been that the resistance of the dominant
groups was too strong, and this answer certainly captures a part of
the truth. A closer look at the political struggles of the time, however,
shows that, beyond the mere assertion of the interests of a 'ruling class',
explicit reasons were given why 'the people' could not actually govern
themselves. One main line of argument located the reasons in the people themselves: they were not capable of acting responsibly, either from
an innate lack of rationality, or for lack of education, or for their dependence on others owing to their lack of property. One or more of these
reasons could be applied to women, to workers, to non-Europeans or
to all the poor (see Chapter 2 for more detail). The other main line of
argument evoked practical limits: the large number of residents on the
territory of existing states made it impossible to deliberate and decide

together about common concerns. There were functional requirements of political decision-making, such as timeliness, authoritativeness and efficacy, that could not be fulfilled under conditions of free and equal participation in large polities (see Wagner 2013 for one recent discussion). Such arguments suggested strong limits to the reach of democracy, but arguably they were not necessarily 'non-modern'. Beyond all of these factors, in the so-called 'new societies' such as South Africa and Brazil many people remained outside of this struggle for collective self-determination. Integration of territories through a central authority, a shared language and internal forms of societal interconnection was fully achieved only during the twentieth century.

This brief illustration bridges our discussion of 'modernity' as a concept that can connect different historical situations to each other with one that is meant to underline our need for elaborating a more complex understanding of 'politics' than can be found in most current debates. Such understandings of politics are themselves highly fragmented between empirical political science and political philosophy in scholarly terms, on the one hand, and, on the other, in more topical terms, split between an emphasis on institutions and their functionality and an alternative focus on political movements and their claims.

This more complex understanding of politics is grounded on a notion of autonomy; in this sense it is a modern concept. But aiming at a wide, historically appropriate understanding of politics, it starts out from a notion of autonomy in the broad sense discussed above, namely as the insight into the absence of external justifications for power. This step helps to avoid the narrowing down of political history over the past two centuries into the gradual realisation of freedom and democracy. In turn, it emphasises two main kinds of ambivalences at the core of the concept: on the one hand, the ambivalence between the primacy of functional efficacy and the primacy of democratic participation; and on the other hand, the ambivalence between the primacy of personal freedom and the primacy of collective self-determination. Neither the one nor the other are strong contradictions; the principles can be reconciled in practice. But there is what we call an ambivalence at their core, a tension that cannot be overcome through any conceptual resolution, but can only be dealt with in contextual political action. In other words, the commitment to political modernity is always open to context-specific interpretation; there are, thus, varieties of political modernity.

In the remainder of this chapter we will try to spell out what such an understanding of politics entails for our historical and comparative analysis. We will approach the ambivalences at the core of the concept by briefly discussing three key elements of modern politics, namely, democracy, the public sphere and the state, along with the transformations their meanings have undergone across the history of the past two centuries, particularly in recent decades.

POLITICS AS COLLECTIVE AUTONOMY: THE QUESTION OF DEMOCRACY

Collective action with a view to bringing about political change was often motivated by discontent. It did not necessarily aim at a transformation of the political order. Often, indeed, it did not question the legitimacy of the existing order and hierarchies, but was based on the view that the current powers that be were falling short of what legitimately could be expected of them. Thus, it aimed at restoring the good political order, to set political matters back on the appropriate track. This orientation characterised events as different as the Glorious Revolution in England in 1688 and the Túpac Amaru revolt in 1780–1, mentioned earlier. Once, however, principled doubt is cast on existing forms of legitimacy, the meaning of the political and the orientation of political action change. When the insight arises that there are no external sources for the legitimation of power that can be taken for granted from the start, then human beings need to autonomously give themselves their rules for living together. This notion of democracy as collective autonomy is known from Ancient Greece, but it reasserts itself strongly at the end of the eighteenth century. Rather than the restoration of a good order, the term 'revolution' comes to mean an action to establish a political order that derives its legitimacy exclusively from within itself. This meaning clearly emerged in the revolutions in France from 1789 to 1799 and in Haiti from 1791 to 1804.

During the revolutionary period, the idea that self-legitimation should take the institutional form of representative parliamentary democracy based on free and equal universal suffrage arose. It was, however, not lastingly implemented in any political order on the globe until much later. During the revolutionary debates, this option was actually consciously discarded in favour of the parliamentarisation of monarchies or of the creation of republics with strongly restricted political participation. Nevertheless, this idea formed the horizon of political institution-building for two centuries to come. A perceptive observer such as Alexis de Tocqueville could assert in the 1830s that a process had been set in motion that would not stop before universal suffrage had been reached. Twentieth-century political scientists have called this phenomenon 'democratisation', but this term suggests far too strongly that there is an unequivocal and linear trend of political change at work in history, which will impose itself sooner or later everywhere on the globe. In this sense, to 'democratise' means nothing but to fully achieve a stable, liberal and predictable political order.

We do agree, as said above, that political action acquired a new dynamics during the revolutionary period. However, we prefer to talk about a democratic political imaginary that arose and that oriented much of political action from that moment onwards. This imaginary is always open to interpretation and resignification. Rather than translating neatly and unambiguously into universal suffrage-based representative democracy, this imaginary entails the normative claim that all those who are affected by a binding decision should have a say in making that decision. Historically, this all-affected principle, as it is now often called, served to ground the claim for equal inclusion of all residents within a given polity. As such, it came to be based on the establishment of (territorial) boundaries that were meant to determine who is affected by a political decision. We will later call this the building of political containers (Chapter 2 below). Today, it is more often used to argue for transnational means of legitimate decision-making. This shift occurred in light of the facts that equal inclusion within polities has often been reached, on the one hand, and that the effects of decisions within one polity more and more often go beyond the polity's boundaries, on the other. At present, furthermore, the democratic dilemma of the always-possible election of a 'racist, fascist, and/or an unpeaceful' leader through 'free and fair' suffrage, as it was once pondered by the US diplomat Richard Holbrooke,[2] is clearly creating the conditions for a transformation of the liberal-democratic view of the all-affected principle. We will have occasion to show in detail below how the democratic imaginary provided for a dynamics of political change in the societies that we look at in both of these senses, but not for a determined path of political 'progress' unlike the theorem of democratisation suggests.

POLITICS AND THE INDIVIDUAL HUMAN BEING: COMMUNICATION AND DELIBERATION

The lack of unilineal direction becomes immediately clear when we scrutinise another element of Tocqueville's prediction: seeing universal suffrage as the telos of modern politics, Tocqueville adopted an individualist understanding of political participation. Looking from today's angle, this can be seen as an amazing capacity for foresight. But in the given historical context, what is striking is the absence of alternative conceptualisations. After all, the classic-republican notion that only male, property-owning heads of households can be citizens because of their material independence and capacity for responsibility was widespread and found its institutional expression in suffrage restrictions. The 'Boer' republicans in South Africa were capable of adhering to republican principles and at the same time excluding the native Africans, who were working for them at home and in the fields, from political participation. The same can be said about Brazil. The establishment of a liberal, representative republic at the end of the nineteenth century came along with the end of slavery. However, the problem of inclusion of the ex-slaves was not at all present in the political agenda of the first and the second republics (for more details see Chapter 2). They were all excluded from political participation, not because of racial laws as such, but because of laws that excluded the illiterate and those without property. Ideas about a family vote still circulated in France during the interwar period. And today considerations about including future generations into the vote are being voiced. Tocqueville had the ability to recognise that any arrangement other than one being based on the 'unit citizen' (Stein Rokkan) would be open to objections of inequality and injustice and thus likely to be successfully challenged sooner or later. But seeing his prediction from this angle, it announces less the triumphant march of democracy than rather underlines the lack of any other foundation for a modern polity.

And this is indeed the more appropriate way of understanding the rise to centrality of the individual human being in modern political thought, which in conceptual terms started long before democratic suffrage rules were institutionally tried out. The encounter with unknown and even unexpected inhabitants of America led Bartolomé de las Casas to probably the first explicit formulation of individual human rights. In his wake, and furthermore shaken by the cosmological uncertainty created by the religious wars in Europe, Thomas Hobbes and John Locke saw the rights of the individual as the only legitimate basis on which a political order could be erected. Thus, the notion that, in the absence of external sources, 'modern' forms of political legitimacy could only be based on the individual human being had been elaborated upon for quite some time when Tocqueville made his institutional prediction.

At the moment when modern republics were indeed starting to be built, however, it became clear that the conceptual solution was hiding a practical problem. Was it indeed plausible to assume that a multitude of free individuals would have the capacity to write up and agree upon a 'social contract' that could sustain a political order, as Hobbes and Locke presupposed they would? Was it not necessary to consider in more detail the ways in which these individuals communicate with each other about the matters they had in common? The restrictions to political participation, mentioned above, can be considered as a partial answer to this question. Thus, the number of citizens was more limited and their capacity for responsible action, so one assumed, more developed. Still, this measure might be insufficient; furthermore, its legitimacy was precarious, as calls for female suffrage and the Haitian declaration of independence already showed at the end of the eighteenth century.

Two additional requirements for sustaining a modern polity were introduced in response to the doubts about the sustainability of a polity on purely individualistic foundations. First, the focus was placed on relations of communication. They had to be of such a kind that one could have reason to assume that the potentially diverse opinions of a multitude of human beings would converge to form a 'public opinion' as the common outcome of deliberate interaction (Baker 1990). Public spaces reaching from coffee houses to parliaments and media of communication such as newspapers were seen to enable such relations of communication. That this hope could not settle the question, however, becomes clear from the fact that concern has ever since been raised about powerful societal forces bringing about a 'transformation of the public sphere' (Jürgen Habermas) that undermined the normative potential of free political communication. Current debates about the effects of so-called social media are just the most recent instance of a long-lasting concern.

The notion of a public sphere is potentially all-inclusive. It does not as such presuppose any limit to the reach of political communication. The second requirement tries to answer the question by different means, namely by a limitation of citizenship that creates an outside. The starting point here is the notion that theorists of the social contract were indeed too optimistic. No multitude of individuals would be capable of reaching an agreement about how to live together. These individuals needed to already have something in common on which to base their deliberations with a view to becoming citizens of a future political order. The main idea about what this 'something' could be was language and culture. To have a common language would provide the basic means for communicating with each other and understanding each other. In an expressive understanding, furthermore, commonality of language also signals a common way of being-in-the-world. In this sense, the concept of culture was very close to that of language.

The rise of nationalism during the nineteenth century must be understood in this context, as an attempt to make the idea of a self-legitimating modern polity more realistic. It suggested the need to bring speakers of the same language together in one polity, and to separate them from speakers of other languages. This idea has been enormously forceful in European nineteenth- and twentieth-century history. It also contributes to understanding why Brazil remained isolated from other American colonies and did not participate in the Panama Congress of Hispanic America[3] (even though it does not explain why the Spanish-speaking states did not form a federation, a question we address below). The idea even informed the apartheid notion of 'separate development' in 'homelands', although it clearly served to hide the relations of domination and oppression there. Joined with the notion of a limited capacity for reasonable action by indigenous people and (descendants of) slaves, it shows how the elites of 'settler societies' could see themselves as new nations, as modern polities of a particular kind.

These brief reflections are intended to show, in conceptual terms, that there is no coherent theory of a sustainable modern polity. To make such a polity sustainable, additional pre-conditions of various kinds needed to be introduced. In historical terms, as we will see in more detail below, this leads to the construction of polities on varieties of these political self-understandings, each expressing a particular mix of conceptual considerations.

Jumping from these reflections to the present, it is easy to recognise that the problem at the core has not at all been resolved. Today, there are many more inclusive democracies on the globe than ever. Within them, the hegemonic understanding of democracy is individualist in the terms that Tocqueville had already recognised: the free and equal participation of individual citizens, institutionally expressed in the 'one person, one vote' principle. Furthermore, it is today widely assumed that the consolidation of democratic practice, where it has occurred over long durations, has made it possible to overcome the concerns of the past, even if practice often falls short of principle: there are basically no restrictions to participation, except for children and imprisoned people; there is freedom of expression and pluralism of communication media; and the boundaries of polities within which communication occurs are rather stable.

At a closer look, though, this common view is not without contentious presuppositions of its own: it looks at the collectivity mainly as an aggregate of individuals and considers public opinion as the mere sum of individual opinions. The rise of opinion polling in recent decades has exacerbated aggregative individualism through the pretence that it can measure public opinion on a continuous basis through surveys or, increasingly, big data analysis. The thus-measured 'preferences' of citizens are that to which political action has to respond. To use recent European examples, the rejection of migration as evidenced by surveys or the exit of the United Kingdom from the European Union, apparently demanded by a referendum outcome, are seen as expressions of a democratic will. Institutional action can only accept and follow this will; the idea that such a will can only reasonably be brought about by prior communicative action has lost persuasive power. This is in striking contrast to historical debate, as briefly shown above, in which public opinion was supposed to emerge through communicative exchanges among citizens about problems at hand. What gets lost in this transformation is the capacity to identify issues as common problems and to join in communication to elaborate solutions to these problems. In our analysis, we will consider this capacity as crucial for the kind of positive political change that we are interested in. For this reason, we add to our understanding of the political, which started out from democracy as the expression of collective autonomy, a second dimension, which we will call problem-oriented reflexivity. Problem-oriented reflexivity requires a relational understanding of political action, which emphasises communication between citizens rather than a merely aggregative understanding of political will-formation.

POLITICS AND POLICY-MAKING: PERSONAL FREEDOM
AND THE STATE

But, one may now ask, what happens to the freedom of the individual in such a relational understanding of the political? After all, the theory of the modern polity assumed that collective self-determination would go hand in hand with the increase of personal freedom. This question leads us to the third dimension of our understanding of politics.

Going again back to the period around 1800, one recognises that the transforming polities became more liberal than democratic. During much of the nineteenth century, the making of authoritative decisions was marked by the 'persistence of the Old Regime', as Arno Mayer (1981) had put it for Europe, in the European Imperial or national states and in Imperial Brazil, while South Africa was undergoing processes of 'settler' state formation in the Cape Colony, the Orange Free State and the Transvaal republic. After the rejection of inclusive democracy, the emphasis was placed on personal liberty, based on a new understanding of freedom as, to use later terms, freedom from interference by the state and by other people rather than freedom towards the pursuit of objectives in common. This shift can be traced by looking at key documents such as Benjamin Constant's speech 'The freedom of the moderns compared to the freedom of the ancients' (1819), John Stuart Mill's treatise *On Liberty* (1859) and Isaiah Berlin's lecture on 'Two concepts of liberty' (1958). Two observations are necessary here: first, the new personal freedom was largely restricted to a minority of property owners, which in Europe largely overlapped with the descendants of the pre-1800 elites and in Brazil and South Africa with the descendants of the settlers, excluding the descendants of the indigenous and slave populations. Second, the role of state institutions was predominantly seen to reside in protecting this exclusive personal freedom, not least against protests and revolts. Towards this end, pre-1800 state structures could well be used and only needed to be somewhat 'modernised'. They did not need to emerge themselves from processes of collective self-determination, not even in the cases of the newly forming republics in Latin America or the new 'nationally unified' states in Europe.

Debates about the limits of state interference were a central topic of nineteenth-century liberalism, but in practice social problems of various kinds were increasingly seen as requiring collective solutions to be brought about by state policies, in particular from the late nineteenth century onwards, as argued and claimed both by social movements and by elites (the classic analysis was provided for Europe by Karl Polanyi in 1944; for a critical appreciation, see Halperin 2004). We will discuss details of these transformations below (in Chapter 2), but it is important to note already here that the existing states were in most cases a kind of 'natural' addressee for dealing with social problems. Societies tended to be seen as quasi-organic entities, and their states as the agents of responsibility for the collective whole. During the first half of the twentieth century, such an understanding came to be expressed in a variety of overlapping ways in Italian fascism, the *Estados Novos* in Portugal and Brazil, Peronism in Argentina, the Swedish 'people's home', and German National Socialism. There were significant differences between these political projects in their balance between individualism and collectivism as well as in their degrees of inclusion and domination, of particular importance for our reasoning (see Chapter 3; the Union of South Africa differed in important respects from this pattern, to be detailed below). But in historical perspective they all had in common that they were based on a rather unquestioned sense of collectivity and legitimacy of statehood.

This situation has radically changed after the 1960s. While many of the early twentieth-century states were powerful, but neither very democratic nor very liberal, some post-Second World War states, especially in Europe, came to be based on inclusive democracy while remaining legitimately interventionist. From the 1960s onwards, however, the legitimacy of state action was increasingly challenged (for details see Chapter 4). In less democratic settings, these challenges were based on the critique of state capacity being usurped by a small power elite. The contestation aimed at greater inclusiveness and intensity of democratic participation while maintaining important collective goals. In societies with experience of pronounced and recent oppression and injustice, such as Brazil and South Africa, the emphasis on a needed major socio-political transformation was particularly strong. In settings in which formally inclusive democracy was more pronounced, in contrast, the challenge was directed at the constraining nature of collectively binding decisions in general. In recent years, this orientation has gained further ground, leading to the contemporary hegemonic understanding of political modernity as liberal, in terms of widening spaces of personal expression, rather than democratic, in the classical sense of supporting collective decision-making. This understanding tends to assume that almost any expression of individual autonomy is self-justifying by definition while any collectively binding rule needs strong justification because it might interfere with individual liberty.

From the preceding discussion, three requirements for bringing about positive political change emerge: all those affected by political change should participate in making decisions about it; the measures to be taken should be generated from communicative processes of reflection about the problems to be addressed; and there needs to be the capacity to transform a decision into effective policy action. The set of political institutions that was historically seen as fulfilling these requirements was the combination of democracy, public sphere and state. In our brief overview, we have maintained that some such set of institutions is indeed necessary, but have also shown that the ensemble has undergone historical transformations which in their sum make it rather unlikely that it can fulfil the demands placed on it. Specifically, we have argued that, in contrast to the past, inclusive democracy is rather widely accepted today, but it is now joined to a highly individualised notion about the formation of public opinion and a strong delegitimation of the creation and enforcement of collectively binding decisions. The latter two phenomena are the effects of an invasion of political thought by a kind of individualism that tends to forget about the need for a balance between individual and collective autonomy. As a result, the idea of democracy seems to be almost globally hegemonic, but in practice political collectivities have increasing difficulties at arriving at reflexively setting their own rules and policies, much less implementing them. In the background stands the problem of determining what a 'political collectivity' is, if we are all foremost individual human beings.

THE QUESTION OF THE COMMON GROUND: POLITICAL
CHANGE UNDER CONDITIONS OF INTERDEPENDENCE

This question can be further explored as the issue of the common ground on which political action takes place, and this in two senses (as an example from recent debates about 'the common', see Gilbert 2014). As mentioned above, first, many of the recent invocations of the all-affected principle concern issues for which a decision has been taken in one polity but the effects of which occur to some extent – in some cases: to a major extent – in other societies. Thus, the assumption that government action concerns only its citizens is clearly much less tenable in the current era of greater interconnectedness than at other times. This assumption has always been a useful – maybe necessary – hypothesis of democratic political theory, namely, that government by the people is government for the same people, to paraphrase Abraham Lincoln. But it has never been entirely sustainable, given not only that boundaries have never been entirely closed, but also in the face of the asymmetry of power between existing, formally equal polities. This is a fact that dependency and post-colonial theories have underlined, but rarely phrased in terms of asking the question of what the common ground of action is and what principles should be derived from it. In these terms, the question of the common ground arises as that which two or more polities, and their citizens, have in common and need to deal with in common despite and beyond the persistence of the principle of sovereignty.

The question of the common ground, however, arises also in another sense. Given the tendency towards ever more emphasising individual liberty, it takes the form of asking what there is that individual human beings have to handle together with others at all. Individualisation is often seen as a key trend of the history of modernity. Mostly it is praised in terms of enlarging the spaces for personal self-realisation, even though sometimes it is also critically seen as generating conformism as well as anomie. Rarely, however, is individualisation considered as a political phenomenon in its own right. The emphasis on individual freedom, however, shifts the burden of the argument onto anyone who sees the need for changes in collective, institutional arrangements. True, collective autonomy can no longer take the existence of any given collectivity for granted. The fact that individual human beings live interdependent lives, however, is central for any notion of solidarity, as argued by Emile Durkheim, for instance. In much current thinking this becomes secondary to the individual's desire for independence. Once such a conceptual move is accepted, it is very difficult to maintain the legitimacy of most kinds of collectively binding decisions.

Thus, interdependence is today a central concept both for polities and for persons. And given that we can neither rely on the effective boundary-setting of states nor uphold the idea that human beings are members of pre-given collectivities, such as nations, classes or cultures, a notion that gave interdependence a determined shape, we need to ask explicitly and specifically what the common ground of action for any group of persons is. This notion of a common ground imparts materiality to contemporary collective action by revealing the limitations of the focus on nations and even world-regions. This is so because we then are asked to specify where we are free or where we could be free. The political sciences have always tended to focus on the place where political rights exist and can be used as a tool for transformation, which entails the assumption that we are always free only in very specific settings, such as within nation states. In turn, the broader quest for the common ground of democratic collective action is twofold: (1) it addresses the limits of the rights-based idea of political freedom within given institutions; and (2) it addresses the question of what constitutes the 'we' of a *polis* or of a collectivity, for which a purely factual answer is often impossible. In other words, the quest for the common ground is a quest for the interpretation of a political subject whose action is not pre-determined by a structure (such as a national boundary, a language, a geography, a gender or a race, even though it may use any of these categories), but aims for specific forms of engagement that happen because of the spatial–temporal configuration of political horizons. The common ground of collective action is not structurally predictable, but neither is it completely conjectural. It is formed because in certain spaces and moments of time subjects recognise historical patterns that they collectively regard as injustice and by their action make the appearance of another political horizon on the agenda possible.

Part I

Trajectories of Modernity: How We Arrived at Where We Are

Chapter 2

HISTORICAL INTERPRETATIONS OF MODERNITY AND THEIR TRAJECTORIES

At the beginning of the fifteenth century, there was no evident connection between the Tupi-Guarani and the Tapuias living in what is today Brazil,[1] the San and Khoikhoi in South Africa and the Portuguese in Europe. But Portuguese ships had begun exploring the African coast southwards, attempting to find a viable sea route to India. In 1487, what is now known as the Cape of Good Hope was first rounded; and in 1497, the first Portuguese ship reached India. After this success, a large expedition was sent out in 1500 and reached – whether by intention or error is not known with certainty – the coast of current Brazil in April of that year, landing in what is now Porto Seguro in the Brazilian state of Bahia. The encounters that followed between people who did not know of each other, not even of the others' existence, spelt the beginning of the creation of an Atlantic world with a slowly but steadily increasing density of exchanges.

The immediate aftermath of the first encounters differed significantly between these regions. The Portuguese had no intention of settling on the southern shores of Africa. Their ships just stopped over on the way to India. It was only in 1652, after the rise of the Seven Provinces of the Netherlands to a commercial and seafaring power, that a first settlement was established in what is now Cape Town, on behalf of the Dutch East India Company, and even then with the limited main intention of growing food stock for the seafarers. In contrast, American soil entered quickly into considerations within the competition between Portugal and Spain. The Treaty of Tordesillas of 1494 divided up the planet along a longitudinal line that hardly had been touched by then, but the interest in having it agreed was significant. As a consequence, the Portuguese crown soon embarked on distributing large areas of land to settlers who managed it on their behalf, paving the way for the creation of large agricultural estates.

Over the longer run, some key features of the emerging societies became rather similar. The relations of exchange between the local population and the new arrivals became increasingly asymmetric. Initial commerce in perceived mutual interest gave way to transformations of the local economies in the interest of the seafarers and colonisers. Furthermore, the colonisers increasingly tried to subject the locals and force them to do domestic and agricultural work. In both regions, the colonisers' experience was that those Americans and Africans who lived in the vicinity of the settlements resisted subjection and forced work. As a consequence, workers were brought in from other regions as unfree people. Slaves were shipped to Brazil from western and south-western Africa to work in sugar plantations and in the settlers' houses and estates. In the Cape region, slaves arrived from Asia, from Madagascar and only to a minor extent from other regions of the African continent, such as current Mozambique. In both regions, the number of slaves was soon higher than the number of free people (with Brazilian numbers of slaves going into the millions, hugely outnumbering those of the Cape).

THE EMERGING ATLANTIC MODERNITY: THE LIMITS OF THE EARTH AND THE ENCOUNTER WITH THE OTHER

The creation of this Atlantic world had a major impact on global consciousness, in at least two key respects. First, one may say that a global consciousness in the strict sense of the term arose for the first time, namely as the experience-based insight into the nature of the planet earth and the limits of its space. From now on there was no longer any radical outside about which European people felt that nothing at all was known. If 'globalisation' means the extension of social relations across the entire planet, then globalisation started at this moment. A 'New World' was added to that which was until then the known world, namely Europe, Asia and North Africa, now to become the 'Old World'. Within that future Old World, it was generally known that regions distant from one's own were inhabited by human beings, even though little was known of them and the space for imagination was wide. The inhabitants of the New World, in turn, given that that world was itself unexpected, were entirely unknown (Pagden 2000). The encounter with the entirely unknown other was the second major impact on global consciousness of the 'era of discoveries'.[2]

These two novel elements had significant, but often overlooked or misjudged consequences for the arising view of modernity. First, the insight into the spatial limits of the earth was accompanied by attempts at claiming complete territorial mastery. The key example for such ambition is the Treaty of Tordesillas signed between Spain and Portugal in 1494, as already mentioned. The actual line of demarcation remained far from being trampled by colonisers for a long time, and the complete division of the earth between the existing powers was much more clearly at issue in the so-called scramble for Africa during the second half of the nineteenth century, the Berlin conference of 1884–5 being a major attempt at settling the claims. By overemphasising the immediate importance of the Treaty of Tordesillas, Carl Schmitt's *The Nomos of the Earth* ([1950] 1997) misreads politico-legal history from a twentieth-century vantage point. However, Schmitt is right in suggesting that global law-making as world-making is on the horizon from this period onwards. Significantly, it is not world-making under the sign of equal autonomy, but by European powers dividing the earth among themselves and setting up different criteria for dealing with each other than with the subjected others (Koskenniemi 2001).

The question of the recognition of the other arose in a radical way when European seafarers encountered human beings they did not expect, and of whom they had not been aware. In contrast to members of other 'Old World' civilisations, who were different in many respects but to some extent knowable and known, the native Americans were seen as the radical other. In a first discussion, at the core of which was the Las Casas–Sepúlveda controversy in 1550, their common humanity needed to be determined, and Christian thought helped towards that end, even though it could also be used for denying equal status. Subsequently, the otherness of contemporaneous native Americans served to construct a dichotomous perception of world history, distinguishing a state of nature, in which the native Americans lived, from civil society, which Europeans supposedly had reached. This distinction was operated in three ways. On the one hand, and first, in social contract theories, it was of a conceptual nature that allowed for the grounding of social life in the co-ordinated action of individuals as the only foundation. What Europeans observed in America was transformed into a hypothesis on the beginning of organised social life.[3] On the other hand, second, the temporal implication in this hypothesis, itself of little relevance for social contract theories, opened the path for evolutionary thinking about human history, modernity and modernisation. Then, the non-European others could be considered as living in an earlier stage of history than the Europeans. They were denied coevalness, to use Johannes Fabian's (1983) apt expression, very often with implications for their status as

rights-holders of an inferior kind. The third layer in which this distinction between Europeans and the New World natives has operated is
found in the so-called 'romantic' view of what those ways of life represent for the human cosmology, as the work of Rousseau about the
'noble savage' and Alexander von Humboldt about the 'cosmos' as a
form of connection between different people illustrates. That which is
often hailed as the beginning of modern political and social theory in
Europe is made up of reflections by European thinkers generated on the
basis of a new experience that was made in America and Africa and in
the encounter with the native Americans and Africans.

At the end of the eighteenth century, social contract theories were
being mobilised in ongoing political struggles. They underpinned the
Declaration of Independence of the thirteen colonies that came to be
called the United States of America, the French Revolution, the Haitian
Revolution and other political events. Against the background of the
Enlightenment thinking of the preceding century, a radical political
imaginary was at work, aiming at instituting a new world on significantly
different foundations. It is important, however, to make distinctions. The
Haitian Revolution had clearly the most radical social commitment; it
aimed at full equality for slaves, the lowest class in the colony. Equal freedom regardless of gender and status was also on the agenda of the French
Revolution, but the radical forces soon lost out. The so-called American
Revolution did little to change the social order in the thirteen colonies; it
aimed at independence from Imperial Britain and created a new political
order, a republican one. But in many respects it was a revolution of the old
kind, grounded on classical republicanism and its notion of political participation based on the responsibility that comes with owning property.

From the angle of intellectual history, this period marked an important transformation in the conceptualisation of political modernity. This
is not the same, however, as saying that it marked the onset of political
modernity *tout court*; rather, it created the space for a variety of interpretations of modernity. To identify how this space was filled, one needs to
go beyond intellectual history and look at the political aftermath of the
revolutionary period.[4]

VERSIONS OF THE OLD REGIME: RESTRICTED SETTLER AND ELITE MODERNITIES

All three regions we look at participated in the great transformations of
the late eighteenth century, but to different degrees and in different ways.
In *politico-economic* terms, this period witnessed the rise of Britain to a

leading world power and the very beginning of the industrial revolution. The former was expressed in terms of Britain taking over the Cape region from the Netherlands, of the Portuguese Empire becoming economically dependent on Britain, and of the exposure of the European continent to free-trade demands. The rise of industrial production in the strict sense started only in the nineteenth century, but it was prepared during the earlier period: through the large plantation providing a model for work organisation that was further elaborated in the industrial factory; and through the – slowly but steadily – increasing importation of agricultural products from the 'South' to Europe (much more from Brazil than from South Africa), thus suspending Malthus's law for Europe and setting Europeans free for work in industry.

In *socio-political* terms, the period similarly witnessed an upheaval in all three regions, but with rather limited immediate consequences. Neither in Brazil nor in South Africa can one speak of a consolidation of the colonial regime when it comes to the issue of mastery of the colonial territory and the native population. Brazil had witnessed numerous rebellions, the creation of rather independent communities of slaves and their descendants (*quilombolas*) and disputes over aiming at independence from Portugal and creating a republic, like the Spanish colonies, or maintaining a monarchy. The establishment of the Empire of Brazil in 1822 meant the end of the formal colonial period, and also the consolidation of the process of opening to trade with other countries, most importantly Britain, that started in 1808 with the opening of the Brazilian ports, but it did not entail a profound socio-political rupture and the elites remained in a dominant position. A liberal constitution was proclaimed in 1824 but it remained very much over-determined by the power of the moderator – a fourth power established in this document along with the executive, the legislative and the judiciary – which was in the hands of the emperor. Also slavery, which began in the colonial period, was not abolished until 1888. The political order foresaw liberties but restricted political participation. Political conflicts centred on the very unity of the country and on the link between slavery and the economy, challenged by British pressure to end slave trading.

In South Africa, the British Cape Colony had imposed itself on the San and Khoikhoi, but it coexisted with other African societies, in particularly conflictive ways with the Xhosa to the immediate east. In conflict with the British administration of the Cape Colony over many issues, in particular slavery, many descendants of Dutch settlers (increasingly called *Afrikaners*) moved east and founded two separate republics, the Orange Free State and the Transvaal republic, thereby encroaching on the territory of African societies, in particular the Sotho, Tswana and Zulu. The second half of the nineteenth century was marked by frequent military conflicts between all societies, be they predominantly African, British or Dutch (Afrikaner). Politically, the African societies were chiefdoms or kingdoms with significant degrees of accountability of the governors to the governed, fostered by high spatial mobility. The Cape Colony abolished slavery and introduced civic liberties as well as restricted, but non-racialised, political rights. The Afrikaner republics saw themselves as inspired by the republican ideology of the US, restricting rights and participation to whites, for some time even to whites of Dutch origin only. They barely recognised the humanness of the Africans who were working for them.

In Europe, the radical political imaginary of the years around 1800 was defeated in the internal and international battles of the early nineteenth century. Instead of being overpowered by the rising bourgeoisie of liberal-capitalist modernity, the old aristocratic elites gradually changed outlook and started building new alliances, containing any radical new visions as created in the French Revolution and in political economy and imposing their power in the novel constellation through violence at home and abroad. The period between the Vienna Congress of 1815 and the reconfiguration of the European state system in 1870–1 was neither as peaceful nor as revolutionary as has often been suggested (Mayer 1981; Halperin 2004; Stråth 2016). Wars were frequent, even though many of them took place outside the European core territory. Rebellions were increasingly inspired by the democratic political imaginary, in particular from 1848 onwards, but they were rapidly suppressed. Most states remained monarchies, even though constitutions came to limit the powers of the monarch. In West and west-central Europe, state formation was increasingly informed by the cultural-linguistic view of the polity, as mentioned above (Chapter 1), with the cases of 'national unification' of Italy and Germany being seen as exemplary. These states also increasingly adopted civic liberties but continued to restrict political participation, mostly to male property owners based on a tax census. At the same time, they started to involve the population more intensely into nation-building, in particular through basic and higher education institutions and compulsory male military service.

Overall, the general interpretation of (much of) the nineteenth century as a 'persistence of the Old Regime' (Arno Mayer) has considerable plausibility, even if extended *mutatis mutandis* beyond Europe to Brazil and South Africa. True, it seems counter-intuitive to speak of an 'Old Regime' for 'new societies' (Hartz 1964) that never had feudalism (even though these were societies whose colonial elites were still connected to their European roots). The point of similarity, however, is that in all three regions highly inegalitarian political orders persisted despite the experience of the democratic political imaginary. In all three regions, furthermore, domination was maintained by broadly the same groups as before 1800, the only major change being the arrival of British settlers in South Africa and their increasing dominance over the Dutch. Third, the domination was by one category of persons over other categories: in Brazil by the Portuguese and their descendants over the native Americans (despite their exemption from slavery in 1758) and the slaves, and in South Africa by the pale-skinned European settlers over the native Africans and the slaves (with the partial exception of the Cape Colony).

One may want to question whether such domination by category also persisted in Europe after serfdom was abolished. We would, however, maintain that this was so, with some qualification when compared to colonial domination. A first confirmation is provided by the fact that equal rights with men were denied to women all across Europe. In turn, the differentiation of political rights by property and tax census may appear to be gradual and, thus, not based on any firm categorisation that individuals could not overcome. Formally correct as that may be, such an assertion would not reflect the prevailing self-understanding in European societies of the mid-nineteenth century. As the later prime minister of Britain, Benjamin Disraeli, put it in the mouth of one of the protagonists of his 1845 novel *Sybil, or The Two Nations*: this country is inhabited by 'two nations; between whom there is no intercourse and no sympathy; who are as ignorant of each other's habits, thoughts, and feelings, as if they were dwellers in different zones, or inhabitants of different planets; who are formed by a different breeding, are fed by a different food, are ordered by different manners, and are not governed by the same laws', referring to the rich and the poor.

THE MOVEMENT OF PEOPLE AND GOODS

This variety of Old Regimes can be described as parallel historical developments in three world-regions at quite some distance and rather separate from each other, creating their own endogenous trajectories after the original settlement. But this would lose from sight the way in which it is precisely their interconnections that provided the basis for their particular regimes. During the formal colonial periods, in Brazil until 1822 and in South Africa until 1910, the regions were governed from Europe,[5] even though, as a matter of fact, this only extended to parts of the respective territories and often without the capacity for full enforcement. As or more important, however, are the interconnections that were created by the movements of people and goods between the regions. These movements underwent important changes towards the end of the nineteenth century, which became crucial for subsequent socio-political developments.

As underlined before, a major part of the Brazilian population were slaves and their descendants. The slaves were brought from Africa, mostly to work on the sugar plantations and in the gold mines. At the end of the nineteenth century, Brazil was by far the largest producer as well as exporter of coffee in the world, providing most of the supply to Europe and North America. After independence from Portugal, the Brazilian government was increasingly subject to pressure by Britain to abolish slavery or at least to end the slave trade, to start with. In 1888, slavery was finally abolished. Given that workers for coffee planta-tions were no longer available under the same conditions as before and that this event coincided with a politics of eugenics in most American territory, Brazil increasingly tried to attract immigration from Europe. During the 1890s, 1.2 million people immigrated to Brazil, mostly from poor regions in Portugal and northern Italy (Belich 2009: 520).

Until 1872, when diamonds were found at what soon came to be called Kimberley, the territory of South Africa was of limited com-mercial importance for Britain. In the early years after the takeover of the Cape region from the Dutch, nevertheless, the insight had already arisen that population movements could be stimulated for the benefit of Britain both 'at home' and 'overseas'. In 1820, facing unemployment and social unrest in mainland Britain, the British parliament supported the emigration of 4,000 settlers to the Cape, selected from 80,000 applicants, to set up agricultural farms on land claimed by the Xhosa (Thompson 2001: 54). After 1872, and in particular after 1886, when gold was found on the Witwatersrand, the relation between work and population became of crucial importance. The population of South Africa increased rapidly, roughly doubling in the British Cape and Natal colonies and in the Transvaal republic between 1890 and 1904 (Belich 2009: 379), including strong immigration from Europe and from neighbouring African states, in particular the Portuguese colony Mozambique. The mines provided work for a large number of people, and the work was organised in such a way as to reinforce the racial segregation and oppression that had been the socio-political order of the Transvaal republic.

The end of slavery in Brazil, the new societal structuration for coffee growing and for gold and diamond mining, and the immigration that followed in both Brazil and South Africa coincided with the rise of explicitly and self-declared scientific racism, for instance as developed by Joseph Arthur Gobineau, claiming the superiority of some races over others, in particular the 'white' one over coloured ones. Such thinking informed deliberate measures to increase the European population in both regions. Brazil had received around 45% of all the African slaves who became part of the Atlantic slave trade – in total, around 4.8 million slaves were brought to Brazil (Lesser 2013). As we shall see later, it is not wrong to say that the first Brazilian Republic saw slavery as a problem created by colonialism and as such a matter of the past, and tried to build up the 'new nation' under policies seeking to 'modernise' the country through white immigration.

In many regions of Europe, in contrast, deteriorating living conditions in both rural and urban settings, at various times and for different reasons, made emigration a plausible means to try to escape from misery.[6] Between 1850 and 1913 more than 40 million people emigrated from Europe to the so-called New World (Hatton and Williamson 1992). In Brazil only, between 1870 and 1930 around 3 million immigrants settled (Lesser 2013). There is an ongoing debate about the main causes of this mass migration. Earlier population growth due to the so-called demographic transition is often cited as a main background factor, leading to scarcity of work. In some instances, European governments explicitly supported emigration, not only in Britain, as referred to earlier, but also in France, with regard to Algeria. The reduction of a 'surplus population' with a view to avoiding social problems and rebellion was an explicit consideration only in a few instances. But across Europe elites were clear about seeing a 'social question' or 'labour question' arising. Karl Marx had assumed that capital needed an 'industrial reserve army' of workers in need of work, who would lower wages in their competition with employed workers. However, this potential reserve army emigrated out of Europe and turned the native population in the 'South' into a global reserve army.

Though the social profile of the emigrants showed great variety, many of them were migrating for economic reasons, and thus belonged to lower classes, with the largest group of emigrants being single young men without skills. Even though not all of them were successful, and some of them returned, they were expecting upward social mobility and often achieved it. This achievement was facilitated by the high stratification of the 'Southern' societies into which the migrants entered at a high level, at least compared to descendants of the native populations and of slaves.[7] From the late nineteenth century onwards, their 'entry level' was furthermore predetermined by the sense of superiority provided by 'scientific racism'.

During the nineteenth century, in sum, the interconnections between Europe, on the one hand, and Brazil and South Africa, on the other, were marked by the movement of goods (sugar, gold, diamonds, coffee, as well as wool and rubber to a smaller extent) from the latter to the former, and the movement of people from the former to the latter. This double exchange clearly enriched European societies. According to then widespread views, it was also supposed to 'enrich' Brazil and South Africa in terms of improving the composition of the population. What it factually did was to increase the proportion of European settlers in both societies and, as a consequence, keep the other members confined to their status of exclusion or very limited inclusion. It provided the background for transforming the relatively similar versions of the Old Regime from the beginning of the nineteenth century into rather distinct interpretations of modernity in the early twentieth century.

To grasp the key features of these interpretations of modernity, it is useful to distinguish two aspects, even though they became salient in chronologically overlapping ways: on the one hand, the creation of a socio-spatial collectivity that became the 'container' for a specific interpretation of modernity, and, on the other, the ways in which the dwellers in this social space became integrated into social practices or failed to do so.

THE CREATION OF A SOCIO-SPATIAL COLLECTIVITY

Brazil, South Africa and Europe underwent major politico-institutional transformations between the late nineteenth and the early twentieth centuries. In continental Western Europe, to limit our examples to this region, the years 1870–1 witnessed the creation of the French Third

Republic and of the 'nation states' of Italy and Germany through the unification of several territories under a common administration. In 1889, the emperor of Brazil went into exile after a military coup and the Federal Republic of Brazil was created. Though the Brazilian constitution admitted that a woman could become the head of state, Dom Pedro II himself and the traditional elitist groups that were in power did not agree with that. In 1910, the formerly separate British and Afrikaner polities were joined together to form the Union of South Africa, a self-governing, autonomous polity within the British Empire. These dates and events are crucial as they mark the moments at which the long-lasting territorial shape of the polities and key administrative institutions were created, or confirmed while reinterpreted in the cases of Brazil and France. In other words, the 'containers' were provided within which socio-political debate was to take place for a long time to come.

The political rupture that this entailed is immediately evident in the cases of Italy, Germany and South Africa. States were created that did not exist before and whose creation was highly contingent; they might also have not been created or created in different form. Nowhere was this a smooth process. In all these cases, prolonged military action was employed to reach the outcome. In Italy and Germany, the process was underpinned by the cultural-linguistic theory of the polity; it was driven by the major prior powers, Prussia and Piedmont; and it had to face contested issues over the inclusion of certain territories, such as Trieste and Alto Adige in Italy or Bavaria and Schleswig in Germany. In South Africa, unification of the territory was a British colonial project, also led through both political pressure and military action, of which the South African War from 1899 to 1902 was decisive. The outcome was a unified state based on the subjection of the African population and on a compromise between the British and the Afrikaners, but dominated by the British.

In turn, Brazil and France underwent a political transformation without large territorial changes.[8] As mentioned before, the transformation of the Empire into the Republic did not entail major changes in socio-political powers in Brazil (we will come back to the question of slavery in a moment). But it entailed a reorientation of the long-lasting issue of Brazilian unity towards an increasingly consensual understanding of Brazil as one nation, building also on the commonality and distinctiveness of the official language, Portuguese, which was not spoken elsewhere in South America. A similar understanding had been created in France since the Revolution almost a century earlier, but it also received an accentuation due to the creation of a republic that turned out to be more stable than its two short-lived predecessors. The Third Republic developed a very pronounced self-understanding of a political order that its inhabitants have in common, 'the plebiscite of everyday', as Ernest Renan called it in a speech given at the Sorbonne in Paris 1882 under the title 'What is a nation?', enhanced by key republican institutions such as the school and the army, and further emphasised by the radical separation of church and state in 1905.

Thus, these politico-institutional transformations created the conditions for a long-lasting coherence between a territory and a political order, thereby enhancing the possibility of an identification of the inhabitants of a territory with the polity – the phenomenon which often far too unquestioningly is called 'national identity' and also 'national development'. More cautiously, we have above called this lasting coherence between territory and polity a 'container'. This container created, in a rather similar way, new possibilities for the relations between the inhabitants of the territory in the three regions we analyse. But how these possibilities were used differed very widely.

THE POLITICAL ORDER AND THE INHABITANTS
OF THE TERRITORY

'After the conclusion of the national question the so-called social question is for us perhaps the most important of the future' – thus spoke Gustav Schöneberg, a founding member of the *Verein für Socialpolitik*, in 1871, immediately after the founding of Imperial Germany, the so-called German nation state (see Wagner 1990: 79–85). In our terminology here, Schöneberg took the building of the 'container' to be completed, but saw much work ahead in developing the relations between the inhabitants of this political space. This was a common view in major parts of Europe at that time. The statement attributed to Massimo d'Azeglio, 'We have made Italy. Now we have to make Italians', expresses a similar view. In both versions, these statements hint at some kind of inclusion or integration that needed to be achieved across the whole political space, even while leaving quite open how and according to which criteria this should be achieved.

Before going on, let us immediately add that many European states at the end of the nineteenth century appeared with a double face, as both nation states and colonial powers. As such, they mostly considered the 'social question' and the making of citizens as a metropolitan affair and regarded the native inhabitants of their colonies as dominated subjects, not as citizens, granting them considerably lesser rights than the residents of the metropoles (Mamdani 1996).[9] The genocide of the Herero, Nama and San people committed by the German colonial army in what was then German South West Africa (today's Namibia) in 1904–8 is an extreme case of hierarchical distinctions between categories of persons, here including the very denial of equal humanness, in colonial settings. It was committed at a time when social integration within metropolitan Germany was a key topic on the domestic policy agenda. As we shall see, setting spatial boundaries of citizenship was turned into a major tool for addressing the 'social question' in Europe.

The 'Southern' societies, such as Brazil and South Africa, did not have such a tool easily at hand. Descendants of settlers, slaves and indigenous people lived together on the same territory, even though not exactly in the same places.[10] The new political orders explicitly aimed at some kind of integration as well, as the terms 'Union' and 'Republic' indicate. But the logics of integration differed considerably from those of metropolitan Europe.

Despite the persistence of slavery until the late nineteenth century, which concerned almost exclusively persons of African origins and their descendants, Brazilian politics made rather little use of racial categories until recently (and now for different reasons, to be discussed later). In the Empire of Brazil, political participation was restricted, but not extraordinarily so in comparison with Europe.[11] It excluded unfree persons, thus all slaves, and women, and it made voting conditional on being Catholic. Property- and income-based restrictions existed but they were low. Even before the advent of the Republic, it became clear to the elites that slavery would need to end, potentially allowing a large number of former slaves to vote. In this light, the Savaria Law of 1881 lifted the earlier restrictions, except those for women, but introduced the requirement to be literate and also raised the required level of income. With this simple, apparently non-racialised move, most slaves, once freed, and indigenous people remained excluded, limiting the right to vote to only about 15–20% of the adult male population.[12]

As briefly mentioned earlier, South Africa before Union showed two contrasting ways of ordering the polity internally. The Cape Colony favoured non-racial, property-restricted political participation,[13] the

British colony of Natal also emphasised property restrictions but added more hurdles for non-whites, whereas the Afrikaner republics used a 'white only', or even 'Afrikaner only', approach to the question. The Cape Colony tried to extend its system to the Union but failed to do so; the differences between the four former polities were basically maintained in the South Africa Act of 1909.

Thus, one can easily see that the political transformation in Brazil and South Africa was to a considerable extent guided by the political imaginary of equal freedom that had been forcefully voiced at the end of the eighteenth century. But this imaginary was also explicitly rejected in some contexts, in our cases with success in the Afrikaner republics. And important modifications were introduced with regard to the implementation of the imaginary to prevent even the possibility of a rapid political transformation that would have endangered the privileges of the established elites. The problem in any case is that equal freedom practically meant equality and freedom for those who were already incorporated as part of the politico-economic structures.

At the time when Schöneberg and D'Azeglio spoke, the situation in Europe was not very different, as pointed out above. Restrictions to suffrage were common and pronounced. Equal universal suffrage was introduced in many European societies only after the First World War. Female suffrage was introduced in France and Italy only after the Second World War, considerably later than in South Africa (1930) and Brazil (1932), even though there it was subject to restrictions. Nevertheless, European societies gradually embarked on a different trajectory than Brazil and South Africa during the closing decades of the nineteenth century.

Gérard Noiriel (1991) has characterised this transformation as a 'nationalisation of European societies'. In its processual form, this expression underlines the fact that European societies had not built 'containers' before. It was only towards the end of the nineteenth century that it was made more difficult to cross boundaries and take up residence and work outside one's country of birth. Seeing like a state, to paraphrase James Scott, one recognises that once subjects start to become citizens it becomes much more important to know who they are and what they think. The 'nationalisation' process largely went in parallel with what has come to be called the 'early welfare state' or the introduction of social rights as well as with the widening of the franchise or the granting of more political rights, to use T. H. Marshall's terminology. Or to come back to Schöneberg's statement, solving the national question had meant building the container, whereas solving the social question would mean creating a close link within the container, so to speak, between the territory and the population. The three regions that we are working with have dealt differently with both the problem of how to build up the container and of how to create solidarity within it. In Europe, importantly, this was supposed to be done in a rather coherent, even if not in an absolutely inclusive way (as we shall discuss below); that is, everyone defined to be a member of the nation was also meant to be socially integrated into the polity. This matching of the 'national' with the 'social' was to become a characteristic of the European trajectory, even though it came close to being realised only after the Second World War. It took much longer for Brazil and South Africa to build up their containers. And as we will keep discussing throughout the whole book, the problem of inclusiveness and integration was still waiting to be fully incorporated as part of the social question agenda.

Chapter 3

AN ASYMMETRICALLY CONSOLIDATED MODERNITY

THE 'MASSES' ENTER THE POLITICAL IMAGINARY

At the end of the preceding chapter we discussed the politico-institutional transformations in the highly inegalitarian societies of the late nineteenth century predominantly from an elite point of view. These elites increasingly recognised that they would need to take the viewpoints and interests of large groups in society more into account, given the high demand for labour in mining, plantations and – still largely limited to Europe – industry, and increasing social problems related to urbanisation and changes in working conditions. But the elites predominantly assumed that they could contain the impact of these social changes by ameliorative public policies combined with the continuity of oppression and denial of equal rights.

During the same period, however, these large groups in society also increasingly voiced their claims in their own way, through strikes, demonstrations, riots and rebellions. For Europe, Karl Polanyi's account of what he called 'The Great Transformation' (1944) has become highly influential. Polanyi argued that marketisation and commodification movements during the earlier nineteenth century created untenable social situations against which movements for the self-protection of society arose. For Polanyi, these movements characteristically came both from concerned elites and from affected social movements who recognised the disintegrative effects of commodification on 'society' and acted against it. As compelling and fruitful as Polanyi's account is, it has rightly been criticised for, in a quasi-Durkheimian way, postulating rather than showing that there is a collective social phenomenon 'society' for which both dangers and protective measures are identifiable. From our angle, Polanyi's work reflects the effects of those measures of creating coherence between institutional containers and resident populations that we discussed above and that Noiriel (1991) described as the 'nationalisation of European societies'. Thus, Polanyi's 'society' is much more based on historical observation than theoretical fiat, in contrast to Durkheim, but this insight leads to another criticism: rather than giving a general account of the consequences of disembedding markets from society, Polanyi provided an analysis of the European case only, a case that is, furthermore, highly particular and not amenable to generalisation.

As is well known, Durkheim assumed that the emerging industrial society would be based on a pronounced division of labour creating an unprecedented degree of interdependence between all members of a social configuration. The reasoning had its roots in both Montesquieu's notion of pacification of social life through 'sweet commerce' and Adam Smith's notion of increasing the 'wealth of nations' through market-driven specialisation and, thus, increased productivity. But Durkheim shifted the emphasis from individual interest to the social bond between human beings that, under the described conditions, would generate organic solidarity. It was often overlooked that this solidarity could only be 'organic' if the social configuration was something like a 'body', a living system with self-preserving functions and boundaries towards the outside. Durkheim's 'society' is exactly this (Wagner 2003), a concept which reflected key aspects of the European epistemic and socio-political constellation of the time. Such thinking permitted, on the one hand, the assumption of a 'central social conflict', namely the one between labour and capital under industrial conditions, and a 'central social movement', namely the workers' movement.[1] On the other hand, it required the setting of the boundaries within which this conflict could unfold, which were gradually being determined as the boundaries of the (metropolitan) nation states (see exemplarily Rabinbach 1996 for the case of compulsory workers' accident insurance; for a more general discussion, see Wagner and Zimmermann 2004), which also led to the 'nationalisation' of European social democracy (Telò 1988).

Even though often hidden or concealed, Karl Marx's analysis of capitalism stood in the background of much of this reasoning. He identified this 'central conflict' and suggested that it would be overcome through the action of the proletariat as the social class representing the universal interest. For the latter reason, though, the conflict did not lend itself to 'nationalisation' in Marx's view. Marx emphasised 'international' rather than 'organic' solidarity. As a matter of fact, this thinking travelled with the workers who were emigrating from Europe and became transformed in light of the immigrants' new experiences. In Brazil and South Africa, socialist, anarchist and communist thinking was most widespread among immigrant workers. This, though, entailed that these workers were pale-skinned and entered the receiving society just because of that at a high level, at least compared to the native and former slave populations. They were welcomed by the existing elites and, often explicitly, meant to replace former slaves (in Brazil) or to make African immigration unnecessary (in South Africa). Rather than being inclined to struggle for social equality because of their class interest, they entered a highly inegalitarian society and became inclined to support – or not to fight against – the existing forms of inequality.

A telling example from South Africa is the strike and rebellion known as the Rand Revolt of 1922. Faced with falling prices for gold and diamonds, mining companies aimed to reduce costs by hiring more black workers, who were paid much lower wages than white workers. White workers rebelled against such attempts and were mobilised and supported by left-wing organisations. The young Communist Party of South Africa entered into the revolt with the slogan 'workers of the world, unite and fight for a white South Africa'.[2] After the revolt was crushed by police and military forces, the protection of the white workers' wages through the 'colour bar' was reinforced and racial segregation became even more of a key tool for organising South African society (Breckenridge 2007).

In Brazil, the event that became historically known as the Revolution of 1930 shows how existing forms of inequality became unproblematically incorporated in the formation of an emancipatory agenda for the masses – namely the working class. The regional political order of the First Republic was broken by a conspiracy formed by political leaders from Rio Grande do Sul, Minas Gerais and Paraíba, including Getúlio Vargas, who became the first president of the Second Republic after the military coup that put an end to the Revolution of 1930. The revolution started as a demand for the incorporation of the workers (the urban masses) as part of the response to the social question that needed to be developed in the country. In a famous speech of 1929, Vargas said that Brazil was constantly in debt to all the other countries of the world who signed the Treaty of Versailles because so far there was no such thing as Brazilian social legislation. However, the 'masses' (*O Povo*) that

were meant to be incorporated as a way of remedying the social question were basically formed by urban literate/white men. Immigrants
that were brought to the country after the end of slavery to work on
new economic activities, such as national infrastructure and the coffee
trade, would be more likely to be accommodated by the newly proposed legislation than the large number of ex-slaves that were completely excluded. The union tradition in Brazil started after the arrival of
European immigrants and it did not challenge the social structuring of
the labour market in terms of inclusion and exclusion of the non-white
worker. This was so both for the phase that Vianna (1978) calls resistance (1888–1919), in which solidarity between the growing number of
wage-workers was built, and for the following moment of adjustment
(1919–34), in which the unionist agenda was linked to demands for the
liberalisation of society.

It has often been remarked that Max Weber's historical-comparative
sociology, pioneering as it was, was marked by a key conceptual flaw.
Weber had detected a highly significant phenomenon in one world-
region and had explored the causes for its emergence, namely
occidental rationalism and its historical roots in the social ethics
of Protestantism. His subsequent comparative search was guided
by the question of whether similar conditions had existed in other
world-regions, and his unsurprising answer was that they had not.
Furthermore, he had assumed that occidental rationalism had world-
historical significance since it allegedly placed the West on a superior trajectory of development. Modernisation theory later extended
this approach to the whole complex consisting of industrialisation,
democratisation and welfare-state building. Thus, it invited historical-
comparative sociology to explore only the reasons for the absence of
key developmental conditions elsewhere. By contrast, our reflections
do sustain that there is a particularity to the European situation, but
they take a symmetrical look. The European constellation is particular,
but it is not exemplary; it is not isolated but interconnected with 'non-
European' situations; furthermore, its particularity may exactly be due
to its way of being interconnected.

In this light, we can return to the socio-political setting of around
1900. It is by now generally accepted that the trajectory of rather
egalitarian inclusiveness that marked European societies in the (later)
twentieth century was embarked upon during the decades preceding and including the First World War. The combination of the need
for workers due to industrial expansion, the need for soldiers due to

intensified warfare and, concomitantly, the need for women to keep up the economy while the men were at war strengthened the bargaining position, to speak in instrumental terms, of the lower classes in European societies and forced or induced the elites to make concessions.[3] The year 1919 stands out: the war was over and societies were re-organising themselves. In many societies, universal suffrage was introduced, often but not always including women on equal terms. Furthermore, the war experience had brought the groups in society more closely together, in the *union sacrée* ('sacred union') or *Burgfriede* ('peace within the fortress') in France and Germany respectively, for example, or at least this was assumed (Didry and Wagner 1999).

While saying this, though, we have to keep in mind the historical background, as portrayed before: European workers and soldiers were also direly needed because there were less of them due to earlier mass emigration. The migrants, in turn, increased the population in the 'receiving' societies and thus contributed to making a similarly inclusive organisation less likely, as the elites used the whitening policies to ensure that they were less reliant on native and black groups for labour and defence. Similarly, industrialisation in Europe was enabled by the provision of raw materials and foodstuffs from the South. In turn, the Southern societies remained or became oriented to agriculture and mining, not only for their own needs but also and even predominantly for exportation.

Contemporaries have described the early twentieth century as the period when the masses[4] entered history. Antonio Gramsci and Leon Trotsky did so from an activist perspective; among those who expressed more sceptical views were José Ortega y Gasset and Elias Canetti. Even though these authors are Europeans and shaped by their experiences, their observations remain valid also from a broader global perspective – provided that the interconnectedness and the differences between the regional constellations are taken into account. In this broader view, one recognises that two elements came together: from an empirical perspective, on the one side, the 'masses' gained more social force in society for the reasons given above and in highly variable ways; on the other side, in the normative terms of justification for socio-political arrangements, the democratic political imaginary came to stand out more and more. From being a view held by few observers and activists by mid-nineteenth century, egalitarian-inclusive democracy came to be seen as almost unavoidable by the 1920s, even though it did not necessarily become more desirable or acceptable among the political and intellectual elites, but rather a claim to be contained or circumvented by some means or other.

THREE INTERPRETATIONS OF ORGANISED MODERNITY AT MID-TWENTIETH CENTURY

Facing the entry of the masses, all the three world-regions witnessed persisting difficulties in stabilising the socio-political constellation in the early twentieth century. But, gradually, the contours of the ways in which the new situation would be addressed emerged and crystallised by the 1930s. They all had in common that they were based on some acceptance of 'mass society'. Furthermore, they all rejected the idea that this new society could be founded on the liberal imaginary of opinion formation through communication and decision-making through inclusive and pluralistic democratic representation. In the dominant view, to put it simply, there were too many people with too different backgrounds and levels of (moral) education to make this imaginary viable. In turn, it was assumed that integration of the masses would need to occur through some combination of organisation and exclusion. Those who for variable reasons could be considered full members of society would be included, but at the same time their behaviour would be channelled through more or less compulsory socio-political organisations. Others would be considered not (fully) includable, again for variable reasons, and would need to be (at least partially) excluded.[5]

European polities came to set strong boundaries towards the outside and build relatively high levels of inclusion inside, two issues historically known as the national and the social question respectively. In America, what we may call 'settler interpretations of modernity' were created that were based on varieties of relations between the descendants of the settlers and native and slave populations, all of which sustained the dominance of the settler group. At the extremes, we find, on the one hand, a modern self-understanding that presented itself as liberal and republican while annihilating the indigenous population and oppressing the slave population until long after the formal abolition of slavery, with the US as the exemplary case (Henningsen 2009); and on the other, the idea of mixing and fusion of the three population groups in the creation of a new civilisation and polity, with Brazil's discourse about 'racial democracy' as the exemplary case (further discussed in

Chapter 7). In comparison with the intra-European interpretation of modernity, both the American and the South African interpretations are distinct in two key respects: both give historically much less significance to the implication of the whole population in any 'project of modernity', and, at the same time, they are much less concerned with the definition and closure of boundaries. To speak in European terms, neither the national nor the social question acquire constitutive significance for the interpretation of modernity, even though in Latin America more so than in North America and South Africa. In turn, migration and social inequality become key features of the socio-political settings of American and African varieties of modernity.

In what follows we will briefly discuss apartheid in South Africa (1948–90/94, with forerunners in the 1930s and 1940s), the Vargas Regime or *Estado Novo* in Brazil (1930–45) and fascism/Nazism in Europe (1922–45 in Italy, 1933–45 in Germany) as three crystallised interpretations of organised modernity, with specific features. We will focus on these crystallisations but also briefly discuss the conditions of their emergence from the earlier decades of the twentieth century onwards.[6]

In South Africa, the constitution of the new polity in 1910 contained some openness and indeterminacy, as the absence of agreement about a common voting system showed. Against this background, the African elites intended to make their claims on the new polity, founding the African National Congress (ANC, then the South African Native National Congress) in 1912, which has been the governing party uninterruptedly since 1994. In 1912, the Congress aimed for equal rights and expected progress on this front given that the more liberal descendants of the British settlers had got the upper hand over the Afrikaners. However, the arrangement between the residents of European descent held, and economic aspects determined institutional decisions. In 1913, the Land Act restricted the Africans' right to possess land, limiting the possibilities of both African-led agriculture and stable urban settlement of Africans. In the mines, a dual employment system existed for what came to be called the different 'population groups', fiercely defended by white-skinned workers, as seen above. Like in many other countries across the world, sociological research in South Africa started as research into urgent social problems. But it is telling that this was research into the 'poor white problem', in particular among Afrikaners, funded by the US-based Carnegie Corporation.

Even though not all events and measures pointed in the same direction, with hindsight it is clear that South Africa was headed towards a dual society, divided on racist grounds. The objective was to build a 'white' society in which every member would be enabled to live in a 'civilised' way, which meant like a bourgeois European, not like an African. Wages for white workers were as high or higher than in many European countries; social institutions were built on the model of the emerging British (and Australian) welfare state (Seekings 2016). But in contrast to Britain, access to these institutions was not granted to all citizens. It was denied to the Africans who at the same time were working for much lower wages and under worse working conditions for white masters and employers at home, in agriculture and in the mines. To secure this domination, South African politics opted for legal arrangements distinguishing between categories of persons, to create first and then be supported by physical separation of the 'population groups'. Apartheid (literally: 'separateness') came gradually to exist from at least 1913 onwards, even though it became explicit under this name and the core of government policy only from 1948 onwards.[7]

In Brazil, what is now known as the 'First' or 'Old Republic' (1889–1930) was similarly, and even more pronouncedly, marked by an initial openness of further development. Moreover, Brazil was sometimes portrayed as a new society leading the way into the future, in particular due to the mixing of what South Africans called 'population groups' and the absence of explicitly racialised regulations after the abolition of slavery. In 1933, the writer, journalist and social anthropologist Gilberto Freyre provided a grand interpretation of Brazilian society in his essay *Casa-grande e senzala*, in which the close interrelations between immigrant-settlers and the native and slave populations were seen as the central characteristic of Brazil. Subsequently, the concept of 'racial democracy' was proposed to characterise Brazilian society, not least in contrast to the US, where racial segregation persisted after the abolition of slavery. The concept is based on the combination of the absence of racialised laws and the frequency of mixing between the 'races' in Brazil, which is assumed to have led to minimal degrees of prejudice and discrimination compared to other societies. It became the core of published Brazilian self-understanding and a source of national pride at a time when concerns for the homogeneity of nation states and for ethnic purity were widespread in the world.[8] However, the persistence of the patterns of exclusion of the ex-slaves from the public sphere and the growing number of immigration policies that favoured white immigrants in the course of the twentieth century shows that we need to be careful with the idea of Brazil as an example of miscegenation (see Chapter 6).

The 'Second Republic' (1930–45) or Vargas regime[9] gave more economically and politically organised form to Brazilian society. Vargas aimed at transforming the state into the key institution of a new understanding of economic and social development. He introduced a social protection system during the period between 1930 and 1934. The organisation of the urban industrial workers with formal labour contracts became a way of organising society so that the supposed 'cultural' openness of 'racial democracy' did not endanger elite domination under conditions of high social inequality and (restricted) political participation. It was a way of delivering benefits to a significant part of the population in exchange for political stability (see Chapter 6 for more detail). Simultaneously, Vargas used the state to organise the national industrial economy, creating state-owned companies in several sectors and aiming at substituting imports for domestic production, initiating the process that would give rise to the idea of a 'developmental state' a bit later in Brazil. Between 1937 and 1945 the previous constitution was changed in a clearly anti-liberal direction, giving more power to the executive and to industrial groups working both outside and inside the state. Suppression of dissent was connected to selective social inclusion and economic development.

In Europe, the restricted interpretation of modernity could no longer be sustained after the First World War. Between 1919 and the 1960s, through coping with civil wars, as well as authoritarian and totalitarian regimes, an inclusivist reinterpretation was created, entailing full and equal political participation, recognition of the workers as producers through the trade unions and as consumers who would buy the products they themselves had produced. The new accumulation regime of mass production coupled with mass consumption, pioneered in the US (Aglietta 1979), was the precondition for the inward turn of European societies that meant the elaboration of a societal self-understanding in which the collectivity became a community of mutual responsibility, overcoming the class divides of earlier eras (Wagner and Zimmermann 2004). The parallel elaboration of the 'national question' and the 'social question' served as 'attenuations' (Mota 2013) of restricted liberal modernity. The approaches generated by these two questions gave rise to nationalism and socialism/communism respectively. They clashed after the First World War, with Soviet Socialism and Nazism emerging as the most radical collectivist interpretations of these questions.[10] In all cases, this internally organised modernity required a political centre, the state apparatus, that was capable of organising political forces through mass organisations and the media, monitoring and steering the economy, and sustaining boundary control towards other societies.

Within Europe, Germany underwent particularly rapid transformations and provided a radical example of the kind of socio-political organisation that emerged during the first half of the twentieth century. From the formation of the supposed nation state in 1871 to the First World War, the German economy industrialised rapidly and outcompeted Britain in many respects, while politically the core German state, Prussia, kept excluding the majority of the population from participation and oppressed the workers' movement. The defeat of the regime in the First World War opened up a period of social, political and cultural experimentation. The Weimar constitution of 1919, passed after the Russian Revolution and the Mexican constitution of 1917, introduced equal male and female suffrage and the social responsibility of property-owners. But this rapid and 'fundamental democratisation' (Karl Mannheim) also led to the mobilisation of politically inexperienced 'masses' and, under conditions of economic depression and unemployment after 1929, to the rise of the Nazi Party. Coming to power in 1933, the Nazi regime resorts to an extreme concept of 'Germanness' and provides full inclusion, including social inclusion at an unprecedented level, to those inside, while persecuting and eliminating those considered as situated outside the national frame. Applying supremacist ideas within Europe, the regime radicalised segregationist ideas that had been developed earlier in southern Africa, including notions that the to-be-excluded others could be pressed into forced work and that their lives counted for little.

There was a great variety of such organised forms of modernity in Europe. Today, it is important to underline that the positive connection of 'national' with 'social' was by no means limited to its use in German National Socialism. In Sweden, the concept of 'people's home' preceded and possibly inspired the Nazi term 'people's community', but was used to refer to a project based on a democratic alliance of workers and peasants guided by Swedish social democracy. In turn, other forms of inclusivist organisation were undemocratic, and some of them outlived the Nazi dictatorship, such as Francoist Spain (1939–75) and Salazar Portugal, the latter also called *Estado Novo* (1933–74; Marcelo Caetano followed António de Oliveira Salazar as president in 1968).

DIVERGENCE IN THE APPARENT CONSOLIDATION
OF MODERNITY

By the late 1930s, the three trajectories of organised modernity seemed to be headed towards consolidation, in their distinct forms. Saying this, we recall that at that moment Nazi Germany was not considered a completely immoral aberration from any civilisational path, as it came to be seen by the 1940s. Many observers rather saw it as one of several responses to the crisis caused by the Great Depression, similar to the New Deal or the Scandinavian worker-peasant alliances, though with some distinct features. That is what makes the question of what Europe would have come to look like if Nazi Germany had won the Second World War, to which only counterfactual answers are possible, intriguing. One then might have envisaged a combination of 'consociational democracy' (Lijphart 1975) based on predefined and hierarchically organised citizen groups with a 'co-ordinated market capitalism' (Hall and Soskice 2001), led by a strong and somewhat authoritarian state. Similarly, apartheid South Africa in the way in which we have come to see it came about only because the National Party won the general election of 1948, something that might well not have happened.[11] One could also have imagined, again counterfactually, that South African society would have embarked on a course of gradual inclusion and integration of the native African population, starting with the educated and 'civilised' black African elites as envisaged by the ANC (Dlamini 2015).

With hindsight one can recognise that such contingent events led to a divergence between the trajectories of modernity in the three regions, with South Africa marking one extreme and Western Europe the other, while Brazil stood in an intermediate position. The National Party made 'apartheid' the centre of its project for societal reorganisation in South Africa. It deprived the 'black' and 'coloured' population of many of the limited rights they had. Political participation was further restricted; rights to land were suppressed; people were removed from the places where they lived. The core idea was to radically segregate the 'white' from the 'non-white' population, settling the latter in predominantly rural 'homelands', which were supposed to become independent states even while being enclaves in South African state territory, and in urban 'townships', settlements at the periphery of cities combining proximity to workplace with ease of control. Public infrastructure was set up in segregated ways, and was of highly inferior quality for the dominated groups.

'Apartheid became the most notorious form of racial domination that the post-war world has known' (Thompson 2001: 189) during the early post-Second World War period. It violated all normative commitments that the winning side of the war against Nazism had entered into. Nevertheless the Union of South Africa remained a member of the British Commonwealth until 1961, maintained intense commercial relations with the UK, the US and other Western countries, and was little criticised for its domestic policies until British Prime Minister Harold Macmillan's 'wind of change' speech of 1960, when the decolonisation process in much of Africa had developed full momentum. It took until the 1980s for measures to induce policy change in South Africa, such as sanctions, to be more widely discussed in Western countries. The reasons for this reluctance go beyond commercial interests and the Cold War climate in which the South African government was seen as an ally against communism. It has its roots in an underlying supremacism and racism that could not even consider that a black majority might be democratically elected and govern a white minority, which was the likely outcome if equal suffrage was granted (as indeed happened in 1994). The benign-sounding official justification of apartheid, namely that people of different cultures could not live together democratically and thus needed to be separated, was only too plausible for many 'Northern' observers.

This had been, as mentioned before (Chapter 1), the main justification for creating separate, supposedly cultural-linguistically homogeneous nation states in Europe. By the late 1940s, the experience of two world wars and totalitarianism had taught Europeans that antagonistic and aggressive nationalism could have catastrophic consequences, but they did not for that reason abandon the national commitment. Rather, they toned it down, combined it with a liberal-democratic commitment, which had been weak or absent in some of the pre-Second World War European interpretations of modernity, and systematically developed the social commitment of the state to care for the welfare of all citizens 'from cradle to grave', as the Beveridge report to the British Government put it in 1942.[12] This combination of commitments became known as the liberal-democratic Keynesian welfare and nation state. By the 1960s, it was hailed as a model even to be emulated by the US, otherwise mostly seen as more advanced and more 'modern', in its 'Great Society' and 'War on Poverty' programmes.

Without denying its accomplishments, several remarks on this 'model' need to be added. First, it was elaborated unevenly across

Western Europe,[13] with the Scandinavian societies coming closest to the model, while southern European societies remained or fell (Greece, from 1967 to 1974) under dictatorships and/or showed enormous regional disparities, most pronounced in Italy. Second, even the formal democracies were not as liberal as proclaimed, banning communist parties or excluding them from access to power and organising public broadcasting media under state supervision. Third, and most importantly from our angle, these societies continued to forge external relations through a combination of economic asymmetry – as described earlier (Chapter 2), but at a higher level of industrialisation – and restrictions to movements of people. Thus, they aimed to maintain a situation of economic superiority even after the end of colonialism, which allowed them to develop their social commitment (more detail on this in Chapter 5).

If South Africa was an increasingly sharply divided, highly inegalitarian society and Europe showed strongly inclusive and rather egalitarian features, Brazil occupied a middle position in several respects. Strong emphasis was placed on forging a new nation that, in principle, included all Brazilians, marking a strong contrast with apartheid South Africa. 'National development' became the main tool through which national integration was to be achieved. At the same time, Brazil persistently maintained high levels of inequality, among the highest in the world together with South Africa (for more detail, see Chapter 7). This indicated that the proclaimed development could not occur in more egalitarian ways without overcoming structures of hierarchy and privilege. Welfare measures remained largely restricted to workers in formal employment and their families. Finally, Brazil after 1945 was a democracy that, even though it maintained suffrage restrictions, did not exclude a majority of the population from political participation like South Africa did. This also entailed that there was a dynamism of political debate that permitted claims to be voiced and, to some extent, to be transformed into government policies. When this dynamism risked challenging elite privileges, a military *coup d'état* intervened (as briefly discussed in Chapter 4).

NOT 'WORLDS' APART

This chapter has tried to show how the varieties of ways into which the interpretative components that were proposed and elaborated in the course of earlier history sedimented into spatially circumscribed interpretations of modernity that had a determined institutional reach. Such processes of sedimentation or consolidation started in the late nineteenth century and continued through struggles and trials to which the wars of the twentieth century, from the South African War onwards, give testimony. By 1960, these interpretations of modernity all appear relatively consolidated, even though ridden with internal tensions that are only temporarily alleviated, to a considerable degree indeed suppressed.

The 'success' of political consolidation was certainly conditioned by rather extended periods of economic boom in all three regions during the post-war period. As we have shown, such political consolidation occurred in highly diverse terms: through limited inclusion under conditions of vote-restricted democracy and neglect of the excluded in Brazil; through racialised inclusion with oppression of the excluded in South Africa, increasingly justified as 'separate development'; and through full 'domestic' inclusion under democratic conditions in Europe, actually fostered by decolonisation, which soon permitted the avoidance of responsibility for colonial domination, and European integration.

At the time, this perception of relative consolidation led to the notion of a well-ordered global constellation, captured by the imagery of the 'three worlds'. As Brazil and South Africa did not belong to the First World of liberal-democratic capitalism, nor to the Second World of existing socialism, they were often considered to be part of the Third World that was undergoing processes of 'modernisation and development'. However, our sketch of their trajectories and snapshot image of their situation at around 1960, in comparison with Europe, should have served to overcome facile contrasts between a First and a Third World, or between modernity and tradition, which were prevalent at the time and the echoes of which are still strong. 'Apartheid' and 'racial democracy', among other terms, were certainly ideological concepts as well as, in particular the former, instruments of power and coercion. But they also provided imaginaries of socio-political organisation that shaped the attitudes and actions of elites in both societies and underpinned the emergence of highly specific interpretations of modernity.

And interpretations of modernity they are. Asking a white South African or an upper-class Brazilian at that time, they may have pointed to problems in their societies, but they are unlikely to have considered them as parts of a Third World. The 1960s were the 'age of the great programmes' (Wittrock and Lindström 1984), and Brazil and South Africa fully participated in the technocratic optimism of the period. We may just point out, as examples, the easily recognisable versions of 'high modernity' in Brazil and South Africa, such as the project of building an entirely new capital city, Brasilia, inaugurated in 1960, a project that was simultaneously a symbol of national integration and of state capacity, or the quality of the top institutions in 'white' South Africa having enabled the first heart transplant in human history to be performed at Groote Schuur Hospital in Cape Town in 1967.

We have shown that the Brazilian and South African interpretations of modernity deviated from their European counterparts, but they were at least as self-consciously, explicitly and also conflictively argued as the latter. Furthermore, the three regions were interconnected to such a degree that both similarities and differences reflected to some extent the particular position in a common global context. All three interpretations achieved some degree of consolidation by 1960, but they were all also ridden with tensions, even though rather different ones. These tensions came fully to the fore from the 1960s onwards through critique and contestation, which again reflected both the specific interpretation of modernity of each case as well as their location in the global context.

Chapter 4

TRANSFORMATIONS OF MODERNITY
THROUGH CRITIQUE AND CONTESTATION

Halfway through the fourth volume of his monumental tetralogy on two centuries of world history, historian Eric Hobsbawm unexpectedly used an extraordinary phrase when he characterised the period between 1945 and 1990 as 'the greatest and most dramatic, rapid and universal social transformation in human history' (Hobsbawm 1994: 288). This assertion was surprising then, given that there was no strikingly signifi-cant event during the period from the end of the Second World War to the end of the Cold War, with the exception of decolonisation in Africa, that would immediately have supported it. Most observers at the time rather underlined the enormous stability of the post-Second World War period, as captured by the widespread use of the three-worlds image: a First World of liberal-democratic capitalism, a Second World of Soviet-style socialism; and a Third World of underdeveloped countries. This imagery was sociologically conceptualised from the First-World point of view as oneself having reached modernity, the status of 'modern society'; the Second World constituting a deliberate and organised deviation but with trends of convergence between those two worlds; and the Third World still needing to undergo processes of 'modernisa-tion and development'. In the preceding chapter, we have modified this view by rejecting any linear or dichotomous view of historical evolution and underlining the coexistence of a variety of world-regional interpre-tations of modernity. But we also suggested that these interpretations in their variety were relatively consolidated by 1960. What, then, about Hobsbawm's strong assertion of major social change?

To make his claim, Hobsbawm indeed did not single out any moment of rupture. Instead, he added up speedy but gradual processes of a consid-erable range, such as the decline of agricultural employment, urbanisation, global shifts in the location of industry, rising enrolments in higher education and the increasing participation of women in extra-domestic, paid work and in public life in general. While all these observations are highly important, another quarter of a century has passed since Hobsbawm wrote, and the changes to which he referred have already moved some distance from the present. We have become accustomed to them, and his assertion sounds today even less self-evident than at the moment when he wrote.

Nevertheless we suggest that Hobsbawm grasped a transformation of global significance, even though he did not fully succeed in providing the adequate focus on it. From our angle, what happened during the second half of the twentieth century, in particular from the 1960s onwards, was a far-reaching transformation of modernity in an unpredictable direction. This transformation was not a straightforward move from a 'simple' to a 'reflexive' modernity or from a spatially contained to a global modernity, or from rationalisation to subjectivation, as much sociological debate during the 1980s and 1990s had it (for example, in Beck 1986; Giddens 1990; Touraine 1992). Rather, it was the outcome of a reinterpretation of modernity against the background of the relatively consolidated versions of modernity that existed in different world-regions, of which we described three in the preceding chapter. Given the differences between the existing varieties of modernity, the work of reinterpretation necessarily proceeded in different ways, addressing the specific forms of incoherence and underlining the unresolved tensions in the respective locally prevailing interpretations of modernity. At the same time, given the degree of global interconnectedness in the late twentieth century, there were elements of a common constellation, to some extent underlined during the work of reinterpretation itself, to some extent emerging in its aftermath.

This chapter is devoted to analysing the reinterpretations of modernity from the 1960s onwards in Brazil, South Africa and Europe with a view to showing both their differences and commonalities. The accent will be placed on the kind of political change that is seen as necessary and desirable in the three world-regions and the form of collective action, if any, that is necessary for bringing the political change about. It is in the course of these reinterpretations that the currently dominant contours of modernity and the current conditions for political transformation are brought about, which we will explore in the subsequent parts of this book.

THREE CRISES OF ORGANISED MODERNITY

During the early 1960s, the Brazilian government headed by President João Goulart was rather well aware of the fault lines in the prevailing interpretation of modernity and willing to address them. For instance, it proposed measures to provide access to land for landless people in the rural regions and to abolish the literacy restrictions to political participation. Together, these two measures would have hit the prevailing forms of exclusion at the core, mitigating both the socio-economic and the political exclusion of large parts of the rural population. At the same time, though, these measures would have put the benefits of those included at risk, in particular the large landowners, but also the urban middle classes who benefitted from the privileges that came with formal employment. The unsettling of the existing arrangement created political tensions that led to the military *coup d'état* in 1964 (which was actually predicted by one sociological observer; see Santos 1962). Even though government under military control was initially conceived as short-lasting, it persisted until 1985, alternating more liberal periods with highly repressive ones, including the torture and killing of resisters. While accompanied by economic growth, the military government could keep relying on the support of those groups in society who reaped benefits from the prevailing interpretation of modernity. But in parallel, resistance to the regime also grew, reaching a first high point with student protests in 1968 and a second one with workers' strikes in 1978, in which future president Luiz Inácio (Lula) da Silva was involved as a leader.

In contrast to Brazil, which despite the restrictions had democratic institutions up to the military coup, South Africa's apartheid regime was a representative 'democracy' working only for the white minority, which dominated over the non-white majority. The difference in the form of domination notwithstanding, the contestation of the prevailing interpretation of modernity in South Africa as well as its temporary persistence can be analysed in parallel to the Brazilian developments.

During the 1950s, resistance to the apartheid regime was increasingly organised by the ANC, the passing of the Freedom Charter in 1955 being a core mobilising event. With its claim that 'South Africa belongs to all who live in it, black and white, and that no government can justly claim authority unless it is based on the will of the people', the Charter drew on the democratic political imaginary and squarely questioned the legitimacy of the apartheid regime. In parallel, socio-economic changes, not least the increasing role of manufacturing relative to mining and agriculture, also led to diverging interests among the dominant groups, with industrialists starting to advocate the integration of the black working class through education, social security and higher wages. In turn, the relatively conciliatory approach of the ANC came increasingly to be criticised, first by its own Youth League and from 1959 by the Pan-Africanist Congress (PAC), which was more in tune with the Africanist decolonisation movements in other parts of Africa. It was indeed this context of decolonisation that changed the political situation in South Africa.

Rather than accommodate the ANC's demands for equal freedom, the regime resorted to both radically increased repression and more explicit justification. A peaceful demonstration of the PAC in 1960, later to be known as the Sharpeville Massacre, was dissolved by the police killing sixty-nine people and injuring over 180, including many women and children, mostly through gunshots and many of them in the back. Rather than opening up to the claims of the protesters, the apartheid regime founded the Republic of South Africa to maintain its policy of racial segregation and domination and subsequently left the British Commonwealth to avoid being excluded from it (post-apartheid South Africa re-joined in 1994). From the Rivonia trial of 1964 and the subsequent imprisonment of leading ANC members to the Soweto killings in 1976 and 1977, repressive measures became increasingly violent and intolerant of every expression of dissent and discontent, on the one hand. On the other hand, the regime strove to enhance its legitimacy and its techniques of social management. In 1961, South African Prime Minister Hendrik Frensch Verwoerd claimed in London that 'we want each of our population groups to control and govern themselves, as is the case with other Nations' (cited in Thompson 2001: 215), suggesting that apartheid was based as much on the democratic political imaginary as Britain. Rather than signalling exclusion, oppression and exploitation, this meant that apartheid should be seen as standing for 'separate development'.

In Western Europe, the period around 1960 was seen as a moment of stabilisation and consolidation.[1] Rapid economic growth, due to postwar reconstruction needs and Marshall Plan aid, was managed with the support of Keynesian demand management. Part of tax revenue was used to finance the extension of the welfare state, in particular by raising pensions and improving public health and education. In some countries, such as Italy and West Germany, there was talk of an 'economic miracle'. Political participation was based on egalitarian-inclusive liberal democracy, while at the same time geared towards 'civic apathy' (a term coined by Almond and Verba 1963). A return to inter-war political mobilisation was to be avoided, and radical political parties were either banned, as in West Germany, or marginalised, as in France and Italy.[2]

Thus, the widespread emergence of protest action by students and workers at the end of the 1960s came as a surprise. It came later than mobilisations in Latin America and decolonisation struggles in Africa, but at least for the students it had a global component, assuming these movements would seize the torch of world-historical revolution after the workers' movement of the First World had dropped it, and thus should be supported. Domestic concerns were dominant, however, as varied as they were. One key component was the revolt against conformism and alienation in 'mass society' with its standardised life-courses, including the homogenisation of world views in 'one-dimensional society' (Herbert Marcuse) and the imposition of discipline at work (Boltanski and Chiapello 1999). Another one was the struggle for full equal rights for women and the recognition of the right to divorce and to abortion.

In these then so-called advanced industrial democracies, the contestations were diagnosed as leading to 'legitimacy problems' by critical thinkers (Habermas 1973) and to a 'crisis of governability' by observers more concerned with stability (Crozier et al. 1975). The former placed the focus on trends in 'late capitalism' that escaped the grip of governments, whereas the latter diagnosed unrest in society that made government difficult (for the connection between the two issues, see Chapter 5). Both, though, agreed on the identification of the key background condition, namely the fact that the contestations took place in a context of full inclusion and equal freedom. This condition allowed the contestations to arise in this form in the first place; it prohibited their straightforward repression; and additionally it made it difficult to find remedies, as such remedies needed to find voters' support.

Such diagnoses could not be very persuasive in either South Africa or Brazil, even though for somewhat different reasons. In hindsight, the political inclusion of non-white South Africans stands out as the key achievement of the struggle against apartheid. During the struggle, in contrast, many protest actions were directed against non-whites receiving lower wages and being subject to worse working conditions than white workers as well as lower-quality provisions of housing, education and healthcare. Equal freedom of political participation was certainly a key objective in its own right, but it was also seen as a means to achieve full socio-economic inclusion. The apartheid regime, with its political support in the white population, was not inclined to pursue policies very far in that direction, since this would mean endangering the privileges and the lifestyle of its supporters. Given political exclusion, further-more, the demands could not be voiced from within existing political institutions; they needed to take the form of strikes, boycotts and other protests. For the same reason, they could also not be denied within these political institutions; if they persisted, they would be repressed by violence. In this constellation, a change of political regime entailing free and equal participation of all South Africans became the common denominator of the protests. If one wanted to use the 'Northern' terms of crisis of governability and legitimacy, one would need to immediately recognise that this crisis was much stronger than in Europe and needed to find a more radical response in a regime change.

In Brazil, the initial situation during the early 1960s had some simi-larity to the European one, given that a democratic condition existed that despite its limitations did not work with an institutionally exclu-sionary system based on the categorisation of persons. Thus, it is pos-sible to argue that the Goulart presidency tried to overcome profound legitimacy problems by addressing concerns of large socially and/or politically excluded groups. One can also suggest, though with a sta-bility-oriented undertone, that the intended measures led to a crisis of governability. But here the 'resolution' of the crisis through the military coup meant a regressive regime change that suspended the restricted democracy that already existed.[3] As a consequence, the regime change that was demanded in subsequent contestations was first of all a return to democracy. In the light of the experience of reforms that failed because they were interrupted by the *coup d'état*, furthermore, the con-testations were aiming not just at a return to the kind of democracy that had already existed. Rather, they were claiming a democracy that would abolish the earlier restrictions and become fully inclusive, and would provide means so as not to succumb to authoritarian regression again.

LEGITIMACY AND EFFICIENCY

Staying for a moment with the question of legitimacy, we might say that European polities encountered 'legitimacy problems' because they were not performing well enough and, additionally, because they were not enhancing the kind of society that was wished for. The Brazilian and South African polities were also contested because they were not sufficiently performing, but their lack of capacity could be – and was – immediately connected with the fact of political restrictions and exclusions. Given their state structures, it could be assumed that policy action was not intended to address concerns of the whole population, but only of those parts of the population on whose support the political class depended. In inclusive democracies this would need to be (some form of) majority support; in less-than-inclusive democracies such support is highly socially pre-structured.

During the period under consideration, one started to reason about this issue by introducing distinctions between forms of legitimacy. On the one hand, democratic legitimacy required explicit support for policy measures expressed through the vote of the citizenry. On the other hand, legitimacy through efficiency could be gained through policy measures that won the support of the population because they provided benefits, regardless of whether they were explicitly wanted.

Many aspects of the attempt at gaining legitimacy through efficiency were shared throughout the three regions. First, as mentioned earlier (Chapter 3), a general techno-scientific optimism prevailed during that period, assuming that technical solutions to many problems could and would be found. Manned space exploration and supersonic air travel were outstanding examples, but the complete rebuilding of a major capital city, the case of Brasilia, or the replacement of a sick human heart by a healthy one, are examples of the same attitude. By implication, this approach assumed that elites know better than the wider population. Technocratic expertise was deemed to be superior to democratic will-formation.

Second, the main way of garnering support for technocratic policy-making was to make the benefits available to the population, or at least that part of the population on whose support elites depended. This could best be demonstrated by securing economic growth and by distributing a part of the increased wealth across society. The main features of the economy were deemed to be controllable, even though more securely in the North, by applying Keynesian demand management. Partial redistribution occurred through taxation and the use of the tax revenues for improving public services such as infrastructure, education and health. For the North, one spoke during this period about a connection between 'welfare state and mass loyalty' (Narr and Offe 1975). Despite the critical undertone, this term suggests that there was a link between elites and majority populations in the North, a kind of contract or compromise that served both sides. In the South, both in Brazil and in South Africa, a rise in public expenditure preceded the democratisation of state structures. It meant two things: on the one hand, the state became present in very repressive forms in many areas and places without the establishment of a political link between the polity and institutions; on the other hand, it meant no creation of political loyalty between the state and the new urban masses.

Thus, for the South, the situation is more complex. In those more dependent economies, control of economic development was more difficult to achieve, even though import substitution policies were widely applied to increase the stability of the domestic economy during some periods. Furthermore, parts of the economic elites fared better producing for exportation rather than catering to domestic demand. Thus, there was no general elite commitment to societal 'development' (for Brazil, see Paulani 2016). Finally, in as far as elites in the South also depended on 'loyalty', this loyalty was required only from those who were enfranchised as citizens, the white-skinned population in South Africa and the formal, mostly urban workers and employees in Brazil. These were minorities in societal terms, not majoritarian 'masses', and they were the only ones whose legitimation seemed to be needed.

In general, the reinterpretation of legitimacy as being based on government efficiency rather than will-formation provided a new expression for the suspicion of democracy that has been widespread throughout the nineteenth and the first half of the twentieth century. In Europe, this reinterpretation was set into a context of inclusive democracy, and thus efficiency needed to be acknowledged and ratified by the citizenry. In the Southern societies with restricted political participation, elitist political reasoning could be voiced more bluntly. Looking back at the 1960s, Brazilian political scientist Boris Fausto (1999: 284–5) writes from a conservative point of view that: 'an authoritarian regime made the government's actions easier. In order to work, any stabilisation plan depended on sacrifices from society. Given the characteristics of Brazilian society and the narrow vision of the political actors, this was hard to bring about in democratic circumstances.' And H. F. Verwoerd, after he had suggested his government was working for the self-determination of the African nations, added in the speech already quoted earlier: 'in the transition stage the guardian must teach and guide his ward'.[4] In this terminology, the restriction of political participation was the answer to the problem of adequate and effective political action.

THE FAILURE OF TECHNOCRACY-CUM-OPPRESSION AND
THE RISE OF CONTESTATION

By the 1980s, the attempt at replacing democratic legitimacy by efficiency had clearly failed. Even though political thinkers argued ever
more forcefully that efficiency as such can provide legitimacy,[5] it became
clear that, on the one hand, governments under given circumstances
were losing the means to secure policy efficiency and security and, on
the other, that such accomplishments, even when they existed, could
not fully replace other substantive concerns. In South Africa, the technocratic intensification of apartheid could not succeed in masking the
denial of collective self-determination and full socio-economic inclusion. In Brazil, the claim to higher efficiency of an authoritarian government was not fulfilled. Economic crises led to dissatisfaction even
among the included groups in society. In both societies, furthermore,
the intensification of oppression through police and military measures
further eroded the legitimacy of the regimes.

If analysed from a policy perspective, both the attempts at implementing and reinforcing apartheid up to the 1970s and those of reform-
ing and moderating it from the late 1970s onwards 'failed' in very much
the same way in which expanded welfare state policies failed in Europe
and the US and were critically analysed as such (Wittrock 1983; see
Wagner et al. 1990 for an overview). However, South African society
experienced legitimacy and governability problems in the presence of a
forceful collective counter-project, most clearly embodied by the ANC
and the United Democratic Front (formed in 1983), which was powerful enough to undermine policy capacity but not in the institutional
position to design state policies. In Brazil, a variety of social movements
with quite different substantive concerns and objectives, reaching from
workers' issues to health and the environment, but all aiming at democratising the society, arose under the military dictatorship and spread
further after its end. Taken together, these movements could also be
interpreted as outlining a project of larger societal transformation. The
Workers' Party (PT) came to be the agency within the framework of which
the contours of this collective project were sharpened (the role of social
movements and other forms of collective action is discussed in more
detail in Chapter 10). Thus, the signs of crisis and failure in Brazil and
South Africa did not lead to conclusions about collective agency in general, of state, nation or class, but in the first instance to conclusions about
the inadequacy of the existing, elite-based institutional arrangements

to exercise planned social change in and on a society which they could 'represent' neither in political nor in interpretative terms.

In other words, while Europe, Brazil and South Africa may all be said to have undergone a democratic crisis during the 1970s and 1980s, this crisis was interpreted in highly different terms in each region. In Europe, the limits of existing democracies were tested by movements of contestation, and calls for further 'democratisation' were made to overcome these limits. However, the medium-term response was a transformation of political and economic arrangements such that performance expectations were lowered. The arguments about the decline of the nation state and the crisis of the welfare state provided exactly this: reasons why governments and the economy should not be overburdened with (democratic) demands they cannot fulfil.[6] As a consequence, after a decade or so of rich and vivid debates, rather than further democratisation, a lower-intensity democracy emerged in which citizen disaffection was pronounced but usually remained rather inconsequential. In South Africa and Brazil, in turn, the fact that the ANC and its allies as well as the PT and the social movements were offering a programmatic alternative to the apartheid and military regimes but were deprived of any possibility of implementing it raised high expectations for the moment at which this situation would change. Here, inclusive democracy was claimed in a non-democratic setting, and its advent was therefore seen as the very beginning of the exercise of collective self-determination in these societies. Political change towards collective autonomy was the precondition for general social change.

With the adoption of free and equal universal suffrage, South Africa moved towards inclusive democracy, and the 1994 election victory of the ANC-based alliance confirmed the expectation that such constitutional change would lead to radical political change due to the sudden enfranchisement of the majority of the population. South Africa is one of very few cases in which such radical political transformation occurred in a society with a world market competitive economy, an efficient central state apparatus and other institutions that are commonly referred to as key characteristics of 'modern societies'. This transformation – utterly unexpected even shortly before it occurred – is often considered a 'miracle', both because of the presumed unwillingness of a long-term successful elite to relinquish power and because of the presumed inability of a majority-based opposition without experience of administering 'functional' institutions to suddenly take power. Possibly the closest comparison in those terms is the transformation of authoritarian and oppressive Imperial Germany into one of the most participatory and most socially committed democracies of the time within a few weeks in the winter of 1918/19, leading initially to electoral majorities committed to socialism. The Weimar Republic, though, would witness the rise of Nazism in the wake of the worldwide economic crisis of 1929 and it collapsed with Hitler coming to power in 1933, after only fourteen years of existence. In contrast, the ANC-based alliance has been re-elected in all national elections until today and has embarked on a profound, even though increasingly contested, social transformation of South African society.

In Brazil, the transition was more gradual but had similar features. The constitution of 1988 also introduced free and equal universal suffrage, but the preceding exclusion had been less strong in quantitative terms and had not been based on racial categories. There was initially no radical exchange of political elites but some continuity from pre-military government times. The major changes at the beginning were the rather full commitment of Brazilian society to egalitarian-inclusive democracy, as signalled by intense election campaigns and high voter turnouts, on the one hand, and the recuperation of a space of critique and contestation that had been curtailed during two decades of military rule, on the other. After a few years of government instability, the presidency of the sociologist Fernando Henrique Cardoso (1994–2002) was marked by a moderate conservative reformism, including not least fiscal-economic policies that led to greater integration into world markets and steps towards widening social-policy commitments. However, his agenda of state austerity led to very low levels of state social commitment – an agenda of social inclusion was not developed during his government. The step that makes 'post-transition' Brazil more similar to South Africa is taken with the election of Lula to the presidency in 2002, after three attempts that showed high mobilisation but ultimately failed, in 1989, 1994 and 1998. Lula was confirmed in office in 2006 and was succeeded by Dilma Rousseff, also from the PT and a former minister in Lula's government, in 2010, re-elected in 2014 but impeached in 2016. The period from 2002 to 2016 is a period of pronounced social transformation in Brazil, not unlike the one in South Africa (to be discussed in detail in the subsequent chapters).

A GLOBAL SHIFT IN DISCOURSE AND ITS DIFFERENT
WORLD–REGIONAL IMPLICATIONS

The political events in Brazil and South Africa can be set in the broader context of, regionally, the success of the anti-colonial movements in Africa and the strengthening of political contestation of oligarchic rule in Latin America. Even though these movements faced strong elite opposition, going as far as military *coups d'état* in Brazil, Chile and elsewhere and the violent oppression of anti-apartheid protest in South Africa, by the end of the 1980s their success was on the horizon. We can thus suggest that a novel interpretation of modernity is being elaborated in American and African societies, featuring inclusive-egalitarian democracy, often with a high intensity of participation, and facing the legacy of high social inequality and, more generally, a hiatus between the elite perception of societal self-understanding and the living conditions of the majority of the population.

In more general, global terms, the whole period from the end of the 1960s to the beginning of the 1990s is an era of major social contestation and of subsequent political transformations. Remaining cautious with over-generalisation, we can analyse this period as the exit from the varieties of organised modernity that existed in the various world-regions. We use the term 'exit' for two reasons: first, because no 'entry' into a new interpretation of modernity can be outlined (yet) with clear contours; and second, because the reinterpretations of modernity may continue to differ considerably across world-regions, given the different conditions at the outset of this transformation. Having said this, we shall now briefly delineate these contours as far as this seems reasonably possible.

The current constellation of modernity did not evolve smoothly from the preceding organised modernity; its emergence was not driven by any logic of capital nor by linear progress towards greater individualisation and inclusion. Rather, the organised modernity of the 1960s was actively contested and exposed to critique, on a number of fronts and often in radical ways 'from below'. In what was then called the Third World, movements for national liberation called for decolonisation and collective self-determination, these struggles reaching a high point around 1960. In what was then called the First World, the year 1968 marked a climax of workers' and students' contestation, often seen as the combination of a political and cultural revolution of which the latter aspect would become dominant. In the wake of 1968, time-honoured issues were returned to the political agenda, with greater force and urgency, by the feminist movement and the ecological movement. During the later twentieth century, new movements of the poor and excluded emerged in response to the consequences of global economic-financial restructuring. Where democracy had been abolished by military regimes, these movements merged with movements for the restoration of liberty and democracy. And where exclusion and oppression had a marked ethnic/racial component, contestations centred on political and cultural claims for self-determination.

These contestations, in their sum, played a considerable part in what we now recognise as the dismantling of organised modernity. Decolonisation dismantled (most of) what had remained of the empires. The women's movement achieved – in many, though not all societies – the abolition of remainders of patriarchal law. Restrictions to information and expression were lifted, partly enabled by new technologies. Party structures, which political scientists thought of as mirroring lasting social divides, crumbled partly because of the formation of movement-parties, partly because of a blurring of those social divides. In other words, and again in very sweeping terms, these contestations proved highly successful, to the degree of bringing about a pronounced social transformation.

Many of these occurrences can be described in terms of normative achievements, of progress: of recognition, of freedom, of equality. This, precisely, is where the success of contestations can be located. There are two qualifications to be added, however. First, other components of organised modernity were dismantled in parallel, but the normative assessment of these processes is much more ambivalent, to say the least: the capacity of states to direct national economies diminished; commercial and financial flows are increasingly beyond control; the institutional frames for collective self-determination have been weakened, partly deliberately in favour of supra-national or global co-operation, partly because of an escape of socio-political phenomena from the view and grasp of political institutions.

Second, one can probably say that any socio-political transformation entails the dismantling of existing institutions, but that this dismantling is often accompanied by building new institutions, or by giving new purpose and meaning to existing institutional containers. The transformation from restricted liberal to organised modernity (discussed earlier in Chapter 3) is a strong example of the building of collective institutions to address problems that restricted liberal modernity had created. The contestations of organised modernity, however, have often had the oppressive, exploiting or excluding nature of existing institutions as their target, and have therefore been aiming at de-institutionalisation in the first place. As a largely unintended side-effect, this orientation has tended to incapacitate collective action: on the one hand, because specific existing institutions are weakened, and on the other, because institutional rebuilding in general is delegitimised in the name of some generic concept of equal individual freedom.

Over the long run, such contestations have been increasing and increasingly successful, even though in some settings they were initially brutally suppressed. Despite initial similarities as well as emerging ties of solidarity, furthermore, these movements of contestation acquired specific forms in the different regions. For our purposes, in particular, we can observe an emerging contrast between Europe, on the one hand, and Brazil and South Africa, on the other. In Europe, the post-1968 'cultural' (rather than 'political') revolution had predominantly 'individualising' effects. Critique and protest effectively challenged restrictive rules and conventions, most explicitly in terms of gender relations and public media. But they also dismantled the capacity for collective action. As Italian historian Luisa Passerini (1996) puts it in her study of '1968' in Turin, in 1968 the question of power was put in abeyance in Western Europe. In Brazil and in South Africa, in contrast, the 1960s saw the emergence of 'collectivising' political projects born in resistance to military dictatorship and apartheid repression, respectively. In both cases, institutional transformation has led to temporarily rather stable political majorities committed to transformative collective action. In Europe, significantly, one rather speaks about 'citizen disaffection' – a topic further discussed in Chapter 10. All that appears to remain of a collective project is European integration with the redefinition of the (enlarged) European Union since the early 1990s. This was clearly a response to the weakening of the capacity of the nation state. However, the political character of the new polity, the EU, created over and above the nation states, was defined hesitantly and incoherently and remains contested in the current crises.

Returning to Eric Hobsbawm, what do our observations now allow us to say about recent socio-political changes across the globe? Have we witnessed a 'most dramatic universal social transformation'? We are inclined to say yes, but not exactly for the reasons given by Hobsbawm.

The core of the recent transformation is something like the full 'entrance of the masses' into socio-political organisation. It has by now become extremely difficult for elites of all kinds to justify the exclusion of members of societies from participation in social and political institutions. Furthermore, their inclusion increasingly has to be provided on formally equal grounds. And in contrast to the period at the beginning of the twentieth century, this 'entrance' no longer occurs in the form of collective action by politically organised 'masses' but increasingly of particular human beings with their diversity of experiences and aspirations. The subsequent chapters will retrace key aspects of this change and will analyse the consequences of this event for socio-political organisation. Importantly, as may be anticipated, this event should not be confused with the arrival of democracy in the full sense of political requirements as outlined in Chapter 1. Under current conditions, rather, collective action faces new, and in many respects unprecedented, obstacles in bringing about positive political change.

Part II

Freedom, Equality, Solidarity

Chapter 5

DEMOCRACY AND CAPITALISM

In the preceding chapter we discussed how the different forms of 'organised modernity' that existed in the North and the South were dismantled through contestation and protest between the 1960s and the 1980s. We placed the emphasis there on political aspects, in particular the rise to hegemony of a certain discourse of human rights and democracy. In this chapter we build on these observations but widen the focus: we now ask how the articulation between the polity and the economy changed in the course of the dismantling of organised modernity.

As seen earlier, the core of the reasoning about legitimating political regimes through efficiency was the capacity to first promote economic growth and then distribute a part of the benefits from this growth to wider society. This reasoning presumed that the state had some grip on the economy, even under capitalist conditions, and that the surplus to be distributed was sufficient to secure the loyalty of the majority of the electorate. Around 1960, there was widespread agreement that a lastingly harmonious relation between the democratic polity and the capitalist economy had thus been achieved in the West. The rise of industrial society with the large corporation and standardised mass production, so it was assumed, had transformed capitalism. The crisis-prone arrangement of market capitalism with periodic recessions due to competition and class struggle had supposedly given way to 'modern capitalism' (Shonfield 1966), which reached stability and growth through organisation and co-operation. Furthermore, due to functional requirements, the viability of this model would not remain limited to the West. There would even be convergence between Western capitalism and Soviet socialism; and 'Third World' countries would embark on trajectories of 'national development' guided by 'developmental states' rather than by market forces. The rather high growth rates of the period, with variation across regions, seemed to confirm these assumptions.

For our purposes here, and as will become important as we proceed, we have to keep in mind that this reasoning was based on notions of functionality, which is what made it apparently equally applicable to rather inclusive representative democracies; to 'people's democracies' with a state-run economy and limited freedom of expression; and to segregated democracies with limited inclusion such as Brazil and South Africa. The capacity of these regimes to efficiently secure growth and distribution was the primary concern. If this was the case, then 'mass loyalty' was likely to follow, but in characteristically different ways, namely majority electoral support for the regime in the so-called advanced democracies; majority consent combined with oppression of dissidence in Soviet socialism; and electoral support among the included part of the population in segregated democracies. Or in other words, the political form had to be adapted to the functioning of an industrial economy in this reasoning, not the other way round.

This was the prevailing interpretation of the politico-economic constellation during the 1960s. In one sense, it seems very far from our current situation; in another sense, very close. It seems far because the notions of organisation and co-operation have given way again to ideas of self-regulation of markets, associated with the terms neo-liberalism and globalisation. But it appears close in its subordination of political possibilities to economic requirements. There is a broad consensus today that we have entered a new phase of capitalism since the 1980s. To emphasise the inherent logics of an industrial-capitalist-market economy, however, as is often done, entails downplaying the impact of other social phenomena on economic developments. From our historico-sociological perspective, we maintain that this is an erroneous interpretation of politico-economic transformations. Furthermore, such one-sided emphasis is problematic in a context in which 'the economy' is marked by dysfunctions, generating crises, poverty, inequality, unemployment and the devastation of the earth, and in which calls for political action to put the economy back on a societally beneficial track are widely voiced. After all, we supposedly live in an era of 'democratisation'; and if democracy means collective self-determination, it should be possible, in principle, to regulate economic action with a view to collective benefit.

This chapter aims to analyse the current relation between the polity and the economy, or more concretely, between democracy and

capitalism in Brazil, South Africa and Europe aiming at both understanding the specificities of the regional constellations and the interconnectedness between the regions. It will start out from observations
on a recent turn in the European – or 'Northern' – analysis of capitalism away from political considerations and back towards an emphasis
on the economy alone (section 1). A critical discussion of this shift
shows that its limitations arise through its temporally and spatially
confined perspective. As a remedy, a longer-term historical perspective shows how democracy transformed capitalism (2); and a global
perspective demonstrates how the current weakening of European
democracy was enabled by spatial displacements of production (3).
These displacements, however, do not have the same political consequences across the globe. Looking at the examples of Brazil and
South Africa, it will be shown how vibrant democracy could coexist
with current capitalism under certain conditions (4). These observations allow a more systematic comparison of the relations between
democracy and capitalism today (5).

FROM VARIETIES OF CAPITALISM BACK TO THE
LOGIC OF CAPITAL

Until the late 1980s the question of whether there is an alternative to
capitalism has been a central concern of critical analysis throughout the
globe. Theories of dependency in Latin America and reflections on the
link between capitalism and apartheid in South Africa were part of this
debate.[1] The collapse of existing socialism, however, seemed to confirm
Margaret Thatcher's provocative claim that 'there is no alternative'. An
important focus of discussion then became the idea that, in the apparent absence of alternatives, there might at least be 'varieties of capitalism', some of them distinguishable from one another also in normative
terms. The phrase belongs to David Soskice, but the idea is found in
many accounts of the 1990s (Crouch and Streeck 1997; Albert 1998;
Hall and Soskice 2001; later: Amable 2005).[2] A distinction was repeat-
edly made between the 'organised' welfare capitalism in continental
Europe, especially Germany, and the liberal market capitalism of the
Anglo-Saxon kind.

Within this debate, Peter A. Hall and David Soskice directly addressed
the question of whether the variety of capitalisms could be maintained
under conditions of globalisation. Their provisional answer was that
it could. Such optimism has since largely disappeared in the North.

To give just one example: Wolfgang Streeck was one of the protagonists in the debate about sustainable alternatives within capitalism as
well as a champion of 'the German model', characterised by strong and
intelligent trade unions, a successful export-oriented economy and a
political landscape in which social democracy, though not always participating in government, remained ideologically largely hegemonic
and in which neo-liberalism was marginal. But since then Streeck has
developed a perspective on capitalism which remains conceptually
open but in which, empirically, he only recognises the forward march of
neo-liberalism with its individualistic-instrumental emphasis on profit
and greed, and in which other social bonds, institutional forms and
normative orientations have disappeared and are unlikely to return –
just as Marx and Engels had it in *The Communist Manifesto* of 1848
(Streeck 2011a; 2012; 2013).

What is significant for present purposes is that Streeck's analysis
is accompanied by observations about the weakening of democracy
as a consequence of the transformation of capitalism. The connection
is made in two steps: the capitalism of the post-Second World War
period, called 'democratic capitalism' (Streeck 2011b), was nationally
organised, with elected national governments taking responsibility
for Keynes-inspired economic steering; it was thus compatible with
democratic expectations. The democratic idea of the sovereignty of the
people identified the sovereign with the nation; this nation in turn
was thought of as a community of responsibility, in which organised
solidarity was an obligation (Wagner and Zimmermann 2003; Karagiannis 2007). However, globalisation and neo-liberalism released the
capitalist economy from the fetters of the nation state, which meant,
in a first step, that governments could no longer meet expectations of
economic regulation and welfare state redistribution. In Europe, the
transfer of competences from elected national governments to central banks and other regulatory agencies such as those of the European Union is an institutional expression of this farewell to democratic
steering. In a second step, as a consequence, citizens turn away from
democracy: because elections do not change anything, participation
is pointless. Falling turnouts or an increase in votes for protest parties
with weak programmes are expressions of this 'disenchantment with
politics' or 'citizen disaffection' (Offe 2009; see already Wagner 1994).
Some analyses assume a fundamental transformation of politics, in
which the democratic element has disappeared and been replaced by
co-operation between oligarchic-technocratic elites (Castoriadis 1997:
64; Crouch 2004).[3]

The transformation of nationally embedded, regulated Keynesian capitalism, based on industry and on standardisation and homogenisation in both production and consumption, into global neo-liberal capitalism, in which services, in particular financial services, creativity and flexibility gain in importance, is accompanied by a political transformation, in the course of which a competitive-party democracy, with a measure of fit between the will of the electorate and national government policy, gives way to a technocratic politics in which political programmes are diluted and in which voters are asked merely to approve measures to which there is no alternative. That at least is the impression given by current academic and political commentary in Europe – and it is hard to deny that European political and economic reality corresponds rather closely to such an image.

To sustain this interpretation, the assumed link between economic and political developments is conceptually crucial because otherwise one would have to ask why, under democratic conditions, there was not a more effective opposition to neo-liberal capitalism. The concept of 'democratic capitalism' suggests, in the first place, that democracy and capitalism are compatible. But the notion of a 'crisis of democratic capitalism' suggests that this compatibility has many preconditions, and cannot be maintained in the long term. It is assumed, quite reasonably, that the latest transformations of capitalism bring with them a transformation of democracy. But here the economic transformation appears as the plain triumph of the ever more effective logic of capital, and the political transformation as nothing other than the weakening or even rejection of democracy.

This account raises more questions than it answers. It is short-sighted in two respects, temporal and spatial. It is historically limited in that it ignores or forgets the origins of the dual transformation. To be sure, there is in Europe a crisis of democratic capitalism, but this is also a democratic crisis of capitalism. That is, the shift from Keynesian to neo-liberal capitalism cannot be explained by the inherent logic of capital; it has to be placed in the context of the political and social demands on the reproduction of capital (see also Hall 2013). Second, the account neglects the fact that the prescribed exit from the crisis has not only spatial consequences – so-called globalisation – but also global presuppositions. In other words, neither was social-democratic Keynesianism an endogenous achievement of north-western Europe, nor can its crisis be understood without referring to worldwide political and economic change. The regional limitation of this account will become especially clear if it can be shown that the relationship between democracy and capitalism is fundamentally different in other parts of the world. In what follows, an attempt will be made to correct the temporal and spatial short-sightedness of such an analysis of capitalism. New questions will then be raised about the challenges facing current democracy and capitalism.

THE DEMOCRATIC CRISIS OF EUROPEAN CAPITALISM: A HISTORICAL PERSPECTIVE

Current analysis concentrates on the decline of democratic capitalism but does not ask if and how capitalism became democratic and what democratic embedding means for the reproduction of capital. Yet across the globe, including most European societies, capitalism developed before the introduction of universal suffrage – if we take this for the moment as a formal criterion for the existence of democracy. Such democracy had been on the political agenda at the end of the eighteenth century as much as free trade and the abolition of serfdom and slavery were, which made possible the expansion of wage labour. In a very broad sense one can say, paraphrasing Habermas, that democracy and capitalism were co-original. But in many countries democracy was introduced only after the First World War. As we saw earlier (Chapter 2), European elites were discussing the introduction of democracy around 1800 but they consciously rejected it. So how does one explain the breakthrough to an egalitarian-democratic idea in the European societies of the early twentieth century?

Capitalism is an economic form with two characteristics that are important for answering this question. First, it is based on the idea – which we have called elsewhere the economic problematic of modernity (Wagner 2008) – that material human needs are best satisfied indirectly, mediated through the interests of producers of commodities on a market (Hirschman 1977). Second, in capitalism there is a distinction between a group of economic subjects who decide over production, and another who are subject to the decisions of the first – for brevity's sake we will adopt established terminology and call them the dominant and dominated classes. For two main reasons this makes probable a discrepancy between economic potential and actual need satisfaction: exploitation in the sense of an appropriation of the products of labour by those who make production decisions; and crises of market self-regulation, which lead to actual production falling short of possible production, or to the destruction of products that remain unsold. The awareness of such a discrepancy leads then to critique (Wagner 1994; Boltanski and Chiapello 1999). Whatever its precise content, critique will be likely to include the demand that all who are affected by this state of affairs should be involved in measures to improve it. When stubborn social problems appear under conditions in which people are excluded from government, egalitarian-inclusive self-determination – democracy – is prima facie a convincing means of tackling the problem in an appropriate way. Such reasoning obviously needs to be made more historically nuanced, but in general terms it allows us to understand the democratic tendencies at work in a capitalist economy.

Nevertheless, the foregoing account only explains the demand for democracy voiced by the dominated class. It does not explain why the dominant class should accede to it. To a certain extent the force of argument may be adduced – under conditions of modernity there is a need for justification (Wagner 2008: chs 12 and 13; Wagner 2012: ch. 7) – but this alone is insufficient. Other conditions must be in place; we can conceptualise them in ways that are compatible with the idea of a 'logic of capital': in historical terms, the dominant class has been tied to the dominated class in two ways: first, industrial production requires a great number of workers who under conditions of wage labour must be willing to work, even if F. W. Taylor tended to separate motivation from results and Max Weber claimed that modern capitalism was no longer dependent on such motivation. Strikes were historically as effective as they were because withdrawal of labour struck at the heart of capitalism. Second, the consumer capitalism that emerged in the twentieth century required workers who purchased the products of their own labour, and this in turn demanded both corresponding purchasing power and the will to acquire the goods produced. Fordism combined mass production with increased wages in order for these conditions to be met.

Because of this dependence on workers, the dominant class in Europe could not resist the demand for democracy in the long run. Its introduction enhanced the legitimacy of capitalism and at the same time ameliorated the problems of profitability associated with the prior regime of accumulation (Aglietta 1976). However, democratic, mass-production capitalism brought with it new problems, which were often associated with democracy: voting rights for workers would lead to policies that went far beyond what was functionally desirable. After the

First World War there was a fear of a socialist or communist revolution, and in general the concern was widespread that the granting of social rights might bring about a major socio-political transformation. At the beginning of the twentieth century the idea of democracy was closely associated with a high level of political mobilisation and with social demands which derived from class struggle and which were opposed to the interests of capital. The move away from supposedly immature democracy and into authoritarian or totalitarian regimes during the 1930s was, among other things, a first attempt by the elites to solve this problem.

After the Second World War democratic political forms were re-established in different ways, a process that can be understood in the light of the experiences with class struggle and civil war. The West German case is exemplary: political organisations with extreme pro-grammes were banned, and the interaction between parties and inter-est groups was organised in such a way as to avoid the dominance of particular interests and to foster the search for consensus. Democratic theory adapted itself to the new reality: the egalitarian form of democ-racy was for the first time in history the starting point for all thinking; at the same time, the problem of the limitation of political passions was central (Almond and Verba 1963). Direct citizen participation outside elections was undesirable, and it was expected that conflict resolution through representative organisations would have a filter effect, so that only reasonable points of view could influence decision-making (Avritzer 2007). This model proved effective until the late 1960s, when it appeared to have reached its limits.

The decade from the late 1970s until the late 1980s was marked by a series of events, briefly already summarised before, that at first sight appear unconnected but which led to an unforeseen great transforma-tion in so-called 'modern societies'. We will name a few of them here and add some more in the next section. Significant for changes in the rela-tionship between democracy and capitalism in European societies were: the student revolt of 1968 and the return, in 1968 and 1969, of spon-taneous labour protest that was not directed by trade unions; the first post-war recession in the early 1970s, which affected almost all societ-ies, called into question Keynesian demand management and led to the 'fiscal crisis of the welfare state' (O'Connor 1973; OECD 1981) that cast doubt on the sustainability of redistribution through taxation; and finally, the electoral victories of Margaret Thatcher and Ronald Reagan in Britain and the USA, through which monetarism and supply-side economics became government policy and trade unions were seen as opponents of governments.

This sequence of events can be presented as follows: the demands of workers and students express a crisis which can no longer be solved through the co-ordinated action of trade unions, employers and the state. Because the crisis persists and is even deepened by counter-measures such as wage increases, which fuel inflation, radical solutions such as monetarism gain increasing acceptance, until they become a central plank of government policy. The protests that stand at the beginning of this sequence of events can be described partly as democratic pressure on the profitability of enterprises (Glyn and Sutcliffe 1972), and partly as an expression of discontent with alienating living and working conditions. But at their end there is neither the socialism that was hoped for or feared in 1919, nor the destruction of democracy of the 1930s, but rather the transformation of both capitalism and democracy.

In the first half of the 1970s the crisis was perceived as such by elites and critical thinkers alike. A report of the Trilateral Commission referred to a 'crisis of democracy', while Habermas spoke of legitimation problems; (Crozier et al. 1975; Habermas 1973, as already mentioned in Chapter 4). But this crisis was not dealt with in the way that was anticipated. The processes that are often summed up as economic globalisation, namely – according to circumstance – neo-liberalism, deregulation, and structural adjustment or shock therapy, mean that capitalism is freed from its embeddedness in national institutions and thereby from the grip of democratically raised demands. That far, the analysis by Streeck and other critics of today's capitalism in Europe appears correct, and their distance from the varieties of capitalism thesis is understandable in so far as, for instance, European banks have opened themselves to the global financial market and major European firms have relocated their production – though mostly not (yet) their research and development facilities – or adapted themselves to global conditions of production.

Our disagreement with these critics lies less in the analysis of European outcomes than in the account of the causes. The presentation so far should have made clear that the recent transformation of capitalism cannot be attributed, at least not exclusively, to capitalism's internal dynamics. Neither the classical Marxist account of the limitless pursuit of profit, to which Streeck surprisingly appeals, nor regulation theory's more historically nuanced account of changes in regimes of accumulation, enable us to grasp the latest changes in capitalist practice. In order to understand both the temporality and the form of that change, the dynamics of democracy need to be considered as well. The effective exercise of democratic rights had threatened the profitability of European capitalism and provoked transformative responses by the elites.

The longer-term historical perspective is important, beyond the time-span of the recent politico-economic transformation. In contrast to the inter-war years, in which democracy still had few passionate advocates, there has been a widespread consensus about the desirability of democratic political forms since the Second World War and particularly since the 1980s. For this reason the democratically provoked crisis of profitability in Europe – in contrast to Latin America, for instance – did not lead to the cancellation of democracy, as it is did in the 1930s. Since this exit option was not open, the flight from democracy's grip, its hollowing out rather than its destruction, provided an alternative for the elites.

DEMOCRACY AND CAPITALISM: A GLOBAL PERSPECTIVE

Flight from the grip of democracy presupposes that there is another place – another spatial constellation – from which capitalist enterprise can be carried out more profitably. Let us add to our list of events during the 1960s and 1970s: at the beginning of the 1970s the post-war monetary system, with the US dollar as its leading currency, collapsed; the so-called oil crises of 1972–3 and 1979 shifted the terms of trade for a central raw material to the disadvantage of the industrial countries; US industry was unprepared when Japanese businesses became globally competitive, and other East Asian countries followed suit. From this point onwards, one began to speak of a 'new international division of labour' (Froebel et al. 1979), in which societies for which the adjective 'industrial' made less and less sense no longer had a monopoly on industrial production, as 'newly industrialising' or 'threshold' countries came to the fore, countries that were at a competitive advantage over the old industrial countries, notably due to lower wages and, often enough, to the absence of democracy.

Why is it worth rehearsing these well-known facts? The point is not only to show that the current discussion about the omnipresence of Chinese industrial products on the world market, or about emerging economies or BRICS (Brazil, Russia, India, China, South Africa) has had a thirty-year-long preamble. They suggest furthermore that the events of the 1980s do not signal the beginning of globalisation but rather presuppose an already-existing global politico-economic constellation.

Neo-liberalism and deregulation did not create globalisation; rather, these policies exploited a situation of globalised production, responding to problematic democratic pressures by circumventing them.

During the 1980s the full significance of the new global situation was not yet appreciated in Europe: it was assumed that only the less desirable forms of production – with poor working conditions and high environmental impact (see Chapter 8) – would leave Europe, where high levels of qualification would continue maintaining competitiveness and living standards (Hauff and Scharpf 1975; Piore and Sabel 1984). In stark contrast to the current situation, relocation of production and migration of labour were seen quite positively, enhancing the comparative advantage of the organised variety of European capitalism. It should be added that this strategy presupposed that national capacity for action would be maintained, and that, even under the new conditions, the sedimentation of European/Western domination, which had gone on for a century and a half, would continue to generate a significant difference in the quality of life and work.

Today it is clear that this line of thought rested on false assumptions, and not only economic ones. For these expectations to be met, all or most of the participants would have had to commit themselves to the project, without considering the exit option (Hirschman 1970). But this did not happen: deregulation opened up the possibility of exit, and gradually – in continental Europe rather slowly – banks and productive enterprises made use of it. We could say that the European bourgeois class bade farewell to the project of societal development.[4] Marx of course had never assumed that they would participate in it. In *The Communist Manifesto* he and Engels attributed to them the destruction of everything national. But in fact, it became the specificity of Europe that the economic development of Europe was carried out by a combination of state and economic elites, joined by the trade unions in the 1920s. Since the 1980s and 1990s, however, European economic elites have abandoned this project.

But the hollowing out of nationally constituted democracy in Europe stands in contrast to developments in other countries. Post-Soviet elites in Russia appear to pursue booty capitalism using national resources under political conditions in which opposition is barely able to express itself. In China the persisting elites pursue an economic development project in which, on the one hand, they themselves acquire unprecedented personal wealth and in which, on the other hand, national resources are used for wealth creation at large, albeit with enormous damage in the form of exploitation of workers and nature. These are variants of capitalism that the debates of the 1990s did not take into account. Moreover, the three remaining BRICS societies – Brazil, India and South Africa – are capitalist societies as well as high-intensity democracies, and so especially instructive for the following discussion.[5]

DEMOCRACY AND CAPITALISM IN BRAZIL AND SOUTH AFRICA

Thus, our reflections on the relation between democracy and capitalism need to gain a wider global perspective. Let us first recall the fact that not all of Western Europe generated the apparently harmonious con-nection of democracy and capitalism in the democratic Keynesian wel-fare state. Spain and Portugal maintained their clerical-authoritarian regimes, which had been created in parallel to fascism and Nazism in Italy and Germany, until the 1970s. The Franco regime in Spain ended only after the death of the dictator in 1975; and the Portuguese ver-sion of the *Estado Novo* succumbed to the decolonisation wars in 1974, when its military officers refused to continue supporting an oppres-sive regime. And in Greece a military dictatorship took power at the moment when the prospect of a centre-left government arose in the mid-1960s. These Southern European experiences bear similarities with some of those in the Global South. Thus, it should not be overlooked that neo-liberal economic policies, while designed in the North, were first practised in the South, namely in Chile, where a military *coup d'état* had brought down the left-wing *Unidad Popular* government headed by President Salvador Allende. This was one of several cases in Latin America in which the military seized power in response to political sit-uations that were analysed by the elites as critical, defined as instability in the wake of contestations and demands for significant socio-political transformations. While in similar situations in Europe, with the excep-tion of Greece, the commitment to formal democracy was sufficiently pronounced to avoid democracy's self-cancellation (see Karagiannis 2016), in Latin America the suspension of democracy, in most cases with the support of the US, was the rule, and the persistence of democ-racy the exception.

The politico-economic developments in Brazil and South Africa from the 1960s to the 1980s fitted the 'Southern' pattern. In both societies, the existing restricted democracies were increasingly challenged from the 1960s onwards, as briefly discussed above (Chapter 4). And in both cases, the reaction was elite entrenchment, in Brazil through the military *coup d'état* and in South Africa through the intensification of apartheid. In both societies, too, the elites tried to foster economic growth to restore legitimacy by efficiency, but by and large failed to do so. To this extent, one might be inclined to say that the logic of capital asserted itself and required the suppression of claims for democratic progress. However, from the late 1980s the picture changes considerably, again in both societies, and demands an enlargement of the perspective on the relation between democracy and capitalism.

In contrast to Europe, Brazil and South Africa have witnessed a strengthening rather than a weakening of democracy, at least until very recently. With the Brazilian constitution of 1988 and the South African constitution of 1996, egalitarian-inclusive democracy and universal civil and political rights were established. Given that these rights and the political form that framed them had existed in the North for some time already, one could be tempted to call the re-institution of the Brazilian and the South African polity a 'catching-up' revolution (paraphrasing Habermas) with little general conceptual or historical significance. However, a closer look suggests that this is not so. Against the background of the long-lasting experience of exclusion and oppression, both constitutions commit the polities to processes of societal transformation, thus acknowledging many of the demands of the preceding protest movements. The Brazilian constitution of 1988 for the first time adopted universal political rights – everyone over the age of sixteen would be eligible to vote and to take part in elections. Even more importantly, a proposal for highly intense political participation was incorporated under the umbrella idea of overcoming social exclusion from the state. These demands for political participation were incorporated as a constitutional commitment to be implemented during the 1990s with specific laws.[6] Similarly, the South African constitution of 1996 expressed equal freedom for all citizens for the first time and contains a Bill of Rights that includes significant economic, social and cultural rights.

In line with the new societal self-understanding expressed in their constitutions, both countries have been governed after the 'democratic transition' by political majorities oriented towards societal transformation. Until 2002, Brazil witnessed a period of governments committed to inclusive democracy and otherwise drawing on mainstream economic expertise and mild social redistribution. During this time, demands for more radical social transformation came to be voiced ever more strongly and were now unimpeded. Coming from a variety of hitherto little-connected social movements, these demands crystallised in the PT and its presidential candidate Lula, who after several unsuccessful attempts was elected president in 2002. Since then, candidates of the PT have won presidential elections four times in a row, and the federal government was formed by the PT in alliance with other parties until President Dilma Rousseff was impeached on highly dubious grounds in 2016. In South Africa, the ANC, the most important organisation of the opposition movement to apartheid, succeeded in immediately dominating the party system from the first inclusive elections onwards, pushing its most significant adversaries, the National Party of the prior apartheid governments and the Inkatha Freedom Party, which was drawing electoral support from the Zulu, to the margins. The ANC has governed the country in alliance with the trade unions and the communist party uninterruptedly since 1994, approaching at times a two-thirds majority, even though on a currently declining trend.

In both cases the government coalitions are a product of the resistance to repressive regimes – the apartheid regime in South Africa and the military dictatorship in Brazil. Members of these governments have experience of armed resistance, arrest, imprisonment and torture: the former South African president, Jacob Zuma, in office until 2018, was a member of the liberation army of the ANC, spent ten years in prison on Robben Island with Nelson Mandela, and then lived in exile until the ANC was legalised. The impeached Brazilian president, Dilma Rousseff, was active in a small, revolutionary guerrilla group and was tortured in prison. The resistance, at times violent, was connected in both countries with the mobilisation of broad sections of the population for democratic and social demands, in conjunction with the trade union movement and parties such as the South African Communist Party (SACP) and the Brazilian PT. Many members of Brazilian governments between 2002 and 2016 came from protest movements and movements for participatory democracy that began in the Porto Alegre Social Forum and then achieved worldwide attention.

Over a rather long period, the government alliances in both societies continued enjoying considerable support, as the 2014 election victories of Dilma Rousseff and Jacob Zuma show. In contrast to Europe, where during the same period governments were frequently voted out of office because they not only took no measures against worsening standards of living but often brought them about by budget cuts and tax increases, the PT as well as the ANC could still rely on electoral majorities, albeit diminishing ones. Pre-empting a common prejudice, it should be emphasised that party competition and media freedom prevail in both countries, and that the political opposition could count on the support of considerable sections of the economic elite and of the media. Electoral success of these alliances, therefore, was not attributable to 'incomplete' democracy, as the 'North' is often inclined to assume about the 'South'. The governments were dependent on the votes of a majority of the electorate, were aware of this dependence, and they took protests seriously enough to keep winning elections until recently (on the intensity of democracy in Brazil see, for instance: Holston 2008; Domingues 2013; Avritzer 2016).

At the same time, these governments, which were not only democratically legitimated but arose out of democratic and social movements – and here is the second objection to the generalisation of observations about Europe – left the capitalist structure of the national economy intact and even encouraged a wider opening to the world market. They have therefore sometimes been described by leftist critics as 'neo-liberal'. In Latin America this was an accusation that saw the Brazilian government as much more moderate than other governments in the region during the turn to the political left in the early twenty-first century. In South Africa it was directed in particular at the economic policy known as 'Growth, Employment and Redistribution' (GEAR), introduced by President Thabo Mbeki, Zuma's predecessor. But it often remained unclear what the term 'neo-liberal' was supposed to mean. It is evident that the PT and ANC governments tried to avoid policies that threatened their credibility in the context of a capitalist world economy (Fleury 2012; Paulani 2016). To the extent that this world economy operates under neo-liberal conditions, such national policies are doubtless compatible with the neo-liberalism of the external economy. At the same time, both governments were pursuing a relatively successful growth policy led by a democratically legitimated, interventionist state that was committed to pursuing its objectives without jeopardising its relationship to the world market.

A core component of both government programmes was an expansionist social policy, guaranteeing to the lower-income strata benefit payments to a hitherto unprecedented degree (for more detail see

Chapter 7). In Brazil the *Bolsa Família* programme, which under the PT's government reached 13 million children, provides poor families with continuous cash payments on condition that they send their children to school and attend to their family's health. In tandem with this, the minimum wage was raised, and economic growth itself created more employment. As a result of these developments an internal economic demand emerged in Brazil, which makes the country – which predominantly exports primary sector goods – less dependent on fluctuations in the world economy, as shown at least by the early developments since the outbreak of the financial crisis in 2008. Similar processes, though on a lesser scale, can be observed in South Africa. The index of social inequality has hardly altered, attributable to the fact that the social and political improvement in the living conditions of the poor population has been statistically effaced by the growing wealth of a small stratum, including now parts of the black population. But 14 million South Africans now receive social grants, alleviating poverty. In both countries the social structure has changed enormously during the period in which these governments have been in office. There are now middle strata whose living conditions have improved markedly. In Brazil this is discussed under the heading of 'the new middle class', in South Africa under that of 'the black middle class' (Seekings and Nattrass 2006; Fleury 2010; Chipkin 2016).

The political situation in both countries, though, has changed rapidly and considerably during the past few years. In Brazil since 2013, contestations that were large in size but initially seemingly limited in scope have broken the hegemony that the PT seemed to firmly hold over the political agenda. Groups of the old elites seized the moment and succeeded in impeaching President Dilma Rousseff and jailing former President Lula, considerably twisting existing rules and laws. In South Africa, ANC politics was increasingly criticised for enriching a small part of the African population instead of providing for a larger societal transformation. Losing electoral support as a consequence, internal debate within the ANC led to the forced resignation of Zuma, who stood in the centre of the accusations of corruption and 'state capture' (Chipkin and Swilling 2018), and the election of Cyril Ramaphosa as new president. We will analyse these recent developments as our reasoning unfolds, focusing both on the kind of criticism that has been directed at the policies of these governments and, not least, on the question of their long-term sustainability. Before doing so, however, we want to pause for a moment and compare these two Southern experiences of the past two decades with those of the European welfare states and draw some conclusions from these comparisons about the general relationship between democracy and capitalism. The main theme of these reflections will be the mixture of scepticism and reserve with which the Northern analysis of capitalism approaches the South: have these temporarily 'successful societies' (see Hall and Lamont 2009) merely been catching up with something that began in Europe much earlier, and thus are destined to run up against the same limits? Or are there reasons to assume that Brazil and South Africa have been asking political and economic questions – and finding answers – that are new and thereby of both analytical and practical interest to the North? At this point, we will restrict ourselves to five remarks.

BRAZIL AND SOUTH AFRICA IN COMPARISON WITH 'THE NORTH'

The first conclusion from the reflections above is that the European welfare state is no model for the link between capitalism, democracy and solidarity (in contrast to Claus Offe's 1998 view). The post-fascist reorganisation of society in Europe was based on concertation at the expense of participation, according to a model that had already been developed in the Netherlands in the first half of the twentieth century (Lijphart 1975). The promise of social security was made on condition that high levels of participation were renounced. During their growth period, the so-called 'thirty glorious years', these societies did not develop a political culture which understood how to devise common political and economic goals under restricted circumstances. The current crisis in Europe makes this clear. In Brazil and South Africa, by contrast, social solidarity programmes, modest though they are, are driven by a democratic movement. Social transformation is the result of a democratic transformation whose radicalism is often underestimated. In South Africa for the last twenty years the government has been shaped by a majority population that was hitherto completely excluded from 'conventional' political participation. In Brazil, political discourse has until very recently – until the demonstrations of June 2013 – been dominated in quasi-hegemonic fashion by what was a radical leftist grouping founded only thirty years ago and which had its first successes in connection with social movements and local participative democracy. True, electoral stability in both countries has also been the result of an 'exchange' of votes for social policies. But the strong democratic impulse that characterises Brazilian and South African politics largely distinguishes both countries from Europe.

The strength of this impulse, second, can indeed even be gathered from the fact that it has turned against the government alliances. The ascent of the PT and ANC to government had raised very high expectations of radical and rapid social transformation. In South Africa there is a rather widespread sense that these expectations have been disappointed. In Brazil, in turn, some of the recent protest urges going further, while others call for a change of direction, towards moderation, and yet others even for a return to authoritarian forms of state action. The fact that government practices are challenged in election campaigns, in the media and in the streets gives testimony to a continuity of high-intensity democracy rather than to a crisis of democracies still in search of consolidation.

But what, third, about the limits of transformative politics in these societies? For Brazil it needs to be kept in mind that the PT, now accused of corruption, adapted to common political practices because it never had a majority in parliament and needed to keep political allies on board. In South Africa the ANC 'inherited' a state apparatus that dealt rather efficiently with the needs of a minority but was ill-suited for equal treatment of the whole population. The amount of politico-administrative transformation that is needed is often underestimated in the critique – also the scholarly critique – of government performance. Nevertheless, there are good reasons to assume that the transformation strategy on which the PT- and ANC-led governments embarked has reached its limits. A main component of this strategy has been the satisfaction of the demands voiced by their core electorates, whether material or institutional. Given the historical legacy of oppression and injustice, such a strategy is highly justified and should not be denounced as mere interest politics. But in the pursuit of this strategy, the alliances renounced both a broader transformation of the state apparatus and a public debate about the kind of society one wants to live in, beyond general statements that suffer from lack of concreteness. Stating this, though, one has to bear in mind two further features of the situation.

Fourth, namely, that unlike in Europe in the post-war period, there is no economic and social model that can be simply applied in a techno-cratic way. European societies, inspired by Keynesianism, rested upon a full employment economy, with one full-time salary enough to sustain a family, and a level of redistribution that financed social security, education and health. Such a productivist conception of economic and social policy cannot be applied to Brazil and South Africa. In South Africa the official rate of unemployment at the time of writing, at the beginning of 2018, is 24%. In Brazil the rate has fallen from 10% a dozen years ago to 6% six years ago, and now, at the beginning of 2018, it has gone up to 13%, but it remains lower than in some European countries. In both cases, how-ever, the figure for those who are actively seeking formal waged work hides the far greater number of those who do not participate in the for-mal labour market. For this reason too, poverty reduction is at the top of the social policy agenda, along with the question of the long-term link between democracy, economy and solidarity. For European societies, in which this once-stable link is at breaking point, the'Southern' discussion should be a matter of great interest (see Chapter 7).

Fifth, Brazilian and South African politics face challenges that Euro-pean elites in the post-war decades did not recognise or did not want to recognise, but which, given the prominence of democracy in both societ-ies, are unavoidably high on the political agenda. We just mention here three issues to which we shall return further later: (1) today's Brazil and South Africa emerged against a background of oppressive regimes. For this reason, the repression and injustice of the past and the resulting – and justified – political expectations and demands of the present are a key component of current societal self-understanding. In Europe, in con-trast, the dominant view is that the past – centrally Nazi totalitarianism and war – has successfully been settled through the creation of liberal-democratic polities allied with one another. Some current debates in Europe, though, show that this is an erroneous assumption, for instance in the emerging North–South cleavage. (2) Brazil and South Africa not only live with the high social inequality that is a long-lasting legacy of European settlement, they also live with cultural plurality in ways that are still unimaginable for many Europeans in whose self-understanding the democratic nation state has cultural-linguistic homogeneity as a core presupposition (on these two issues, see Chapter 6). (3) It may appear as if concern for ecological sustainability first arose in the North and was successfully dealt with in environmental policies. It seems more appropriate, however, to consider the North as having exported environmental problems to the South through the relocation of industries and the intensification of resource extraction, while at the same time placing the burden of future policy change on the South as well. This can be seen in the debate about climate change as well as in the responsibility placed on Brazil and South Africa for protecting the Amazon rain forest and the rhinoceros, respectively, for the sake of all humankind (see Chapter 8).

Chapter 6

INCLUSION AND EXCLUSION

In its own predominant self-understanding, twentieth-century European modernity has achieved inclusivity in the scope of all institutions. However, this image neglects important facts. From the late nineteenth century, social inclusion in Europe was premised on strong boundaries to the outside through mechanisms of control over the amount of international labour regarded necessary for national development. In stark contrast, in Brazil and South Africa societal institutions were much less inclusive, internally separating inhabitants along lines of skin colour, employment condition, race and place of origin/residence. One way of grasping these quite dissimilar trajectories is to look at the socio-political and symbolic significance of the relevant devices of social identification and of citizen inclusion. These mechanisms are still relevant and they were all implemented for the first time in the period of organised modernity, that is, the first half of the twentieth century. In this chapter we go back to this period of transition from the nineteenth to the twentieth centuries as a way of addressing the present political constellation in which we are living, and we also make an argument that challenges the stigmatised representation of these societies. We look at forms of solidarity that have been transformed in light of (re)interpretations of experiences of historical injustice. These experiences reveal another side of the issue of how, in specific contexts, subjects were differently regarded as deserving to be included and what compromises the elites are willing to commit themselves to in order to establish social cohesion. Following the general argument of the book, our exploration here moves beyond the point in which Brazil and South Africa would be presented simply as less inclusive than Europe, or 'behind' in historical processes of recognition. Rather, we return to the question of boundaries and the creation of an external other and the challenges of inclusiveness under present conditions in both North and South.

DIVERSITY AND SOLIDARITY IN HISTORICAL CYCLES: CONTEXTS OF STRUGGLES OF BELONGING IN BRAZIL, SOUTH AFRICA AND EUROPE

The form and scope of political, economic and social institutions are determined by different interpretations of historical injustices elaborated in each of the three regions we are looking at. The constitution of an idea of what a common world is and how it should be organised relies on the uniqueness of historical trajectories. Keeping the metaphor of the container in mind (Chapter 2), in this chapter we also address the issue of how each unit can be related to the other, and how the formation of external connection is an important factor for understanding in each context who gets what and in which conditions. A medium-term historical approach is the method we use to analyse the issue. Our aim is to understand how social integration is produced and reproduced over time and whether historical injustices can be mobilised as a source of collective political action. Both the reproduction of injustice and the struggles against it can be understood when one looks at the acceptance of non-material systems of values that are established differently in different societies, as expressed by the ideas of *deservedness* and *commitment* that will be further explored in the next chapter. Social cohesion, democratic development, and the legitimacy and crisis of an established order need to be understood in the light of meaningfully constituted social structures in which people are inserted, without losing sight of the embeddedness of modern history.[1]

Consequently, the notion of a historical constellation remains relevant for current political transformations. After the long period in which national identities were defined and linked to a specific idea of the role of the state, European social-democratic capitalism after the Second World War was expected to eradicate unemployment and to define economic inclusion around the idea of full employment. The history of Europe as a place of emigration that marked much of colonial history and also the beginning of the twentieth century started to change due to these policies of inclusion through employment and to policies for controlling the entry of immigrants in countries such as the US. On the one hand, to pursue a different life in other parts of the world became less attractive to poor Western Europeans than it was before.[2] On the other hand, the special route of European emigration to the US that accounted for 58% of the total of overseas European emigration was partially blocked with the Emergency Quota Act of 1921 (Tomka 2013). Brazil and South Africa were also prime destinations for Europeans and it remained like that until about 1960.

Reaching a climax in the period immediately after the Second World War, the flux of European migration was gradually weakening by the 1950s. Since 1960 the balance of migration in Europe has been positive, which means more arrivals than departures (Tomka 2013: 35). One of the reasons is that in the middle of the twentieth century (the late 1940s to the early 1970s) European colonial powers were proactively encouraging migration from their ex-colonies to bolster national economies (Buettner 2014). At the same moment, in Brazil and South Africa, by contrast, precarious work situations outside or at the margins of the formal economy separated 'native' and 'ex-slave' populations from whites and formal workers. In both societies societal cohesion, though in different forms and degrees, came to be determined by racial categories. In these Southern societies, forms of inclusion/exclusion were much less open to the internal other than in the European system.

European modernity became inclusive in terms of the scope of formal institutions for European citizens themselves and in terms of the acceptance of social and economic rights for legal immigrants – though deficient in terms of political rights for legal migrants despite their time of residence in a European nation state. This is, again, relatively accurate for the post-Second World War period in Europe, but is nonetheless short-sighted. It neglects the discourse on parallel developments inside given societies since the nineteenth century, which became famous in the image of the 'two nations' that was born in Victorian England and exacerbated later in the Union of South Africa. It above all neglects the enforcement of strong boundaries and mechanisms for excluding those from other countries when European societies in need of workers created policies for welcoming immigrants from the ex-colonies.[3] In the late twentieth century, the question of boundaries towards the outside and the 'borderlands' created inside European territories was a challenge for inclusiveness (Agier 2016).[4] In the South, following the principle of whitening or 'civilising' the population, immigration campaigns were adopted as a way to avoid the problem of internal inclusion through the inclusion of what was regarded as the 'good other'.[5] Until the problem of the working class in Europe was solved, these policies adopted in the Southern countries were quite successful. When the European social democratic model of inclusion became based on the full employment of the population, working displacement started to be less attractive for the European poor. Still, as central as it is, the fact that the European model of inclusion truly aims to include all citizens does not mean that it succeeds. Social justice remains a significant challenge to most European states, as it does to the European Union itself.[6]

In historical terms, Brazil's and South Africa's societal institutions were much less internally inclusive, separating and segregating inhabitants through lines based on skin colour, an urban–rural divide and/or distinctions between formally employed workers and informal workers (to use current terminology). The exclusion of the internal other is in striking contradiction with policies of welcoming international labour. In both countries we find legal mechanisms that encouraged specific groups to enter these countries while explicitly prohibiting others. Generally, these mechanisms were implemented as part of eugenic policies. Religious and ethnic criteria were used to define who could inhabit these countries.[7] The interconnectedness of both the North and South and the variances between them when it comes to the issue of inclusion and exclusion is represented by the adoption of formal devices attesting a person's designated category (as included or excluded). Devices have been used to guarantee to the holder access to a prescribed system of solidarity: the worker's record book (*carteira de trabalho*) in Brazil; the black pass-book ('*dompas*') in South Africa; the passport, the paperwork of legal immigrants, and the national identity card in Europe. Put in context, these mechanisms of regulation and control show how solidarity in, and within, countries has been bound to specific societal self-understandings of what constitutes a desired society.

For the comparative framework that we are interested in, it is important to go back in history to see how different actions gave rise to different trajectories of inclusiveness that are still important in the present. The issues that we want to highlight include: links between nation, state and the rise of the 'social question'; separateness as a desired form of state-driven development; and informal practices of exclusion formalised by the absence of large programmes of inclusion. In Europe the nation state became the privileged body for the establishment of a solidarity system and the modern policies towards the other. Even when it comes to the support for European integration, one sees that it has been driven by national interests (Delanty 2018). In Brazil and South Africa, a system of solidarity based on separateness of the *closer-other* was structurally linked to the emergence of both the state and the nation (in the South as separate entities).[8]

Brazilian Solidarity: The Slow Recognition of Diversity as a Social, Political and Economic Issue

Brazil as an independent country was founded by a very peculiar combination of liberal principles on the back of a monarchical, conservative state (Scantimburgo 1980; Mota 2013). A country composed of different societal matrices, clearly separated when it comes to the access of public goods, Brazil reached a basic territorial unification achieved in the absence of a wider system of social integration by the colonial regional powers when independence was proclaimed in 1822 (Ribeiro 2000; Carvalho 2005). The first Brazilian Constitution of 1824 was normatively influenced by a conception of liberalism and power organisation that comes from Benjamin Constant's conception of the liberty of the moderns compared to the liberty of the ancients. The liberty of the ancients demanded the existence of a large group of those excluded from the polis – slaves, for instance – to carry on with the practical obligations that the citizens could not do because of their involvement with state affairs (Constant [1819] 1988).[9] As this explicit example shows, in terms of state norms and principles (horizons) and concrete forms of solidarity, the history of Brazil since independence from Portugal in 1822 is the history of the antagonism between what is normatively proclaimed and what is practically executed.[10]

The political imaginary that emerged in independent Brazil was in contradiction with the entire organisation of the state around slavery, land concentration, racial exclusion and the marginalisation of the majority of the population.[11] This contradiction is still a major feature of Brazilian inclusiveness and exclusiveness. But it is in light of these discrepancies between norms and practices that important social transformations will unfold. Many revolts and rebellions against this exclusion happened during the Imperial period (1822–89),[12] as ex-slaves, indigenous groups, small farmers and the lower classes tried to fight for their inclusion in regional political and economic systems. It is important to highlight that we are talking about regional forms of struggle because up to the period of independence Brazil as a national central body did not exist. Always when the word 'homeland' appeared in historical documents up to the middle of nineteenth century, it was specific provinces that were mentioned (Slemian and Pimenta 2003; Carvalho 2005).

On the one hand, it was the exercise of power against the revolts and rebellions of the nineteenth century that helped the Empire to somehow consolidate a primordial feeling of 'being Brazilian'. Nonetheless the country was still lacking much regional integration and means of communication between the different parts of the territory. On the other hand, this feeling of becoming a subject that was part of a political body called 'Brazil' was also constructed around the opposition to the image of the Portuguese (a subject from Portugal). The Brazilian was the non-Portuguese (Carvalho 2005: 237). The Brazilian population had accepted the language and the religion, but had not become recognised as Portuguese. Despite this, the Imperial state would come to an end, not because of the denial of Portuguese belonging and rule, but because of the strategy of keeping power concentrated in the hands of an elite with a very conservative view of the society. Dom Pedro II, the last emperor of Brazil, was still respected by the elites and also the urban population, but it seems that the costs of keeping the Empire would require compromising core conservative values. The successor of the last Brazilian emperor was his daughter, Princess Isabel. Though the Brazilian constitution allowed a woman to become head of state, Dom Pedro II himself and the traditional elitist groups did not agree with it (Schwarcz 1998). A military coup instituted republicanism in Brazil in 1889 and sent the emperor and his family into exile. It marked the end of the Brazilian Empire, but not of the mythic image of the powerful man controlling the institutions of the country by any means. In this way the Old Regime persisted.

The republican period emerged along with the promises of full inclusion through the proclamation of the new federal constitution in 1891. This moment represents a key point for understanding how exclusion and inclusion marked the conception of justice and solidarity in the country. Despite the willingness of the society to emancipate the black population, the abolition of slavery at the end of the nineteenth century is actually better interpreted as a liberation for the whites from the burden of racial slavery (Costa 1986). It was also part of the development of modern capitalism, which had no use for non-wage-earning workers who were not part of the market economy. For blacks, however, in the absence of a politics of inclusion, of education and the granting of social, economic and political rights, abolition meant that they were free to go nowhere and they did not know what to do with their new-found 'liberty'. Thus the foundation of the republic came without an agenda of how to incorporate the ex-slaves into Brazilian society and without granting them social, economic and political rights.

The republican state considered itself responsible for boosting the immigration of groups of people that would develop the sciences, arts, agriculture, industry, trade and commercial activities in the country. In fact, this was a eugenic public policy that sought to encourage mainly white Europeans to come and develop the country. Brazilian immigration policies of the twentieth century were mostly created at this time and were based on the promise of welcoming northern immigrants and offering them a place of 'equality' and of 'plenitude' (Lesser 2013). The issue of historical justice for the Afro-Brazilian population as well as indigenous and mixed-race groups appears as a central theme only with the social struggles that became visible in the period of re-democratisation and the constitution of 1988. Around the informal exclusion of the black population, the elites fabricated an exclusionary ethic of inferior moral attitudes towards work and social activity by blacks; this purported ethic was based on the idea that the black population were poor because they deserved it and never fully wanted to be included (Cardoso 2010).

The period that became known as the First Republic (1889–1930) introduced an unparalleled power for the colonels and the patriarchal elites, but otherwise it was very much a continuation of the Imperial system of rule. As in the previous period, beside a shared language and the large-scale adoption of Catholicism, there was no evidence of a generalised feeling of belonging and unity of the Brazilian people beyond the feeling of not being Portuguese (Carvalho 1990). We would suggest that this was due to the absence of a broader discussion about the social question and the exclusion of the masses. It was a liberal republican moment which the Brazilian landlords took to mean an absence of state interference in their private interests – nothing more than that. Prevailing until 1940, a sort of 'structural inertia' dominated the political and economic elites when it came to the understanding that the state should be no more than merely a capitalist developmental institution (Cardoso 2010). By then, the significance of devices of inclusion developed during the Vargas era in Brazil became a watershed when it comes to this question. Urban workers were the group that was first targeted by a politics of inclusion of the masses. By the implementation of devices of regulation and laws to protect workers, this system represented also a form of political inclusion of the poor. Collective workers' rights were incorporated side by side with the institution of a social protection system that aimed to include people that could not lead an autonomous economic life, such as children, the disabled and the elderly/retired people. It was at this moment that labour courts were instituted. Through the idea of 'regulated citizenship' we can understand how such forms of inclusion happened (Santos 1979).

During the Vargas period, through action from inside the state, the national developmentalists saw themselves as the vanguard who should bring about social protection and assume responsibility for the construction of a welfare state. The development of the country through integration into the global capitalist economy was a project both to bolster national industry and to create a structure of rights to regulate the access of the poor to market society. Regulated citizenship during the Vargas period expresses a form of inclusion that is based on the occupation that a person has, not on her status as a political citizen. It is not a step in the direction of inclusiveness and a universal system of socio-economic rights that is at stake. It is by the recognition of specific groups' or workers' entitlements to rights that the poor first become recognised as full citizens in Brazil. The symbolic weight that the worker's record book acquired in Brazil is a product of this transformation.

Showing evidence of an ongoing work contract by a stamp in the worker's record book meant that you were someone who was included, which entailed both being included in the masses and occupying an elevated status within this multitude. The *carteira de trabalho* never had the status that the passes had in South Africa – as a document that a person should hold all the time – but a holder of it could hand it over to show that they were not a 'vagabond' whenever needed. The issue of inclusion of the unemployed and others who had experienced historical disadvantage and because of that fell outside of the system of inclusion remained very much untouched. From the 1930s to 1960s a structure of universal social rights first became established. The main tool that an individual had to access these rights was entrance into the formal economy through work. To be formally accepted in the capitalist system as a worker meant that the person could fight for the achievement of social, political and economic rights. This meant that collective action from below, as long as it was concerned with issues of class struggle, became a legitimate form of political action in Brazil.

South Africa's Cohesion: A History Constructed through Separateness

Though placed in the cognitive map of the known world as part of trade routes that preceded the first appearance of the New World, the first experience of Dutch colonialism in South Africa started only by the middle of the seventeenth century – much later than in Brazil. Until the unification of South Africa at the beginning of the twentieth century, internal wars between Dutch, British and local powers (such as the Zulu) were responsible for the configuration of a colonial picture that was harder to define both in terms of geographical domain and in terms of who rules and what/who is ruled. Colonialism in South Africa did not create a unified territory dominated by a shared language and a central system of rule. Furthermore, compared to Brazil, colonialism in South Africa was much more volatile and difficult to determine in terms of the imposition of power over a dominated group. The Union of South Africa was established after the end of the South African War[13] (1899–1902) when, under British Imperial rule, policies of segregation based on white supremacy were continuously implemented. Though formally initiated with the victory of the National Party in the election of 1948, the roots of apartheid can be situated in segregation polices initiated under the process of unification of South Africa under British rule (Dubow 1989). What colonialism did manage was the formalisation of a racialised administrative machinery that worked as part of a global capital dynamic of exploitation and dispossession. Because of this, South Africa always appears as a unique example of historical injustice and exclusion towards a group created and imposed through a racial criterion.

Nevertheless, it needs to be highlighted that the history of segregation in South Africa goes beyond the dual antagonism between blacks (natives) and whites (European settlers). This history also is marked by the place of 'Asians' in the development of inclusion/exclusion policies in South Africa. Slaves from the different parts of Asia were first introduced into Cape Town in the seventeenth century. The majority of the 'Asians' brought to South Africa at the beginning of the eighteenth century were taken from India. In certain Dutch colonial areas, the Asians were composed of slaves, ex-slaves, shopkeepers, manual workers and assistants of Cape officials (Bose 2014). The transformation of the legal status of these Asians and the struggles for the recognition of these 'mobile individuals' as having a special place in the composition of southern African systems of solidarity is connected to transformations that happened in colonial India as part of the British Empire during the nineteenth century (Bayly 2012). Internal factors also play an important role in this history, such as enforcement laws that closed down businesses owned by Asians, deported some to their place of origin, and imposed the use of '*passes*' – for the black population – that would record the status of the person. The Natal Indian Congress, founded at the beginning of the twentieth century, fought to abolish some of the laws that excluded Asians in colonial South Africa. Gandhi was one of the leaders of this Congress. However, as Bose (2014) shows, Gandhi and the others involved in struggles for the inclusion of Asians in South Africa did not base their claims on the idea of the equality of all. They did not want full inclusion of all people living in South Africa; they wanted to have the same status as whites.[14] In the liberal circles of the Cape, it became an influential idea that rights should be granted to all *civilised* men (Dubow 1989). The allocation of rights in South Africa was imagined at this moment as part of the debate between civilised and uncivilised groups that inhabited the same territory.

In 1894, the Glen Grey Act reserved the area north of the Cape to be used exclusively by (black) Africans for their development. The meaning of this act was subject to many different interpretations,[15] but it is recognised as one of the first institutional measures of what became a basic characteristic of South African segregation polices of the twentieth century. In 1903–5 the South African Native Affairs Commission (SANAC) was created. It endorsed the view that, though Africans should be entitled to land ownership, it should be done through a different system of justification, not through the general structure of individual rights and duties. Following from that, the Native Land Act of 1913 came to be the first expression of a very complex system of segregationist policies implemented before apartheid. This document restricted the ownership of land by Africans, who constituted a majority of the population by a considerable measure, to around 10% of the territory of the Union of South Africa. The law created reserves where blacks could own land and prohibited the trade of land between Africans and whites (South African History Online 2018).

It would not be wrong to say that South Africa came to be the most visible expression of the Victorian idea of two nations developing apart. However, unlike in Britain, in the Union of South Africa segregation polices prior to apartheid came to consolidate the idea of race[16] as requiring strict separation between societal groups when it comes to the structure of rights in which each category of person should be inscribed. As Beinart (2001: 62–3) points out,

> The incorporative elements of Victorian liberalism were being jettisoned in British and colonial thinking, replaced by the loose amalgam of ideas sometimes called Social Darwinism. [. . .] Biological ideas of supremacy justified European pre-eminence and there were fears that this might be diluted or corrupted by intermingling with 'lesser' races.

Nothing good could come from this understanding, but pre-apartheid segregationist policies in South Africa worked out because they entrenched white supremacy without completely dismissing the possibility of autonomous black development.[17] That is why many Africans tried to build up their demands in the language of policies of segregation that would allow them to take control over different areas of the Union; even in the discourse of moderate groups, known as 'liberal segregationists', the notion of the Union's development through 'parallel institutions' was regarded as the best option for all in South Africa (Dubow 1989: 44).[18]

Policies of segregation in South Africa were, however, intrinsically implicated in the formation of capitalism, social classes, centralisation of state power, racism, and capital accumulation centred principally on the mining sector and downstream industries. After the South African War, with the Dutch losing their political and economic power, the Afrikaners wanted to become the working class *par excellence* of the Union. To this end they implemented measures such as, for instance, the industrial 'colour bar', which was introduced to protect the white tribe of Africa – the Afrikaners, also known as the Boers – against the entrance of black labour into the market. The Rand Revolt of 1922 (discussed in Chapter 3) paralysed the Union and made clear to the British that they needed to integrate Afrikaner leaders in order to maintain the power relations established after the First World War. In this way, race was assumed as the central category for the crystallisation of political and economic power (Beinart 2001).

As we saw above, during the 1930s Brazil initiated a politics of economic integration through the assimilation of the urban population into the labour market. In the absence of an explicit racial mechanism of exclusion, in the Vargas era inclusion through work aimed to create the conditions for the emancipation of the urban population that had already gained some technical abilities and attained a minimal educational level. In South Africa the formation of national capitalism was addressed above all in terms of who the proletariat of South Africa should be. The question was whether the 'natives' were ready or entitled to fulfil this role. The Native Administration Act of 1927 answered this question by seeking to 'retribalise' the African population, at the same time making clear that whites should be the structural agents of capitalist modernisation. It also clearly assumed that the state was the agent that should control labour forces on the market. In Brazil urban masses were incorporated into the national development ideal initiated in the Vargas era through their work conditions (in accordance with whether they were formal or informal workers). Some forms of everyday exclusion of the non-white population did exist but they have never been institutionalised. In South Africa, on the contrary, a system of formal, exclusionary racial hierarchies was introduced and enforced throughout the twentieth century. At the moment of the formation of South Africa as a united political territory, inclusion meant granting the Afrikaners similar standards and rights as the British, along with the exclusion of all others (Leubolt 2009).

Apartheid was the outcome of different social processes initiated by white colonialism and at the juncture of global capitalist interests. It has become the epitome of segregation, racism, state-driven inequality, and social engineering applied to humanity. Though part of the capitalist developmental agenda, in 1948, when apartheid formally started, the National Party had not set up a long-term programme.[19] The prevailing ideology was of unity (*volkseenheid*) for the full realisation of the superior race (Beinart 2001). H. F. Verwoerd is probably the name most strongly associated with the engineering of apartheid, first, when he was appointed as Minister of Native Affairs (1950–8) and later as Prime Minister (1958–66). It was by his hands that the Population Registration Act, which made racial classification compulsory in 1950, was created. With this act, documents establishing which racial group an individual belonged to were issued. Rights became completely associated with racial assessment. Additionally, when he was the Minister of Native Affairs, both the Pass Laws Act (1952), which instituted the 'dompas', and the Reservation of Separate Amenities Act (1953) were implemented.

The enforcement of these laws came with the expansion of bureaucratic structures and violent retaliations against black resistance. The '*dompas*' exacerbated conflicts and increased resentment against apartheid. However, a decade after the Pass Laws Act was implemented,

> nearly 600 labor bureaus had been created. Four million men and 3.6 million women had been issued with new pass books. Convictions under the control laws increased from 164,324 in 1952 to a staggering 384,497 in 1962 – a total of three million in ten years – with hundreds of thousands of foreigners deported. (Beinart 2001: 158–9)

Revolts and resistance were a mark of apartheid struggle. Many Africans were killed, exiled, and put in prison during these years. The controlled 'inclusion' of the black population only happened through the violent imposition of state forces. Despite that, the institutions of apartheid lasted until 1994. Even now, after almost three decades of its formal abolition, apartheid is more than a shadow in the history of South Africa. It is important to be clear about the causes and consequences of a system of racial segregation in order to be aware of its presence.

Europe, Internal Integration and Displacement of Conflict

By now it should be clear that the formation and the support of the welfare state in Europe cannot be fully grasped without assuming links and global connections that extend far beyond Europe itself (Dussel 2007; Delanty 2013; Stråth and Wagner 2017). Though unique in terms of the social, political and economic achievements that this phase of organised modernity brought about, the welfare state in European countries was made possible because of the movement of capital, goods, persons and ideas from all around the globe. The discrediting of the notion that markets were self-regulating actors and the national integration of European states, along with the prolonged economic stagnation that marked the end of the nineteenth century, are factors that explain the emergence of the idea that the state should be responsible for creating the rules that would make possible global market exchanges and individual freedom. It was at the end of the nineteenth century that the idea of 'unemployment' first emerged – a term created to 'reflect a prescriptive approach closely aligned with a desire to improve industrial performance in the face of increasing competition on foreign markets' (Stråth and Wagner 2017: 151). The social question in Europe and the debate about inclusion and exclusion only became completely transformed when policies of full employment were implemented in the course of the twentieth century – after 1945. The success of the welfare state in Europe was due to the development of industrial economies based on the extraction of raw materials from parts of the still-operating European colonial system[20] in Africa and Asia and of South America's entrance into global capitalism through 'enclaved economies' (Cardoso and Faletto 1979). The development of social nationalism in Europe was accompanied by the increased struggle for international leadership under conditions of capital and industrial expansion. This impacted even on the international effect of German National Socialism, as Hobsbawm (1994: 117) shows. The rise of Germany as a world power gave visibility to Nazism much quicker than other forms of fascism.

Democracy was first achieved in Europe in a historical scenario marked by the construction of an imaginary of a nation trying to define its geographical internal boundary, and by the imaginary of an empire whose power could not be consolidated only by internal developments.[21] To answer the demands of the working and new middle classes, there emerged in Europe a widening of the political horizon in the direction of a compromise between groups with different socio-economic power. Internal solidarity and social rights were achieved through the displacement of exploitation of natural and human resources to other parts of the globe. What we have shown before about the configuration and change of the social question in Europe (Chapter 2) is, among other things, the outcome of this displacement that happened in the transition from the nineteenth to the twentieth centuries. A displacement that literally meant the moving about of people, goods and ideas or a reallocation of social borders by the use of legal means.[22] Anti-Semitism had existed since the second half of the nineteenth century in many countries, especially in France. The politics of hate, exclusion and elimination of Jews was linked to National Socialism and fascism because these views expressed the counter-side of what the national community and racial state-driven development wanted to become: the Jews were very much internationalised, sharing a general commitment to values of individual freedom and enlightenment. They were easily targeted as the 'symbols of the hated capitalist/financer' or as 'rootless intellectuals' (Hobsbawm 1994: 119). They were actively displacing people, challenging by their very existence the increasing connection present in nationalist discourse between race and territory (boundaries).

The apparently contradictory existence of exclusionary practices and the institutionalisation of a social state based on the affirmation of social and economic rights for the masses marked the inter-war period in most of Europe. However, an exception needs to be made: Spain and Portugal. Portugal held an impressive colonial territory for the greater part of the twentieth century. In contrast to Northern European countries, the long-lasting dictatorships in the Iberian Peninsula undermined the widespread social model of development and regional integration through welfare-state rights, thereby isolating these countries in terms of the history of democratic learning, with consequences that still can be seen.[23]

THE PRESENT: BORDERLINES AND THE CHALLENGES OF A POLITICS OF INCLUSION

What has been discussed so far should be enough to correct the widespread view of modernity as an attempt to homogenise societies based on a particular Eurocentric project of pretentious universalism (Quijano 2005; Mignolo 2011). We suggest that a diversity of both normative principles and societal integration has been a constitutive part of the modern world. By the second half of the nineteenth century, under conditions of the expansion of capitalism and of rational principles applied to the modern state and national organisation, Brazil, South Africa and Europe have experienced different forms of solidarity based on specific self-understandings of how autonomy and determination should happen. Though eugenic politics as well as ideas of white supremacy are widespread practices at the beginning of the twentieth century in both North and South, it is going to be in the discourse of autonomy and equality between human beings that inclusive discourses and institutional mechanisms will emerge. Brazil, Europe and South Africa experienced and locally reinterpreted global development in terms of cohesion and exclusion. Initiated as a struggle against apartheid, dictatorships and historical injustices, major transformation will most likely occur in the present. Still, it is in the modern commitment to the creation of a better future and failures in the realisation of promised social progress that the different responses will be found.

During the last military dictatorship in Brazil (1964–85) the country went through a period of rapid rural–urban transition. This process was accompanied, on the one hand, by the formation of new forms of controlled political and economic solidarity; and on the other hand, by the concentration of power in the hands of very small groups associated with the military, such as the industrial bourgeoisie, who were already becoming a very powerful group due to the policies developed by previous presidents Getúlio Vargas and Juscelino Kubitschek. The model of regulated citizenship became even more regulated during the military period and much less citizen-oriented than before.[24] The dictatorship was a period that saw the accumulation of economic and political power; it is linked with a slight improvement in the lives of the urban middle classes and a worsening condition in the lives of the excluded poor. Brazilian cohesion patterns came, more than ever, to be based on the misrecognition of historical injustices against vulnerable groups. It was a situation in which solidarity was not based on a feeling of commitment towards the 'other', but on the refusal to look at the other as one's immediate equal.[25] With the growth of the metropolitan centres and the expansion of the economy, the unrecognised poor and the very rich were living in close proximity but without sharing much more than a language and a physical space.

On the one hand, the military dictatorship of the 1960s to the 1980s created new forms of exclusion to prevent disadvantaged groups from benefitting from the economic boom of the period. Nonetheless, during the dictatorship programmes of inclusion of the formal working class with the incorporation of new rights did occur. On the other hand, it was in this turmoil that marked the mid-twentieth century in Brazil that new forms of solidarity emerged and became institutionalised, initially outside of state institutions and later inside them. Even when it comes to the organisation of groups that were silenced by the public political discourse around social integration – such as groups pressing for elevating the status of rural workers and combatting the exclusion of Afro-Brazilians – it is in this period that under the umbrella idea of 'neighbourhood associations' many collective local political actors pushed public institutions in new directions (Avritzer 2009). It was by denouncing the lack of equality among the citizens that new struggles and forms of collective action emerged.

With the gradual recovery of democracy by the 1970s, Brazilian society was still based on a structure of non-commitment to the poor by the elites. However, one can say that in the last decade of the twentieth century a new Brazilian self-understanding based on the slow transformation of the historical pattern of exclusive solidarity began to emerge.

This change was due to the action of important urban and rural social movements that sought to press public debate into addressing topics of vital concern. These included: addressing the concentration of land and the necessity of land reform; public health as a matter of state responsibility; and racism as a characteristic of Brazilian society, as against the fallacy of racial democracy as a feature of the country. As Avritzer (2009: 41) argues, understanding democratisation in Brazil demands a strong consideration of how 'associative life' developed in the country. Social movements and civil organisations found in the participatory mechanism created by the 1988 Brazilian constitution an entrance into state institutions and a way of transforming democracy from the inside (we will come back to this topic in Chapter 10).

The spirit behind the constituent moment and the constitutional commitment that arose in Brazil and South Africa in the last decades of the twentieth century expresses a new historical understanding of past injustices. In Brazil, the re-democratisation of 1988 was accompanied by a feeling that the constitution would back the actions of multiple actors with very different interests and all of them could somehow be processed democratically within the relevant state institutions. It is possible to see that for the first time homogenisation was not understood as the driving principle for the formation of cohesion in Brazilian society. The general imaginary that emerged was that the transition from dictatorship to democracy finally opened the doors for the realisation of the promises of full inclusion. Brazilians created a normative constitutional framework that would back a new form of participatory democracy as a way of solving de facto inequality among formally equal citizens and eliminating social, economic and political exclusion. However, it was not until the early twenty-first century that inclusion/exclusion became finally recognised as an issue of historical justice, and a public commitment to the excluded 'other' appeared on the horizon of what seemed to be a new Brazilian social articulation. Due to the conjunction of pressure from civil associations and participatory institutions and of the effort made by sectors of the PT during the years when the party led the presidency of the country (2002–16), groups historically silenced recognised their condition and started to build up alternatives together with other actors previously included.

In South Africa, the movement that would become the ANC was formed in 1912 as a collective organisation fighting for the political rights of black and mixed races. Along with the PAC, the ANC became a key political actor in the struggle against apartheid. In 1960, following the promulgation of the Unlawful Organisations Act, both the PAC and ANC were banned. Nelson Mandela, the historical ANC leader, won the election of 1994 and since then the ANC has ruled the country. The inclusion of the majority of the South African population was achieved along with polices for the reduction of poverty and, occasionally, of social inequalities. As in Brazil, South Africa also experienced economic growth during the apartheid era. However, political rights were even more limited there and completely marked by the exclusion of the African. The institutionally racial and racist capitalist model[26] developed in South Africa under apartheid started to shows signs of exhaustion by the late 1970s. The combination of growing international pressure, pressures from inside coming from a variety of collective forces, and economic crisis need to be all taken together to understand the passage to a non-racialised system of inclusion (Leubolt 2015).

The Rainbow Nation project of 1994, seeking to create a nation in which racial and ethnic difference would be harmoniously combined, had overcome racial laws and focused on the process of peace and reconciliation, without a deep economic and social redistributive plan to avoid the creation of new social conflicts with the former ruling class. Liberalisation policies and the new fiscal plan introduced first in the Reconstruction and Development Programme (1994), followed by the GEAR plan in 1996, obtained success in areas such as social security. However, these plans did not robustly challenge the main sources of inequality in the prevailing system of solidarity by, for instance, creating new taxes on heritage and income.[27] The ANC has held political power since 1994 in an alliance with the SACP and the Congress of South African Trade Unions (COSATU). This alliance has guaranteed the improvement of rights and working conditions of formal sector workers. In 2005 the Accelerated and Shared Growth Initiative for South Africa (ASGISA) was created to replace the GEAR plan. Again, some important objectives in terms of social inclusion were set up, but these objectives were pursued in isolation from a deeper programme aimed at the correction of historical injustices by targeting patterns of historical reproduction of inequalities.

In Europe, the fact of immigration has put strains on the self-understanding of societies that had conceived of themselves as culturally homogeneous. Debates about what it means to be French or German have intensified since the end of the twentieth century. Explicitly xenophobic political parties have emerged all across Europe. Their significance has increased with recent migration driven by the desire to escape from misery and poverty, mostly from sub-Saharan Africa, and from warfare and violence, mostly from the Middle East. In the face of this recent migration in particular, and despite the effectiveness of human rights discourses and actions in European societies, institutions do not guarantee, and even violate, the rights of 'others' in European territories – as epitomised by the evictions in the Calais migrant camp and the confinement of sub-Saharan African migrants without assuring them basic living conditions in a penitentiary in Malaga by Spanish Government authorities.[28] In Europe borderlands became a place for the emergence of a new subject who is both included (in the life of the borders themselves) and excluded from the world of which they want to be a part (Agier 2016).

One cannot adequately talk about inclusion and exclusion under conditions of diversity and solidarity without taking the issue of migration and the politics of boundaries fully into account. Human history is a history of displacement. Different societal self-understandings and reflexive action towards autonomy have been strongly associated with the pressure made to change the borders (physical and imaginary) of modern societies. The others of our contemporary society – be they the excluded poor and/or immigrants – are a political manifestation of the need for change in the patterns of global inequality. This was Gloria Anzaldúa's claim in her 1987 work *Borderlands/La Frontera*, when she first asked for history to take into account border thinking and action as a source of political transformation.

In Europe the problem of the border clearly touches on the politics of national immigration and home affairs inside European states. In South Africa and Brazil borders are more concerned with internal limits that split societies and reproduce an unequal system of solidarity. With different historical backgrounds and nuanced contexts of solidarity which reveal the specificity of global movements, Brazil, Europe and South Africa challenge universal discourses of inclusion that are accompanied by exclusionary practices. To understand the improvements, challenges and dilemmas that we find in these different trajectories, there is a need to overcome analytical perspectives that approach societal processes by starting from the separation of structural and superficial patterns of reproduction. From an analytical point of view, inclusion and exclusion from the perspective of global history show that cultural patterns and structural constraints are much more imbricated than established sociological history is open to accepting. For instance, Göran Therborn (1995), in his analysis of the European trajectory of modernity, splits structure (the boundary and morality of a social system along which that which happens inside the system is regulated) and culture (a system of identity, a shared knowledge about the world, an ethical-moral communicative system that determines what is good or bad). By doing so, his analysis of modern development relies on processes of *structuration* of different organic systems of solidarity that come along with improvements in the system of rights; and of modern *enculturation* that shows how human cumulative knowledge has been shaped by the system of values expressed in different societal configurations. Under modern conditions of entangled production of global inequalities (Costa 2011), regional disparities are formed by both internal and external factors that cannot be explained through an analytical system that separates structure from culture. From what we have shown in this chapter, in Europe, Brazil and South Africa the 'system of values' that marks who deserves what and the existence of concrete internal and external boundaries were shaped together through social actions. A system of solidarity is historically shaped and transformed because human beings are, at the same time, both agents and structures of their own action.

CONCLUSION

If we then compare Brazil and South Africa today with Europe, would it be appropriate to say that the first two are finally 'catching up' with the last in terms of creating an inclusive-egalitarian society? This would confirm the notion that, under conditions of modernity, the normative horizon is equal inclusion of all members of a society. Societies may avoid facing this issue for long periods, due to entrenched hierarchies and interests, but they will not be able to do so forever. Critique and contestation will keep bringing full inclusion onto the agenda until the task is accomplished. If this were the conclusion, then our analysis would have confirmed, at least for this topic, a rather linear understanding of modernisation processes. It would also have confirmed that Europe has been 'ahead' on this modernising trajectory, and that Southern societies were 'lagging behind'.

However, the picture is not that clear. Without doubt, European societies have developed a highly egalitarian-inclusive self-understanding and corresponding institutions over the past century. As we also showed, though, this development was accompanied, and arguably necessarily so, by a closure of those societies' boundaries. Immigration into European societies was limited and tightly controlled during much of the twentieth century. When the post-Second World War economic boom led to labour shortages by the 1960s, limited entry of workers was encouraged but again highly regulated. The most notorious case was the euphemistically named 'guest workers' in West Germany, mostly young men from rural Turkey, who were meant to stay for a few years but then 'rotate' with a new group of again only temporary immigrants. These men were supposed to work but not to settle, even though eventually many of them stayed and Germany, like many other West European societies during the same period, became a country of immigration without wanting to be so.

At the time of writing, it is unclear whether Europe will be capable of developing an adequate response to the new challenge to its borders. While a basic political intuition is to keep the borders shut, given the prevailing European self-understanding, there is also increasing humanitarian activism, often pointing out the earlier periods during which Europeans were refugees in need of help and support in other world regions, in particular when fleeing war and totalitarianism in the mid-twentieth century. More rarely, though, is it underlined that millions of Europeans emigrated to America and Africa during the nineteenth and early twentieth centuries, as we recalled earlier (Chapter 2). Both in absolute terms and in relation to the population of the receiving societies, their numbers were much higher than those of the refugees arriving in Europe today. In a way, Europe faces in the current wave of immigration the reverse of the earlier emigration. But European consciousness has, by and large, not risen to make this connection.

Chapter 7

POLITICAL EQUALITY AND SOCIAL INEQUALITY

In capitalist societies, one might expect to see a decrease in social inequality under an inclusive democratic scenario. This is because democratic conditions should enhance the capacity of the majority (namely, the poorest) to exercise power through autonomous institutions and periodic elections. In what follows we explore further the relation between political equality and social inequality along three axes: (1) we will look at how the actual reduction of social inequality under democratic conditions depends on the politico-economic self-understanding of a given society; (2) we analyse how governments that seek to reduce poverty succeed or fail, and in which way; (3) we reflect on the problem of the use of policies to reduce inequality as a means for transformation-oriented governments to stay in power. The problem here is to understand how liberal democracies in both the South and the North deal with the challenge of enhancing structural change that would target patterns of reproduction of inequality under conditions of a representative system and electoral competition. This examination will proceed by offering a picture of how Brazil, South Africa and Europe appear when it comes to inequality and how their internal configuration has transformed (or not) in recent decades. Moving closer to the contemporary scenario, tax systems, revenues, political contexts and different societal self-understandings will be discussed to present how in each society the idea of *who gets what* is connected to notions of *deservedness* and *commitment*. Furthermore, this chapter provides an analysis that shows how social inequalities are produced, reproduced and become a significant source of collective action in the modern history of both North and South.

UNDERSTANDINGS OF EQUALITY: LIMITS OF FORMAL EQUALITY UNDER HISTORICAL CONDITIONS OF SOCIAL INEQUALITY

The prospect of full equality between different human beings marked the constitution of modernity at its beginning and is still a key motor of collective action in the present. Positive political and economic outcomes have been achieved because of the reflexive response to the experience of social disadvantage in different temporal-spatial configurations of modernity. In its short history, the modern principle of equality between all human beings who belong to a political community has become almost sacrosanct. Its sacralisation derives from a striking antagonism of modern societies: the principle of equality has been used to justify different forms of inequalities in public and private spheres. This is apparent when it comes to the relation between humans that are regarded as possessing different moral aptitudes. In historical terms, this antagonism can be discerned in struggles over which humans were regarded as part of humanity in different temporal-spatial contexts.[1] In contemporary capitalist, democratic societies, as we will further argue in what follows, the general principal of equality has also been used to create an idea of *deservedness* and *commitment* when determining who should be equal, how equality should be achieved, and to which realm the equality principle applies.

In the process of the transformation of ideologies by concrete practices experienced in everyday life, the aspirations for universal forms of equality between all human beings were converted into struggles for the achievement of equality in different realms.[2] These struggles constitute a significant aspect of modern, political collective action as we understand it. In modernity, as with inclusiveness, what we have observed is the subtle vanishing of a political project fully based on universal equality. This has given way to specific forms of struggle leading to specific achievements in different fields: for example, equality between men and women; equal rights for rural and urban workers, or for people with different skin colour; and political equality between the rich and poor. And even with this change, such achievements are uneven and always subject to resistance that can halt a process of social equalisation.

In this chapter we will focus on the prospect of the establishment of democratic justice in different political communities as part of a still-important agenda that focuses on struggles for political, economic and social equality. The hypothesis that we depart from is that a decrease in social inequality should occur under inclusive democratic conditions. This is because, first, such conditions enhance the capacity of powerless economic actors to exercise power through the vote and the system of liberal representation. Second, democracy should lead to an increase in public expenditure based on a fair tax system that would charge higher rates to those who can pay more to distribute public services (Lindert 1994). This idea has underpinned the aspirations of many democratic revolutionaries and political leaders throughout the nineteenth and twentieth centuries in different parts of the world, both in the global North and in the global South.

However, these aspirations have proved to be very limited. Experiences of political inclusion in Southern societies did not necessarily give power to the majority when it comes to accessing the two other core modern, democratically constituted powers: the legislature and, above all, the judiciary.[3] In general, in modernity there is no single example of a successful, long-term programme for fighting social inequality that was not accompanied by a full democratisation of state institutions.[4]

In both Northern and Southern societies that have undergone modern democratic transformations, durable changes in the direction of a reduction of inequality are connected to improvements of formal institutions. Profeta and colleagues (2013) have developed an analysis that shows that stronger democratic institutions and the protection of civil liberties go hand in hand with improvements observed in the tax system and in public expenditure over time. Still, formal political equality has its limits. In this chapter we want to explore some of these limits, taking into account both contexts of crude social inequality and contexts in which social inequalities appear in a more smoothed-out manner. In doing so we shall keep in mind the distinction between 'equalising' and 'disequalising' as that which can explain variations in historical patterns of income, distribution and redistribution in the global context (Firebaugh and Goesling 2004).[5]

To explore the relation between political equality and social inequality, there are three lines of inquiry that need to be pursued. The first relates to politico-economic conditions and the reduction of social inequality. There is of course great variance between Europe and present-day Brazil and South Africa, but we hope to be able to show that these differences can be explained by moving beyond modernisation approaches to explaining institutional differences when comparing societies. Second, there is the problem of political outcomes and electoral competition. This became clear when we came to analyse how governments that seek to reduce poverty or to improve the lives of those on the 'bottom', such as the policies recently pursued by Brazilian and South African left-wing governments, can count on, and use, poverty reduction mechanisms to also create and maintain electoral support. The issue at hand here is whether policies directed to the poorest in society, where this group represents a huge electoral force, can be carried out while still keeping democratic institutions functioning according to democratic principles – which means, in this case, not making use of populistic or paternalistic tools. As we see it, the problem does not concern the relation of government majorities to particular groups in society as such. Rather, and this is the third part of our examination, what needs to be proved is whether adopting polices aimed at the reduction of inequalities by transformation-oriented governments leads to the actual full democratisation of political institutions and durable economic changes. Thus, if political equality shows itself only in an aggregative understanding of political will-formation, much less is gained than the grand term 'democracy' might lead one to expect – just because autonomy is not achieved at all. In the long term, this means that the gains obtained in the economic realm by the poorest will not be converted into structural power inside democratic organisations.

The next section of the chapter looks at the impact of the different tax systems found in Brazil, Europe and South Africa on the patterns of reduction (or enlargement) of economic and social inequality between groups. After that, the discussion will move on to the problem of inequality and poverty reduction as political programmes and the process of democratic will-formation under present political conditions in Brazil and South Africa. In this way, we hope we will move a step forward in the direction of an analysis of global inequalities in the contemporary period by identifying how given historical conditions allow (or block) the possibility of social justice through specific programmes of social equalisation.

PRODUCTION AND REPRODUCTION OF INEQUALITIES IN DEMOCRATIC SOCIETIES

Tocqueville ([1840] 2003) has famously situated inequality as the main cause of social convulsions, both of the richest trying to 'enslave' the poor and of the poor trying to challenge the rich. Much earlier, Aristotle defined democracy and oligarchy by considering the share of rich and poor people among the rulers. In very simple terms, democracy is determined, for him, by the rule of the poorest while oligarchy means the rule of the richest. Making use of similar arguments in the present, Santos (1962) follows this line of thinking, adding to the definition of democracy the moral obligation that democracies have to provide rights that would enable underprivileged groups to fight for justice. Thus, for him, democracy is both a product of the social struggles to make a society more equal and a cause of a wider equalisation of a social order.

The very idea of a bureaucratic state is based on the rational organisation of a tax system, revenue, and expenditure by providing services that meet people's needs in the most efficient way. In some parts of the Western world, the idea of a fiscal state was accompanied by a change in the idea of good governance – understood as the control of a people's wealth for the sake of the well-being of the people itself. In the linear modernisation view that Schumpeter (1991) has developed in an essay that became widely known and used to think about the rise of the fiscal state, we can find a questionable historical explanation about the connection between economic growth, a nation's wealth and the principles of democratic distribution (Schumpeter 1991: 129–30). His view is problematic because it assumes that the attainment of an efficient tax system is a question of going through pre-determined historical steps in the direction of establishing efficient democratic machinery. The implication of this view is that we would need to agree with the claim that war and power through violence are the mothers of democracy. Despite its limitations, we can agree that Schumpeter is probably right when he asserts that an autonomous and fair resource collection system is the backbone of modern democracy. This does not, however, necessarily entail the formal implementation of principles developed in Western societies. Democracy can function even under circumstances of a very unfair fiscal regime that also makes possible the very reproduction of an unequal situation. This is a point we want to explore further.

In the Democracy Index of 2017, which measures democracy through indicators of civil liberties, political culture and pluralism,[6] both Brazil and South Africa are regarded as 'flawed democracies'. Both societies are similarly situated: Brazil is ranked as 49th and South Africa occupies the 41st position. This means that they have a functioning democratic system but experience limitations. Regardless of which data source we work with, southern Africa and Latin America always appear among the most unequal regions in the world;[7] Western European countries are in a more comfortable position among the less unequal countries.

According to the Gini index, in 2006 South Africa was on the top as one of most unequal countries in the world, with a score of 64.08. Among the countries we are looking at, it is in South Africa that we observe the strongest variation from 2006 to 2016. This variation, as we will see, it is due to the adoption of different fiscal and (re)distributive polices. Also in 2006, Brazil was in a slightly better position, with a Gini index of 55.9 – unlike in South Africa, we do not observe strong variations from 2006 to the 2016. For the same period, from 2006 to 2016, most Western European countries had a Gini index around 30.00–36.00.[8] These data give us a general picture of the state of inequality in those regions just before the financial crisis of 2008. Europe was one of the regions of the world most affected by this crisis. Brazil and South Africa were not regarded to have been as affected as Northern countries. Democratic transformation, economic expansion and the social policies developed in those Southern countries were accepted by politicians and experts as the main causal factors used to explain why they were not as badly affected by the crisis as were the main economies of the Western world.

The electoral successes of left-wing governments in Latin America and Africa at the beginning of the twenty-first century, along with the global (high) price of commodities, created a favourable situation for the expansion of social policies in both regions. As mentioned above, the struggle against social inequality varies in relation to the political and economic context into which one is inserted. Thus it would be fair to expect that recent aggregated economic data for the period would show an overall improvement in the picture of inequalities in the Southern countries that we are looking at. This hypothesis is based on the assumptions that the 2008 crisis affected the patterns of social equality and inequality in Europe and that the democratic innovations experienced in Brazil and South Africa would have positively created strong structures to avoid the collapse of the social achievements of the period. However, it seems like the situation is much more nuanced than that. The later speculative crisis confirmed the hypothesis that without economic structural transformation no local economy can remain untouched by the global waves emanating from financial markets.[9]

In 2016, using different data sources, the United Nations Development Programme (UNDP) released the 'Human Development Report 2016: Human Development for Everyone'. This report works with indicators that show how, despite some important developments in global human development levels, these achievements were not evenly distributed among different countries and also within countries. Both in the North and in the South, so-called 'vulnerable groups' – such as indigenous groups, ethnic minorities, immigrants and refugees, blacks, women and children – still experienced disadvantages when compared to traditionally empowered social groups (UNDP 2016). But keeping for the moment to the comparison of the general picture of the relation between democratic mechanisms and the production and reproduction of inequalities, despite expectations, Brazil and South Africa did not manage the economic and political situation in a manner that would allow them to achieve a better position in terms of social inequality; and the picture of Europe did not change as much as one might have expected in the wake of an economic crisis. Income concentration did become stronger in Spain – moving from a Gini index measure of 32.5 in 2006 to 35.9 in 2016 – but the situation in Germany has improved – in 2006 the measure was 31.8 and in 2016 30.1. Brazil and South Africa both saw income inequalities become stronger during this period. (See Table 7.1.)

Table 7.1 General Inequality Indicators (2016)

	North		South	
	Spain	Germany	Brazil	South Africa
Human Development Index (HDI)[a]	0.884	0.926	0.754	0.666
Overall loss in HDI due to inequality (%)	10.5	7.2	25.6	34.7
Inequality-adjusted HDI (IHDI)[b]	0.791	0.859	0.561	0.435
Income inequality (Gini)	35.9	30.1	51.5	63.4

Source: UNDP 2016
[a] Human Development Index: a composite index measuring three basic dimensions: long and healthy life, knowledge, and a decent standard of living (UNDP 2016).
[b] Inequality-adjusted HDI (IHDI): an adjusted version of the HDI for inequality in each dimension (long and healthy life, knowledge, a decent standard of living) of each population section. The IHDI accounts for inequalities in HDI dimensions by discounting each dimension's average value according to its level of inequality (UNDP 2016).

This picture is not just a general statistical expression of what we already know about economic justice in these countries. To understand what these data mean, it is necessary to develop the idea of 'path dependence' further as a method of analysis that needs to pay attention to both historical trajectories and critical (reflexive) interpretation. For us, the main explanation for the differences between Northern and Southern countries relies on an understanding of the manner in which diversity and belonging have historically been (de)linked in each context to the idea of social *deservedness*. Above all, when it comes to moments of transformation when an established social order is subjected to reflexive action. The interpretation needs to move from statistics and mechanisms to the context of production, reproduction and moments of change in prevailing self-understandings of *who deserves to get, who should pay*, and *what should be provided* in each context.

Historical evidence has shown that in the global North – mainly in Europe – democratisation enticed public expenditure and made possible the development of the welfare state and thus democratisation of the social question (Lindert 1994; Castel 1995; Yun-Casalilla and O'Brien 2012). The appearance of what Castel has called the 'social state' in Europe is a consequence of a transformation of the *social question* into a public problem, not a private one. Between the nineteenth and the twentieth centuries it happened to be the case that the state started to see itself as a 'regulator' between different classes (Castel 1995). When it works well as a regulator of social relations, the modern state tends to act in favour of underprivileged groups. Thus, following this perspective, twentieth century European history, which is as uneven as any regional history can be, shows how the state managed to retain this function of regulating class interests under conditions of wider and stronger connectedness.

The understanding of *who deserves to get what* and *who should pay for what should be provided* is completely marked by the formation and transformation of the social question in Europe. Unlike in the South, European solidarity has been transformed when it comes to the *commitment* of the better-offs to assume their share in supporting social security schemes. At least for those regarded as citizens with political rights, and still connected to the historical transformations of the eighteenth and nineteenth centuries, the idea of the poor as a group of people who deserve to live under much worse conditions has been strongly challenged. In this process of ruptures, the tax system of those Northern countries, along with the regulation of concentrations of wealth – as well as land – was slowly transformed by the introduction of more egalitarian policies. In the South, by contrast, it seems to be the case that public expenditure grew prior to democratisation and was used as means to build political support (Seekings 2014).

This is not the same as saying that the continental European model fully attained an ideal way of targeting those who can (and should) pay more for the provision of public structures and services for those who pay less. It is this change in the conception of solidarity and belonging that led to the rise of the 'social state' in Europe (for a broad recent debate, see Karagiannis 2007). The social question in Europe is under a process of transformation and the issue about the inclusion/exclusion of immigrants and how they should be placed in the structures of right in the European countries in which they come to live plays a central role. Another issue to bear in mind is that, at the present moment, it seems to be the case that this regulatory function of the state when it comes to the relations between citizens is moving from a class-based one to a care-based approach in which underprivileged individuals in different social strata have become the focus of state redistributive polices. This is clear, for instance, when it comes to the creation of policies to fight informal, unpaid child labour and to ensure elderly care as part of a gender equality agenda across the class structure in Europe today (Bettio and Plantenga 2008).

There are still many ways through which social inequalities are reproduced in Europe. Rather than to say that in Europe democracy has led to full equalisation, the point is just that the idea of economic, social and political disadvantage has not been justified in terms of identifying a group of people who deserve to be in that situation. Legal immigrants can access social and economic rights in Europe. How this happens varies from country to country. However, what does not vary much is that the immigrant is largely much worse off than the national citizen – even within a similar class position – and that this is so because they do not have political rights. In Spain, for instance, a European resident can vote in municipal elections, though not in national ones, while immigrants from any other part of the world cannot vote at all. The only way to access political rights is to become a national citizen.

The trajectory of institutional transformations is reflected in the perceptions of citizens. As Cardoso (2010) shows, if one compares perceptions of justice and of equality among citizens in countries such as Germany and Switzerland with those in Brazil, one finds that the poorest 40% in the Northern countries recognise that they are inserted into an unequal situation and want to change it. In Brazil, by contrast, the poorest 40% tend to pay less attention to structural inequalities when explaining their social position. This is so even though the rich in Brazil recognise Brazil as marked by the existence of strong social hierarchies and pronounced inequalities.[10] In South Africa, poor people also do not agree with the idea that all of the poorest deserve to be the focus of public policies. Seekings (2014: 16) shows how this works by demonstrating how the poor themselves create criteria of deservedness to justify why some individuals should not get state support.

In Brazil the focus of the PT government was the empowerment of the poorest, but without a major political change in the redistributive and tax system (Silveira 2012). Brazil still has one of the most unequal tax systems the world. Theoretically, the country has a progressive tax system in which people with higher incomes pay 27.5% tax; people in lower income brackets pay 7.5%; while at the middle-income level taxes range from 15.0% to 22.5%. However, income tax represents less than 20% of the tax revenue in Brazil – in 2015 it was exactly 18.27%. In practice the Brazilian tax system is in fact a regressive one. What really counts for the Brazilian tax system is the tax paid on goods and services (VAT), which has been around 50% of tax revenue (Vianna 2000; Silveira 2012). In 2015 goods and services were responsible for 49.68% of all tax revenue collected by the government. In South Africa tax revenue relies more on income tax – called Personal Income Tax (PIT) – representing 34% of tax revenue in 2016. VAT revenue represented 26.4% and other tax, such as company taxes, represented almost 40% of revenue (SARS 2017). In Europe, too, VAT has become increasingly important for state revenue due to the competition among societies for business and highly qualified, high-wage employed and self-employed workers.[11] But those developments have not gone as far as reaching the levels of Brazil or South Africa. European countries are all members of the Organisation for Economic Co-operation and Development (OECD). In OECD countries, personal income tax participation in 2015 was responsible, on average, for 24.4% of the state's revenue; general consumption taxes account for 21% on average of total tax revenue in OECD countries (OECD 2017).

Even under the PT's leadership there was no structural transformation of tax legislation to make it move in the direction of a fully progressive model in which the richest would pay substantially more than the poorest. If what is aimed at by left-wing governments is to distribute and redistribute wealth and services to all members of a political community, it is quite telling that even under a progressive regime it was not possible to push through a reform of the tax system that would rely on direct taxation of income. If a tax system relies on consumption and on taxes on the circulation of goods, both the very rich and the very poor contribute to the structural upkeep of state services – or proportionally more the poor, who probably end up paying more tax than the rich as they have much lower incomes and only have the internal market available to them.[12] Thus, while there was an improvement in the quality and in the amount of public service provided to the population between 2002 and 2015,[13] a conclusion that we take from the years of PT rule is that, without a re-organisation of the tax system, the poorest who improved their lives indirectly paid for the state-provided services they received themselves.

Brazil has managed to foster economic growth without a significant transformation in social inequality (OECD 2010). From 2001 to 2015 what has happened was that the top 10% of earners increased their share in the distribution of wealth, accompanied also by an improvement of the bottom 50%'s income share. However, the share of the top 10% grew much more than the share of the bottom 50%, while the middle income class that represents 40% of the population decreased their share in the general growth of the period (Morgan 2017).[14] During the years of the PT rule, the extreme patterns of reproduction of inequality were not really challenged, neither by a reform agenda advanced by the government nor by civil society actions.[15] There was an improvement in the income of the poorest, while the richest increased their wealth even more in the period and the working middle class became squeezed in the middle of both groups who had experienced some growth. The improvement in the general conditions of life of the poorest was not strong enough to change the high level of income inequality historically developed in the country.[16]

The ANC came to power with the promise of promoting a 'better life for all' in post-apartheid South Africa. In the process initiated in 1994, mechanisms for the reduction of poverty and improving the inequality gap have been tried by implementing changes in the tax system. Such initiatives have slowly progressed in the direction of directly targeting the income of the richest and redistributing it through social policies. This does represent an important step towards the reduction of social inequalities. Economic growth due to high commodity prices and the improvement of welfare programmes was responsible for the reduction of poverty observed especially since 2002 in South Africa. According to data provided by the World Bank, a general decline in poverty from 2006 to 2011 was observed; in 2014 it dropped to one of the lowest levels in history, with 16.5% of the population living in extreme poverty; by 2015 the level of the population living in poverty started to rise again.

In 2014, an improvement in the indicator of the state of social inequality was also observed, with a fall in the Gini index to 59.00. As we saw above, this had stood at 64.8 in 2006. In 1996 only 58.2% of South African houses had electricity; in 2016 the percentage of households connected to the electricity grid reached 90.3% (STATS SA 2017b). The poorest benefitted much more than the rich from the widening of such basic infrastructural policies. However, as Seekings (2014) shows, the general improvement in the living conditions of the poorest did not substantially reduce poverty levels more broadly and the distribution of income became more unequal. This is so because the ANC did not manage to create the promised structure for job creation and maintenance of economic growth along with an accelerated programme of expansion of structural services.[17]

As in Brazil, the policies developed in recent decades in South Africa did not change the situation of these societies as exceptionally diverse and unequal. Unlike in Europe, in Brazil and South Africa state institutions did not show themselves as able to function as long-term regulators of market relations. Distributive and redistributive polices in Southern societies show that the problems of *who gets what* and *how to get what is needed* can only be addressed if historical injustice is democratically faced. In terms of racial injustices, it seems like South Africa is recovering from the apartheid legacy. There is no doubt that blacks should get as much as whites from the state. However, much needs to be done in terms of economic and social injustice. This applies both to class-based issues and to issues regarding minority groups inside the country. Brazil has also strongly challenged the idea of a racial democracy in which racism was not a mark of this society due to the politics of inclusion embraced by the PT in recent decades.[18] The same can be said about gender and ethnic rights. However, as in South Africa, much needs to be done in terms of redressing full inequalities related to class and securing economic and social justice. Without a broader democratisation of state institutions and democratic powers it seems like the gains are going to be very conjectural and vulnerable.

REDUCTION OF INEQUALITY AND REDUCTION OF POVERTY IN BRAZIL AND SOUTH AFRICA

It seems to us that the most plausible explanation for the production or crystallisation of inequalities one can find is through analysing major historical changes in regimes for the regulation of forms of wealth such as income, the tax system, land acquisition, inheritance and land concentration. Of particular importance, in the social settings that interest us here, is the tax configuration and its impact on the social organisation of a society. The effects of such regulation need to be studied side by side with programmes for the reduction of poverty and the process of democratic will-formation.

The reduction of poverty and the improvement of human development indicators can occur without an expected reduction in the gap between those at the top and those at the bottom, as we have shown in the previous section. In 2003 the cash transfer Family Allowance Programme, the PBF (the abbreviation for its Portuguese name, *Programa Bolsa Família*), was launched by the recently inaugurated PT government. The programme aimed to transfer a direct amount of money on a monthly basis to families in situations of poverty. It was announced as the first attempt in Brazilian history to target poverty by allowing working members of poor families to have a complementary income which would be conditionally linked to social rights in the fields of education, health and social assistance. The core innovation of the PBF compared to others that appeared since the Brazilian System of Social Protection emerged in 1920s is that those targeted did not lose their productive capacity. Even after the promulgation of the 1988 constitution and the impetus that it gave to the development of social programmes, social policies tended to focus on retired and disabled people (Paiva et al. 2013). As such, the PBF aimed to challenge poverty as a social problem by pursuing social and economic integration even of families who had work and income (Campello and Neri 2013). The programme also aimed to economically empower women by assigning responsibility to the mother for the handling of PBF family grants. In the case of couples, women were also charged with managing PBF payments. In practical terms, this means that it was the women who received the bank card used for the withdrawal of the monthly allowance.

By 2011, PBF was connected to other poverty-reduction programmes under the umbrella auspices of the 'Brazil without Extreme Poverty Programme' (*Programa Brasil sem Miséria*). There is strong evidence demonstrating the success of the programmes to reduce poverty developed by the PT government under Lula's presidency. According to the Brazilian Institute of Statistics and Geography (IBGE) and the annual National Sample Research of Domiciles (PNAD), from 2003 to 2011 it was possible to observe an improvement in the general conditions of the population living under the poverty line and in extreme poverty.[19]

The outcomes of these programmes seemed to be so positive that in 2012 the eradication of poverty was envisaged as a viable scenario in the near future (Sousa and Osorio 2012). However, the political and economic situation has changed, and it has been accompanied by a reconsideration of the path that the country should take.

The social policies implemented by the PT were regarded by political opponents as part of a populist programme that would allow the party to remain in power. By the end of Lula's second term, the press released news on an almost daily basis about how the PT's electoral support was much more concentrated in the poor zones of the country. By then it was assumed that the main cause of the election of Dilma Rousseff in 2010 – the first woman to become president of Brazil – was that the party was the only organisation capable of keeping the cash transfer programmes to reduce poverty running. She herself was regarded by the press at that moment as an 'inexpressively tough administrator' without much political appeal. In that year, this idea was corroborated by the fact that the PT won significant victories in the poorest parts of the country – while losing support in traditional middle class areas. In the election of 2014 the situation remained mostly unchanged aside from the fact that the PT was losing support even more rapidly in the more developed regions of the country.

Going in a different direction to what has been generally said, we would like to argue that three factors explain the PT's loss of power, which had as its final act the very controversial impeachment of president Dilma Rousseff in 2016. The first is the loss of economic and social power of the 'squeezed' middle class – the 40% that did not gain much economic and political power through the government's project. Second, the regional traditional elites believed their programme of redirecting developmental economic growth incompatible with struggles for the implementation of real redistributive polices in the country – such as the reconsideration of the tax system. Third, and probably more importantly, Dilma Rousseff revealed her intention to target the rich and the traditional elites by revising the pension and inheritance system that is responsible for the maintenance of a form of aristocracy inside Brazilian society.[20] This aristocracy remains in power latently through their position in key state institutions such as in the judiciary. On its own, the defence of poverty-reduction programmes as a populist project that worked to keep the PT in power does not explain the four consecutive victories of the party.[21]

As in Brazil, South Africa also has a social security system that has been in operation since the 1920s. However, it used to be strongly biased along racial lines even while still targeting the poorest members of society (Brockerhoff 2010). Only with the Social Assistance Act of 1992 were racially discriminatory conditions finally abolished. The social security system and the cash transfer programmes put forward by the ANC in South Africa have the poorest and most vulnerable groups (such as the elderly, children and disabled people) as targets, but women, the unemployed and the working poor have not been subject to an extensive programme of economic and social justice (Plagerson and Ulriksen 2015). Post-apartheid South Africa has based social security policies on cash transfer programmes. By 1998, with the introduction of Child Support Grant (CSG), we observe an improvement in public expenditure due to the amount of cash transfer programmes, such as the Old Age Pension and the Disability Grant.

Social assistance grants have been widely used by the ANC as part of programmes focusing on people who do not contribute directly to government revenue. Most of these grants work based on some light conditional criteria. But it has not been always like that. The CSG, for example, started with some conditionalities. They were challenged by studies showing that the conditionalities were excluding those who most needed the programme (Woolard and Leibbrandt 2010). In 2000, the Committee of Inquiry into Comprehensive Social Security – known as the Taylor Committee – recommended that the CSG should be unconditional. They also recommended a universal basic income grant.[22] President Thabo Mbeki argued at the time that the main tool used by the government to fight poverty should be social grants.

In April 2010, out of a population of 49 million people, 14 million were benefiting from this kind of social assistance grant (Woolard and Leibbrandt 2010). The impact of these programmes was quite strong. In 2014, the data showed that in South Africa 3.6 million people escaped poverty and this was accompanied by a reduction in income inequality (World Bank 2014). The social uplift achieved by these means was much better than what we have seen in the same period in other Southern countries such as in Brazil. Along with the tax reform implemented in the country, the implementation of cash grants constitutes the basic general feature of the redistributive programmes implemented in South Africa in recent decades. It seems like ANC rulers recognised that to increase expenditure to challenge inequality and poverty could not be done without a re-structuration of state revenue.

However, as happened in Brazil, it is the case that income inequalities have also worsened in South Africa (Seekings 2014). Both poor and rich have been benefitting from economic growth in South Africa. The poor, however, are still much more vulnerable and dependent on the existence of distributive and redistributive polices to keep them from dropping below the poverty line again. As argued earlier, one of the reasons why we argue that economic inequality is still a huge and persistent problem in South Africa and Brazil is because social injustice was historically incorporated into the social imaginaries and institutions of those societies. There is clear evidence that progressive governments in these Southern countries have improved the social security system to fight poverty, not inequality. And they have been successful in doing so. Diverse programmes have been implemented in these countries, not as political platforms to run elections, but as measures to fight poverty. They try to address historical injustices that have locked underprivileged groups into a very vulnerable position. The problem arose because both countries did not convert the introduced structure of social security into a system of guaranteed social rights.

In 2012, South Africa developed a programme (the National Development Plan – NDP) in which the government formulated its goals for the reduction of inequality and poverty by 2030. The challenges facing this plan are great: to reduce the proportion of persons living below the lower-bound poverty line from 39.0% in the base year of 2009 to 0%; to reduce poverty-induced hunger from 21.4% in 2011 (base year) to 0%. The programme also aims at a small reduction in terms of income inequality – to reach a Gini index of 0.6. Despite the big challenges in terms of improving the living conditions of the poorest and the impressive task of reducing income inequality, what needs to be highlighted about the NDP is the maintenance of the social question as a key political agenda in South Africa. The situation in Brazil is entirely different. Since 2016, with the presidency of Michel Temer, there is no political plan in sight to continue advancing policies for improving the life of the poor and challenging social inequality. On the contrary, the government is dismantling important programmes such as the PBF by cutting the share of the public budget assigned to it. To compare both scenarios, in 2017 social expenditure was responsible for 3.5% of GDP in South Africa; in Brazil, for the same year, only 1.5% of GDP was designated to social programmes.

It is informative to parenthetically illustrate how these policies were expressed through government and political slogans in Brazil. During the first and the second terms of PT rule, with Lula as president (2002–10), the slogan was 'Brazil, a country for all'. In the continuation of PT rule with Dilma (2010–14), the first slogan adopted was 'A rich country is a country without poverty', and later (2014–16), 'More changes, more future'.[23] When we compare these ideas with the following ones the sense in which they represent a broader change becomes clear. As soon as Temer was proclaimed president, he changed his political slogan to 'Brazil, order and progress' – the positivistic idea stated in the Brazilian flag of the nineteenth century – thereby resuscitating the imaginary of the military order and the idea of progress as an economic condition that will come only with the hard work of the 'good poor'. The launch of this slogan comes along with regressive politics in terms of inclusion of historically excluded groups: one of the first presidential orders imposed by Temer on 12 May 2016 was the abolition of the Ministry of Women, Racial Equality and Human Rights, for instance,[24] followed by a labour reform in 2017 that deepens the precariousness of working conditions and removes important workers' rights.

Another problem that we would like to highlight refers to the manner in which inequalities have been increased through the concentration of land and land dispossession, along with the stratification of different ethnic groups according to their deservedness to occupy (or not) specific spaces (Stavenhagen 1969). Land seizure and division also constitutes an important common ground for the formation of collective political action for both Northern and Southern societies. The uses of land and the forms of appropriating it are in themselves a form of materialisation of social, economic and political power. In the middle of the twentieth century the redistribution of land was seen as a key aspect of the struggle against social inequalities (Kling 1956; Gonzáles Casanova 1980). Progressive governments in Brazil and South Africa did not challenge the structures that make possible the reproduction of inequalities through land possession (Gotlib 2015). Doing so would be an important step in the direction of fighting inequalities in a more comprehensive manner.

CONCLUSION

If in Brazil and South Africa the improvements with regard to social inequality have not been as significant as one could have expected with the introduction of political equality, the erosion of the attained level of comparatively low social inequality has not been as pronounced as feared with the arrival of austerity politics. While social inequality has been increasing, the commitment to social welfare has remained rather high at the level of European nation states, that is, at the level where governments depend on voters. Still, there is considerable concern about whether these commitments will be sustained in the near future. Large areas of Europe have witnessed de-industrialisation with losses of employment; and employment creation in other sectors has often not been sufficiently strong to compensate for losses and/or the quality of the new working conditions, in particular contract duration, which is lower. One sociologist talked already in the 1980s about the 'Brazilianisation' of Europe, meaning an increase in the share of precarious, informal employment (Therborn 1989). Rather than pitting one society as a 'unit of analysis' against others, however, it is more important to recognise that the increasing porousness of economic borders, which has led to relocation of industry from Europe to other world-regions, in particular East Asia, entails difficulties in upholding levels of solidarity in Europe that are higher than elsewhere. One tentative response to this question has been European integration, if seen as both the creation of a larger market but also as the formation of a polity committed to solidarity. The recent Euro-crisis, with the imposition of stark austerity measures on Greece and other South European societies, followed by the very limited capacity for regulating Europe-wide the acceptance of refugees, however, have cast strong doubts on this strategy of social Europeanisation. Rather, the predominantly national link between political class and citizenry favours solutions of national closure, finding support and inspiration outside and at the edges of Europe with US President Trump's 'America First' policies and the UK's vote on leaving the EU.

In both Brazil and South Africa, but also in Europe, in very different situations, the racial and the regional issue came to form some of the main foundations for the formation of specific societal self-understandings of deservedness. For Europe, the racial bias of our times can best be discerned by observing the practical exclusions informed by the social and juridical division between immigrants (legal and illegal) and *deserving* and *committed* national citizens. Keeping to the differences that we have explored in this chapter, unequal historical conditions in patterns of income, wealth concentration, and distribution/redistribution have formed everywhere in the North and the South and they have been transformed by the interplay of equalising and disequalising factors.

Part III

Enlarging the Scope of Political Action

Chapter 8

THE AMAZON, THE RHINO AND THE BLUE SKY OVER THE RUHR

A TRULY GLOBAL ISSUE

What we now call environmental concerns used to be most treated as local issues. Industrial factories and urban agglomerations were sites of high emissions of pollutants. These pollutants usually stayed close to the sources of emission and caused environmental impact there, mostly endangering human health. The air pollution in London in 1952, called the Great Smog, using the neologism coined by combining 'smoke' with 'fog' in the early twentieth century, was among the first events that both caused a public outcry and triggered quick and rather effective action.[1] After this, environmental issues rose quickly to become an important part of public debate in Europe. In 1960, the Social Democrat candidate for head of government in West Germany, Willy Brandt, included into the national election campaign a slogan about 'the blue sky over the Ruhr', a river in the main coal and steel region of the country, referring to the ambition to reduce air pollution. Thus he made environmental concerns a key issue of the national policy agenda (we return to this campaign below).[2] In 1962, Rachel Carson published her book *Silent Spring* in the US, pointing to the large-scale consequences of the use of pesticides, even far away from the source. In 1972, the Club of Rome published its report 'Limits to Growth', emphasising the risk of depleting the natural resources of the planet earth, thus developing a fully global perspective on the consequences of industrialisation.

These two last-mentioned publications are often referred to as turning environmental issues global, the one in terms of large-scale damaging impacts on the environment, the other in terms of resource extraction. In 1986, the accident in the nuclear power station at Chernobyl (Soviet Union, now Ukraine) had radioactive fallout that stretched far beyond given state borders. From the 1990s onwards, and increasingly so, the effects of emitting so-called greenhouse gases into the atmosphere have moved to the centre of attention. Climate scientists now largely agree that a long-term change of the planetary climate due to human-made emissions is occurring. Current environmental phenomena such as the increasing number and strength of hurricanes, or the steady rise of average temperatures in some world-regions, are attributed to human-made climate change. With this debate, a point has been reached where a diffuse global phenomenon, not traceable to a single source such as a nuclear power station, has a diffuse global impact. Thus, the identification of causes and the assigning of responsibilities has become as complex an issue as the assessment of damages. At the same time, there has been a drastic increase in the significance of the problem, namely the risk of making large areas of the planet uninhabitable together with the long-term nature of the process and the difficulty of halting it, not to speak of partially reversing it. Climate change has become a prime example for demonstrating the high degree of interconnectedness among world-regions today.

SHIFTING RESPONSIBILITY: THE RHINO AND THE AMAZON

It is peculiar, though, that the apparently recent 'globalisation' of ecological issues along the main lines of debate was preceded by a specific North–South discourse. After 150 years of industrialisation in the North and domestication of Northern flora and fauna, well-intended Northern observers recognised that nature was at risk in the South. An early example is the engagement of the German veterinarian and zoo director Bernhard Grzimek and his son, who focused on the Serengeti region in what is now Tanzania. They did not deny the marvels of civilisation, including industrial civilisation, but underlined that everything human-made could be reproduced whereas natural wildlife, once extinct, could not.[3] Their film *Serengeti Shall Not Die* from 1959 was a great public success and won the US Academy Award for Documentary Feature in the following year. It had the form of a documentary and an appeal, suggesting the need for outside intervention, thus implying that the local authorities – both colonial and post-colonial – would neither have the intention nor the capacity to do so. This kind of Northern ecological discourse that focuses on Southern regions that require intervention for reasons of environmental protection has since become very common.

Two of its more recent examples, addressing Latin America and southern Africa, are the Amazon rainforest and the rhinoceros.

The Amazon region contains the largest contiguous area of rainforest on the globe. It is inhabited by a great diversity of fauna and flora, with many species being unique to the area. Furthermore, it acts as the 'lungs' of the planet by reducing the carbon dioxide content of the atmosphere. Thus, there are good reasons to see the region as of global interest, and not of interest for Brazil and neighbouring countries alone. At the same time, the forest is threatened by deforestation and dispossession of small land-holdings to allow for large-scale agricultural use and for mining. In the course of these acts, the livelihood of indigenous communities is also threatened. It is common to see reports about the threats to the rainforest and their global impact in Northern media. Often it is accompanied by the observation that the national authorities – with Brazil at the centre – are unable or unwilling to stop the destruction. However, it is less often added that much of the invasive production is oriented towards exportation to the North, the incentive thus being provided by Northern economic 'pull'. Nor has the fact been much observed that the close connection of the environmental movement with the Lula presidency resulted in a considerable slowing down of deforestation.

Something similar can be said about rhino poaching in South Africa, in which there has been a sharp spike over recent years. Some 80% of the 80,000 rhinoceroses in the world live on South African territory. While in 2007 thirteen of them were killed, the number rose to 1,214 in 2014 and has not fallen below 1,000 since. The spike is connected to rising demand for rhino horn, in particular in Asia, where it is believed to have aphrodisiac and medicinal qualities. The demand is driven, in turn, by rising incomes in Asia and by the fact that, with greater market integration across the globe, such demand is relatively easy to meet in today's world. While the rise in killings has been associated with corruption of government officials, South Africa did intervene quite forcefully in suppressing poaching and has been able to stabilise the rhino population.[4]

If we look at Northern discourse on these topics, we recognise that Brazil and South Africa are seen as being responsible for key aspects of global sustainability. At the same time, especially the left-leaning PT and ANC governments have been critically observed with regard to their capacity for enhancing economic activities. In the latter regard, the material, substantive core of natural-resource extraction and land dispossession disappears behind the numerical, statistical contribution of these processes to economic growth. Thus, these governments are placed under the dual prerogative of protecting nature for the whole globe's sake on the one hand and enhancing economic performance on the other. They risk being criticised for succeeding at neither to the required degree. To paraphrase what former president Dilma Rousseff, then still in office, once said to the Spanish newspaper *El País*: here 'they detain you for having a dog and for not having a dog'.[5]

NORTHERN COMPLACENCY: THE BLUE SKY OVER THE RUHR

In these discourses, Europe holds multiple positions. First of all, its voice is that of the guardian of the common good. Europe recognises the peril of environmental destruction and urges action. This voice is often not free of paternalistic, neo-colonial overtones: it is Europe that recognises the necessity, and it is the South that does not fully recognise it and/ or fails to efficiently act according to this insight. Second, Europe may contribute to solving the issue, but it would do so voluntarily, since this is not within its domain of responsibility. This is so for two reasons: firstly, both the right and the responsibility for environmental protection action resides with the sovereign powers over the respective territories; and secondly, even in global terms, the responsibility to act lies elsewhere because Europe has already done its duty.[6] The London air is relatively clean because effective action was taken in the Clean Air Act of 1956 and subsequent initiatives. The sky over the Ruhr is blue again (and one can even swim again in the river).[7] Generally, air and water quality has considerably improved in Europe since the beginnings of explicit environmental policies. More and more, materials are recycled for re-use, and energy production is increasingly based on renewable sources.

Statements like the above can be found abundantly in official publications from the local level of municipalities to the supra-national one of the European Commission. And they are largely true. They allow European governments at all levels to present themselves as 'at the forefront'[8] of all action to save the planet and to improve human living conditions on it. However, this discourse is also extremely complacent. It seems to say, true, we have created the problem due to industrialisation, but we have also recognised it in time and, insofar as we are responsible, have largely resolved it.

However, it ignores – or claims to ignore, since the knowledge is not lacking at all – that the reasoning only holds if the results of environmental policies are attributed to individual world-regions and their state actors and, at the same time, the chains of action that cause environmental damage are ignored. If we look again at the case of the Ruhr river, the first successes were reached by using so-called end-of-pipe technologies, such as filters placed on the chimneys of coal-fired power stations and steel production plants, but they were very limited. Breakthroughs in the improvement of environmental quality were achieved when the German iron and steel industry was largely closed down. In public and scholarly debate, such closing down of plants was seen as part of a general tendency towards 'de-industrialisation', a radicalisation of the earlier theme on the transition towards 'post-industrial society'.[9]

Globally, though, there is no evidence of de-industrialisation at all. Global industrial output has been steadily rising over the past decades, the only exception being a fairly minor dip in 2009. However, the sites of industrial production have changed radically, being almost stagnant in Europe after a steep decline in 2010, at only slightly higher levels in the US after three years of decline from 2007 to 2009, and demonstrating uninterrupted growth at high rates in China.[10] Thus, rather than 'de-industrialisation', what happened was industrial relocation from sites in the formerly so-called 'advanced industrial societies' towards other regions, predominantly in Asia (in a way, already starting with Japan much earlier), but increasingly also elsewhere. The observation of these shifts has given rise to the term 'emerging economies' and also to the acronym BRICS, followed even by the creation of an association between those five countries, indicating a possible shift in economic power relations. Our concern here, though, is that the industrial relocation also entails an externalisation of environmental damage.

Looking more closely, the improvement of environmental quality in Europe is directly related to the deterioration of environmental quality elsewhere. While producing less, Europe remains a high consumer of industrial products, and they are produced elsewhere with most of the environmental discharge occurring at the site of production or earlier at the site of extraction of raw materials. The sky over the Ruhr is blue because iron and steel for industrial products used in Germany are no longer produced in Germany. Such externalisation occurs across the whole chain of production and consumption.[11] Thus, Europe uses an enormous amount of global soil for the production of foodstuffs required to feed animals for European consumption of meat. Decades after the end of formal colonialism, it keeps 'occupying' space outside its own territory for its needs and purposes. At the other end, from the early 1990s, China accepted a large part of European recyclable waste materials, mostly paper and plastic. But it has recently refused to continue to do so, taking European policy-makers by surprise and leaving them without any effective response. This is an indication that relations of power have started to change to such an extent that externalisation seems to have become more difficult or less straightforward.

CLIMATE CHANGE AND HISTORICAL INJUSTICE

The problematic of asymmetric externalisation becomes particularly clear when one looks at the debate about climate change and policy action with regard to it. This is so because the global dimension is immediately central with regard to the contemporary consequences of the instrumental transformation of the earth. Let us briefly summarise the argument, introduced earlier. Industrialism in all its aspects – mass production, mass consumption, transport infrastructure – is the main cause for climate change and its likely consequences in terms of deteriorating living conditions on the earth. It was developed by the early industrial powers in north-western Europe and later North America for their own benefit, but dependent on the creation of an Atlantic division of labour involving African labour and American soil in the European 'take-off' of industrialism. When the environmental effects of industrialism were recognised from the 1960s onwards, they were seen as health risks caused by pollution in the vicinity of industrial production and consumption. Remedial action through environmental policies was effective, but it stayed close to these sites. In addition, the emerging new global division of labour from the 1970s onwards entailed the relocation of heavily polluting industries as well as nature-transforming extractive industries to other parts of the world.

This is the constellation that we have outlined. For a long time, it was largely assumed that it could be analysed in politico-economic terms, underlining not least that the industrial relocations were an important cause for economic growth in the so-called 'emerging' societies and the dangers to the environment a 'price to pay' for this growth. Then, 'externalisation' would be nothing other than the application of market logics. The 'comparative advantage' of many societies of the South would accordingly be the fact that they have the soil available to provide the North with raw materials and foodstuff as well as to dump their garbage. The earnings from these activities might lead these societies to 'emerge' in the future and then deal on a par with the earlier industrialised societies. Once climate change comes into the picture, however, that interpretation, doubtful as it always was, can clearly no longer be sustained. Climate change radically alters the perspectives for the future. As such, it imposes an interpretation that recognises that the instrumental transformation of the earth is strongly related to past domination and appropriation.

Therefore, the interpretation of the issue as temporal is what is new in the present. 'Modernist' and colonial discourse had relegated the colonised societies to a 'not yet', had denied them coevalness in the present, as anthropological and postcolonial scholarship has long pointed out (for example, Johannes Fabian, Dipesh Chakrabarty). The argument had been displayed in a variety of forms – reaching from immaturity to be overcome by education to the missing institutional preconditions for an industrial take-off. It did not normally include the notion that the 'backwardness' was induced by the relation of domination between colonisers and colonised (as dependency theory would underline). Whatever the past had been, the discourse of the 'not yet' suggested an exit from this situation in the future. But the climate change debate has changed this situation: because of the urgency, so the argument goes, emissions in the South cannot be allowed to rise to Northern levels. Apparently, the benefits of industrialism that were historically reaped by the 'advanced' societies need to be denied to the 'emerging' societies for the sake of keeping the earth inhabitable. Thus, societies that had been confined to the 'not yet' during colonisation and the hegemony of modernisation discourse are now condemned to a 'never'. If so, then, in this respect, historical injustice can no longer be remedied in the future.

As of today, the debate on climate change has two official points of reference. The state of knowledge on the phenomenon is monitored and summarised by the International Panel on Climate Change (IPCC), which brings together the common assessment of the overwhelming majority of competent scientists in the field, opposed only by a small number of persons who deny the existence of climate change, or at least its human-made nature. And the state of action has been formulated in the so-called Paris Agreement of December 2015, by now signed by almost all states on the globe and in effect since November 2016. The

Paris Agreement is in many respects an amazing achievement. It brings together almost the entire global political community to agree on a complex scientific diagnosis, itself operating with considerable degrees of uncertainty and indeterminacy, and to accept the urgency of acting in common by radically limiting so-called greenhouse emissions and thus avoiding significant future increases in global temperatures. All signatories to the agreement, furthermore, commit themselves to quantitatively specified targets for emission reduction. The agreement does not foresee any mechanism to enforce these targets, but it includes not only a monitoring process, but also further steps to be taken to increase the target levels and to concretise them in line with future observations and estimates on climate development by the IPCC.

Next to praise, the agreement has also received criticism, mostly because of setting the targets too low and lacking enforcement mechanisms. While both of these critical observations are pertinent, emphasising them risks losing sight of the enormous change in discourse brought about by the contract. With this document, the international political community has moved away from the assumption that all states are equal and are equally called upon to act in this highly urgent matter. Rather, it is recognised that 'developing countries' need to take longer in reaching the moment when emissions will fall, and it commits 'developed countries' to providing resources for developing countries to protect themselves from, or compensate, damage due to climate change. Even though the agreement avoids being explicit, this is *de facto* a recognition of historical injustice done by developed countries to developing countries.[12] A sense of this may have provoked the fury of US president Donald Trump, his announcement of the withdrawal of the US from the agreement, and the insistence that a better deal for 'America' was needed.

The problems with the agreement reside less in its quantitative insufficiency and its non-binding nature, because both of these are recognised within the agreement itself.[13] Thus, they are part of the explicit monitoring and adjustment process set in motion by the agreement. The problems reside rather in that which is significant yet not recognised. Three such elements are easily identifiable.

First, the Paris Agreement counts emissions according to the territorial site where they occur. This seems reasonable in light of the fact that governments can more easily control that which occurs on their territory. However, this way of accounting attributes the emissions for products always at the site of their production, not that of their consumption. This means, as hinted at above, that the commodities exported from China for use in Europe are 'counted' in the environmental balance sheet of China, whereas it would be more appropriate to count them where the realisation of their value (using Sadian's 2018 terminology) occurs. In the externalising 'consumer societies' of the North, the difference between 'consumption emissions' and 'territorial emissions' is considerable.[14]

Second, there is a rather great reliance on voluntary action in the agreement, certainly due to the fact that the explicit and specified commitments fall short of what is considered necessary. However, voluntary action by unspecified volunteers is difficult to achieve, particularly in situations in which the advantages and disadvantages fall to different actors. We can give one example that also goes back to a theme addressed earlier. Globally, it should not be too difficult to renounce the exploitation of some oil reserves, given that oil is at the moment rather abundant and that the climate objectives foresee an exit from the use of fossil sources of energy. It is a much more difficult question to decide which reserves are to be exploited and which not, given that they are found in states with very different forms of government and levels of wealth and inequality. Reasonably, one should aim at renouncing such resource exploitation wherever important counter-arguments exist. This is the case in Ecuador, where considerable exploitable oil reserves were discovered in a territory that is both an important natural reserve – a rainforest area of very high biodiversity – and an area in which two indigenous 'isolated' societies live, the Yasuní National Park. The government of Ecuador, headed by then president Rafael Correa, proposed in 2007 that the area be left untouched if the international community provided half the income that the state would renounce. The proposal was active until 2013, when Correa withdrew it after only a tiny fraction of the requested money had been promised.[15] These reserves are currently being exploited by the Ecuadorean national oil company Petroecuador. Hardly any Northern volunteer felt a sense of responsibility for contributing to reach this sensible and rather feasible objective.

Third, quite understandably given its nature, the agreement underestimates the possibilities of displacing the issue. Once signed, and even before, many of those concerned by it started considering what can and needs to be done to continue doing the same and living the same way. A case in point is the German motor industry. Cars built by nominally

German manufacturers are predominantly up-market products, which contain numerous special features. They are rather heavy and expensive, but are successfully sold on world markets to more well-to-do customers. It had been known for a long time that it would be difficult to make these cars meet more strict emission standards. Successive German governments intervened at the European Commission to avoid standards getting too tough, but this was apparently not successful enough. In 2015, the US Environmental Protection Agency detected devices to manipulate emissions under test conditions and started investigating the cases. Currently, numerous legal cases are still ongoing in various countries. Beyond imposing considerable fines, however, little attention has been given to the increased number of casualties and illnesses due to air pollution and the contribution of millions of cars to climate-change emissions. All of this was happening while the international negotiations that would lead to the Paris Agreement were ongoing.

ENVIRONMENTAL ACTION UNDER ADVERSE CIRCUMSTANCES

Thus, as we see, environmental crime in Europe is very much 'white-collar' crime. It happens in the managerial offices of the large companies, and the intention is to secure sales and profits despite existing regulations that aim to protect the environment. As the recent car emission scandal shows, some of this activity is truly criminal, and once discovered, it is prosecuted by the competent judicial institutions. While some executive officers violate environmental laws, others merely ignore or neglect the rising environmental concerns. They pursue projects of resource extraction or of environmentally and/or socially detrimental agricultural production, often on a large scale and with high impact. Much of this activity is planned in the North but executed in the South because both the enforcement of environmental law and social protest would make them impossible in the North. Thus, the politics of externalisation operates by a territorial displacement of conflicts.

Environmental protection laws in Brazil and South Africa are today very similar to those in Europe. The high degree of global interconnectedness has given many environmental threats a global significance, as argued at the outset of this chapter, and it has also facilitated the rise of global environmental consciousness. The – relative and temporary – success in slowing down deforestation in the Amazon region and protecting the rhino in southern Africa is testimony to the strength of environmental action in the South. But such success is achieved under highly adverse circumstances. Illegal deforestation and illegal killing of rhinos happen every day. These are not white-collar crimes; they are committed by local people, often in need of the resources being made available through those deeds. Often a picture emerges, therefore, in which the combination of poverty and social inequality with the inability of Southern states to enforce their laws, in particular in more remote regions, are seen as the cause of uncontrollable anti-ecological activity. Put like this, the issue is firmly placed in the South, and the North is nothing but a concerned onlooker.

However, this is a highly distorted picture. True, in some cases deforestation and poaching are driven by local interests. In many more, however, a global chain of responsibility is attached to them. This is particularly clear in the cases of assassinations of environmental activists, an increasingly frequent phenomenon of which knowledge and awareness have risen not least thanks to the systematic reporting of the UK-based daily newspaper *The Guardian*. In most of these cases, the killers acted not on their own behalf but for the interest of companies, often with a base in the North, developing large-scale agricultural or mining projects.[16] Thus, the picture above, while not false, needs to be inserted into a larger frame in which two elements of the global context become visible: the capacity of Northern societies to displace environmental damage to the South while maintaining corporate profits and a general way of life, and by and large the incapacity of Southern societies to effect a similar displacement, because very often there is no space within reach towards which the conflicts could be displaced.[17]

LITTLE INNOVATION ON THE PATH TO 'SOCIAL PROGRESS'

In Chapter 6, we discussed the rather successful social-policy programmes of the PT and ANC governments in Brazil and South Africa, reducing poverty and – to a minor extent – social inequality and creating a new 'middle class' among the formerly poor and excluded. We have also shown the social limits of these programmes due to the failure to address the entrenched structures of inequality that date from the long historical periods of formal hierarchy and exclusion. In light of our observations in this chapter, we need to discuss further limitations inherent to the projects of political transformation as designed by these actors.

As discussed in Chapter 5, one pillar of the transformative programme was economic growth. Such growth was meant to increase
tax revenue, and a part of this revenue was to be redistributed with
a view to alleviating poverty and enhancing the income of the lower
classes more generally. Given the world market conditions in the
early twenty-first century, economic growth in Brazil and South Africa
could mostly be achieved through the intensification of ecologically
'heavy' production in the primary and, to some extent only, secondary sectors. In Brazil, there is even talk about a 're-primarisation' of
the economy after the relatively successful industrialisation through
import-substitution policies earlier in the twentieth century (Paulani
2016). This observation concerns the production side, and another
problematic feature emerges from the consumption side. A considerable part of the social-policy programmes consisted in increasing the
amount of money in the hands of the lower classes. This emphasis has
some sound reasons. On the one hand, handing out monetary benefits
is relatively easy. It does not place high demands on public administration. On the other hand, it is immediately positively perceived by
the beneficiaries. Thus, as argued above, it is likely to enhance 'mass
loyalty' towards the government. However, the increased availability of
money leads to an increasing demand for consumer goods, especially
durable consumer goods. Both in Brazil and in South Africa, private
cars have come to be seen as a sign of upward social mobility, enhancing life satisfaction and serving as a status symbol, the latter particularly in South Africa. In production and even more so in use, though,
cars are a significant contributor to environmental damage. This aspect
of the political transformation, therefore, has generated negative ecological side-effects.

The alternative would have been to achieve social progress by placing
the emphasis on the improvement of public infrastructure. This objective could equally have been financed by the revenues from economic
growth, but achieving it would have required the development of the relevant administrative capacity, and possibly not all of it would have been
as immediately recognisable as a benefit as the increasing availability of
money. We need to underline that both the PT- and the ANC-led governments have invested considerably in public infrastructure, thus we
talk about an imbalance rather than an absence. And this imbalance is
more pronounced in Brazil than in South Africa, where significant effort
has been made to improve the infrastructure in the residential areas of

the black African population, systematically disadvantaged by the prior apartheid governments. Nevertheless, the imbalance is telling for the overall design of the political transformation effected in these societies. We want to illustrate this in the form of an anecdote which we have good reason to believe is true.

The first large demonstrations against the PT-led governments in Brazil were the protests against the fare increase in urban public transport in June 2013. These protests became significant because they were the beginning of a larger series of protests that ended up breaking the hegemony that the PT programme of political transformation had acquired over more than a decade. Known as *Movimento Passe Livre* (the Free Fare Movement), the protests started out as a clear single-issue contestation, and as such they could have been addressed rather easily. Even before the rise of these protests, a proposal had been made by a leading member of the PT to keep the fares stable by subsidising the cost of public transport through raising the gasoline tax. The proposal came fully budgeted, demonstrating its feasibility and even calculating the effect on the official inflation rate – a constant concern for governments – to be minimal. Nevertheless it met full and immediate rejection by the PT presidency, and a refusal even to discuss it.

AN UNHOLY ALLIANCE

From the late 1970s onwards, sociological value research suggested that material values would give way to post-material values once material needs were largely satisfied (Inglehart 1977 and elsewhere). This has been seen as another step of 'modernisation' and was congruent with the ecological debate, assuming a linear trend towards greater ecological consciousness. Like other aspects of global social change that we have encountered throughout our reasoning, there is considerable validity to this insight. At the same time, the picture gets distorted owing to the fact that the survey research findings on which the theorem is based work with data from individual societies that are treated as if these societies were moving separately across global history.[18] As we have shown throughout this book, though, this is not at all the case.

To again provide a larger picture, we need to, on the one hand, read the findings on the move to post-materialism as something that has indeed to some extent – which should not be exaggerated either[19] – taken place among the global rich, who live predominantly, but not exclusively, in the North. And they live there with the 'false consciousness' of having changed their societies and ways of life by having improved the quality of the environment and decreased their burden on the planet, while as a matter of fact they continue to live beyond the means the planet can sustainably provide and have displaced the immediate effects of this way of life onto the global poor. Framed as an evolutionary theory of modernisation, on the other hand, the findings, without intending to do so explicitly, also sustain the expectation of the global poor that they would first reach the level of material satisfaction that the rich have now, and from there move on to post-material values. In South Africa, for instance, where the benefits of material affluence had formally been denied to the majority of the population for a long time, any suggestion of 'jumping over' the material phase is easily denounced as a new form of neo-colonial imposition. In a very implicit way, such evolutionary staging is expressed in the assumption of the Paris Agreement that the peak of greenhouse emissions will occur later in the 'developing' countries than in the 'developed' ones. It is difficult to object to such an assumption, since it marks a recognition of historical injustice, as argued above. But at the same time, it shies away from any attempt at a more profound rethinking of the ways in which material needs can be met, a rethinking that is urgently needed.

The capacity of the North to displace its ecological impact onto other regions of the globe combines with the incapacity of the South, until now, to develop a different path to social progress than the one regionally taken earlier in the North to an unholy alliance that endangers the living conditions on the planet earth. The 1972 report on 'Limits to Growth' did not lead to reduced consumption of resources, but to an intensified search for extractable raw materials. The current risk is that the climate change debate will not do so either, and that instead technical solutions will be searched for that, on the one hand, protect those who can afford to install them but not others, and on the other, mark another step in the combination of technological hubris and economic expansion for expansion's sake.

Chapter 9

VIOLENCE, AUTONOMY AND EVERYDAY LIFE IN DEMOCRACIES

The integrity of human life and how everyday practices perpetuate democratic behaviour vary a lot in each world-region we are working with. Though the possibility of building a different future has arisen in recent decades, it still does not matter from which angle we look at it, both in terms of safety and the public structure that makes quotidian practices flow, life in Brazil and South Africa tends to be much harder than in Europe. This difficulty is expressed clearly when it comes to issues related to violence. Ever since violence has been studied at a global level, countries such as Brazil and South Africa have contributed a comparatively large number of violent incidents to global crime levels. This chapter will make clear how both the idea of the integrity of life and violence as a problem are lived according to specific societal self-understandings. We see this variety especially when we consider the extent to which different categories of persons are exposed to violent situations. The variation is also expressed in the feeling of being 'safe and protected' (the perception of violence and safety) and of actually being secured by a system that exists to preserve the lives of the members of a society. Here we argue that attending to violent practices and constraints is essential for coming to a broader understanding of how democracy can be realised (or not) in everyday practices. Violent actions are taken here as a political matter with strong consequences for the actual exercise of autonomy. In this chapter, we will explore both the perception of safety and the idea of the integrity of life and how it affects different groups in each world-region differently. The discussion goes from simple everyday practices which show that violence means different things in different contexts to a more political treatment of the subject that aims to understand how sustainable a social system based on the continuous use of violence against specific 'others' can be. In so doing, this chapter hopes to shed a different light on the topic of violence in modern democracies.

VIOLENCE, INTEGRITY OF LIFE AND AUTONOMY IN MODERN DEMOCRACIES

Thomas Hobbes's concern with self-preservation is often seen to mark the beginning of modern political thought.[1] The moral and practical transformations in the direction of assuming integrity of life as a political condition is a development of the Hobbesian idea applied to the study of modernity. The constitution of moral systems aiming at the preservation of human dignity is historically connected to the formation of a sense of the individuality and worthiness of each member of a political community (see Taylor 1989). With strong variations when it comes to each societal trajectory, the integrity of human life and its connection to the idea of human well-being has become a normative element of modernity. However, this is less because modernity brought about a process of universalisation of the meaning of humanity that is present everywhere; it is mainly because, in each context, the idea of autonomy became connected to a specific understanding of what constitutes humanity and how to live a fully realised human life.

It is the *demos* itself that perpetuates the cycle that makes it possible to express life integrally, in terms of the perpetuation of both individual and collective ways of life. Under conditions of modern autonomy, the idea of self-preservation and the integrity of human life have become connected to the issue of violence as a problem. Western political self-understanding has been marked by the transformation of violence as a form of 'social status' to 'status' (hierarchy between citizens) as a form of violence against the principle of equality between humans (Malešević 2013: 278–82).[2] They are both related to the degree to which human self-realisation can be achieved by the establishment of a right and fair system of law that emanates from all but should equally affect and protect all.[3] Around the world, though, there is a great variety in how individuals experience violence, human integrity and well-being. We see this variety especially in the different levels of everyday forms of violence and criminal actions to which individuals in different regions are exposed. We also see it in the different ways through which different persons express the feeling of being safe and of being protected by a system that exists to preserve the lives of its members.

Modernisation approaches have solved the problem of connecting violence and social self-understandings concerning the integrity of life with democracy by creating the minimal standards of human rights that should be granted everywhere for a society to be considered fully democratic. In these approaches, it has been widely accepted that a decrease in forms of arbitrary violence and an improvement in terms of how the integrity of human life is guaranteed is directly related to the degree of democratisation of societies (Lijphart 1999). The correlation between these variables is probably right. However, when taken only in aggregative terms (statistical measurements), it can lose sight of strongly anti-democratic, violent practices that, for instance, are continuously applied to minorities or even powerless majorities that cannot express by democratic means the violation of their rights. Even in places regarded as highly democratic, such as the US, the incarceration rate for black people is much higher than for white people (more than five times higher). These statistics get worse when one looks at surveys showing that blacks and whites consume illegal drugs at similar rates, yet blacks are incarcerated on drug charges six times more than whites.[4]

A general explanation of the use of the 'slippery concept of violence', as Kilby (2013) regards it, is quite important. The World Health Organization (WHO) defines violence as 'the intentional use of physical force or power, threatened or actual, against oneself, another person, or against a group or community, which either results in or has a high likelihood of resulting in injury, death, psychological harm, mal-development or deprivation' (WHO 2002). This definition is helpful for the delineation of actions that are counted as violence in modern societies. However, as a political matter, the debate about violence includes the debates about who uses power against who – can an institution that uses violence to achieve its ends be considered legitimate?

The use of force by the state, seen as a legitimate body *par excellence* that can rely on violence as a means to assert political power, has received great attention in the social science tradition, especially in the field of historical sociology. Following a Weberian tradition, in historical-political terms, Tilly (1990) has developed his large process analyses of the formation of nation states as a product of the 'legitimate' use of force domestically and power struggles through ballistic warfare between states in Western Europe. Focusing more on the question of power and structures for the state to impose itself over other forms of political organisation and in class conflicts, Mann (1993) is also part of this tradition that looks at the inter-relations between violence, state-formation and modern politics. These analyses have been brought to other parts of the world in which there is a less clear relation between wars and the use of inter-state violence as engendering modern political order, as in Centeno's (2002) analysis of state formation in Latin America. Inspired by different practices and ways of thinking, another important reference for the debate about violence under modern conditions comes from Arendt (1970). She was especially shaken by the experiences of violence in Northern societies in which violence had been presented as a 'progressive' tool in specific scenarios of power struggle, such as war, civil war or rights movements that based their actions on the exercise of some form of violence. However, violence, for her, can never be a source of power; on the contrary, violence appears where power is absent.[5] The topic is still very much present in contemporary analyses of violence as a global political problem that calls for more attention, and for systematic analysis (Butler 2004; Bernstein et al. 2008).

In general sociology, the topics of violence and social cohesion have received the attention of classical thinkers such as Durkheim, Elias, Merton and Foucault. Nonetheless, there is still a lack of a theoretical discussion that would define more precisely what the term 'violence' encompasses (Kilby 2013). To make a very complicated matter workable, one needs to define the concept of violence in relation to the specific problem that it implies. For us, violence designates a symbolic, discursive and/or physical political relation in which autonomy becomes harder to achieve because one imposes one's desire onto another, compelling them to act in a manner that would otherwise be different. Violence implies a lack of autonomy for the one who suffers the consequences of another's violent action; and it shows the weakness of the violator and his or her inability to relate to the violated other by communicative exchange through reflexive means. As a global phenomenon, we argue that it is exactly the constraints on political autonomy that make violence a highly problematic issue for contemporary societies. That is why violence is a political matter that can be used to study forms of constraint on democratic collective action. One of the consequences of it, one can argue, is that there should be no distinction between the legitimate and illegitimate use of force – as long as they all imply the suspension of autonomy for an individual or collective person through generally violent means.

We want to show the strong relation between the levels of everyday experiences with violence and historical injustices against specific groups. Violence often serves as a means of reproduction of injustices and repression. This is manifested in the institutionally differential treatment of specific categories of persons and also in the way societies regard the 'loss' or the 'suffering' of specific subjects as a matter (or not) of collective sorrow. As we have shown in Chapter 7, equality became a guiding principle in modern democracies and this would lead us to expect that violence, when it exists, would equally be a problem for everyone. A democratic political life is supposed to rely on the equality of human beings, both as free individuals and as members of a political community, and entails a dynamic tension between the benefits and burdens of being part of the same democratic society. If this is so, then it should be expected that violence would affect all individuals exposed to it more or less to the same degree. But this is not the case.

That is why violence is treated in this book as a political matter, not as a matter of public policy of repression and control; or as a matter of defining who is the criminal and who is the victim solely based on a formal, legal assessment of justice. We are connecting everyday practices that cause harm, exclusion and the deterioration or elimination of life as they have been practiced against specific political subjects, seeking to understand them as challenges to democracy. The exercise of autonomy demands equality, at least in terms of the integrity of life and security. When violence is continuously applied against specific groups of society strong limits to democratic action are imposed. And, very unfortunately and in different degrees, that is the case in the three world-regions under discussion here. In Brazil violence is worst for young black men; in South Africa, for women and also for youth living on the periphery of the big urban centres; in Europe, for refugees, immigrants and their descendants, and racial and religious 'minorities'. In this chapter, experiences of violence and shared conceptions of the integrity of life are understood in terms of their impact on political self-understandings in Brazil, Europe and South Africa. We want to emphasise the meaning of violence and of the integrity of life in each particular context, showing how they impacted, differently, on the social 'status' that different categories of persons acquired.

VIOLENCE AND EVERYDAY LIFE: A PICTURE OF BRAZIL, EUROPE AND SOUTH AFRICA

Though Brazil, Europe and South Africa all have a functioning system of justice, sustained by democratic laws and rights based on a universal conception of equality between all human beings, and they all have institutions that claim to guarantee the security and well-being of their members, when it comes to the translation of these into everyday practices things change a lot. Being at home, leaving home to go to work or to school, or just to have free time outdoors, mean completely different things in the three world-regions we are working with. To be at home and feel safe inside one's own house also varies a lot in each context. By addressing the familiar theme of violence and integrity of life by other means, we want to explore whether everyday social practices are connected to the possibility of exercising autonomy and collective action within the actual circumstances of Brazil, South Africa and Europe.

Most Southern individuals that get to experience Western European life are always asking themselves why it is the case that just the simple act of walking around the cities gives one the feeling that the integrity of one's life is more likely to be preserved than in their places of origin. It is part of a somewhat consolidated imaginary about life in Western European societies. An opposite imaginary penetrates the minds of Northerners. When they decide to have the experience of going to Brazil or South Africa they need to digest a lot of safety instructions. Their perceptions are always corroborated by advice along the lines of making sure that the place where you are going is not 'dangerous' and also showing the advantages of, whenever possible, taking a 'local' with you who knows the social rules of the space well and can translate them for you. That would be one of the formulas that could assure some safety in that foreign space. To be in Brazil and South Africa, quite the opposite of being in Europe, demands that the general rules need to be translated into 'specific' practices. So, it seems to be the case that democratic Europe has become a place in which space can be inhabited and experienced by any inexperienced person that is able to detach themselves from specific contexts by knowing and accepting the general rule of law and of peaceful coexistence. After all, both in terms of the quality of life and of the possibility of suffering quotidian violence, Europe has become a better place to be when compared to Brazil and South Africa. No one would argue against this. The question for some is how it came to be like that,[6] and, for us, how this plays out in everyday life and how it can be connected to the functioning of democracy and democratic institutions when it comes to the exercise of autonomy.

Thus the occurrence of crime and violent actions against individuals and groups of persons is used to differentially characterise the quotidian in Europe, Brazil and South Africa. These characterisations normally split the 'perception' of violence and 'the real data' about crimes and violent actions. The perception of violence is both a combination of real experiences with crime – either as a victim or as an offender – and of a shared interpretation and communication about the meaning of specific relations between individuals. Such perception is formed of a combination of media information and other modes of communicative exchange. The 'real data' about violence is expressive of shared understandings of what integrity is and when it is violated, which become officialised mainly through institutional channels.[7] More than that, data collected by institutions from both within and outside state organisations reveal who is actually more exposed to violence in each context. As we see by now, the general perceptions about the state of violence in Brazil and South Africa as compared to Europe are quite close to the 'real data'. However, as we will see in the next section, violence does not affect everyone in the same space equally.

According to the official statistics, in 2016 there were 61,619 intentional homicides registered in Brazil. This means that, every hour, seven people were murdered in the country – a rate of intentional homicide of 29.9 to 100,000 inhabitants.[8] The profile of the killer and of the victim tend to be very much the same – young black men with very low income and education who live on the peripheries of the cities. What makes this statistic even more astonishing is the fact that it excludes a measure of police assassination because, in many administrative regions, they do not count in the statistics about murder. Nonetheless, considering only the official, countable data, police homicides are increasing sharply due both to interventions in cities such as Rio de Janeiro and to other repressive policies implemented by the state in the last couple of years. The official data about police homicides show that 99.3% of those killed by the police were young men (between twelve and twenty-nine years), and 76.2% were black (Fórum Brasileiro de Segurança Pública 2017).

While in the European region the intentional homicide rate is on average 3.0 (three murders in 100,000),[9] one of the lowest levels in the world, South African data are very similar to Brazil. In 2016 the intentional homicide rate in South Africa was a bit higher than in Brazil – with 34.1 murders to every 100,000 inhabitants.[10] On average, 52.1 people were killed every day. When it comes to homicides, in South Africa the most vulnerable groups are those who live in the poorest areas of the big cities – such as Cape Town and Johannesburg. Apartheid spatial segregation is a legacy that makes it possible to connect the high level of homicides and violence in the areas occupied by the black poor with the absence of basic public service and of structures of communication with other parts of the big cities (GIZ Inclusive Violence and Crime Prevention Programme 2014). Violence against children and violence followed by murder against women are especially high in South Africa. According to the Medical Research Council (MRC 2010), every six hours a woman is murdered in South Africa, and in many cases they are raped or suffer sexual assault before dying.

In terms of the political consequences of violent actions, it is impossible to not regard murder as an extreme point on a continuum of human rights violations. It is so because homicide, above all when it is highly concentrated among specific groups and categories of persons of a given society, completely annihilates the possibility of the victim to be present as a political voice by themselves. For the society in question, the person killed becomes a statistic or, in some cases, they are taken as examples of the existence of political disputes. Though differing significantly when it comes to the statistical data and perceptions about violence, Brazil, South Africa and Europe all show that violence does not happen in a random manner in democratic societies. Violent actions show that there are lives that count as worthy of being preserved in their full integrity and other lives that do not.

In Brazil generally, the universality of the idea that all persons are equal is challenged by the fact that the black poor people have been victims of intentional homicide much more than the white population (Waiselfisz 2015). Most of the murder cases in Brazil are not resolved by judicial means, as there are many unresolved trials that do not result in conviction. The percentage of open, inconclusive murder cases is much higher when the victim is black; the judicial system works better when the victim is white and/or belongs to the middle or upper classes. Impunity, in this case, conforms to a conception of which lives matter most even when it comes to justice. Another face of this phenomenon appears in the fact that 40% of the Brazilian imprisoned population remain incarcerated without trial. And, as one might expect, more than 60% of the imprisoned population are black.

The political and economic changes of 2016–18 were accompanied by the growth of another form of violence: the killing of political activists. Brazil is one of the most dangerous places in the world to be an activist, with little significant difference between fields of engagement – be it over matters concerning the environment, urban segregation, racial issues, or what have you (see Chapter 8 for environmental issues). Among many others, two dreadful cases of political execution happened at the beginning of 2018. Marielle Franco was murdered in Rio de Janeiro on 15 March. She was a young, black, feminist and lesbian activist who also became a political leader and was elected as councillor of the city of Rio de Janeiro in the election of 2016. During the time she worked as a councillor, she became well known for denouncing crimes against human rights by the state on the periphery of Rio de Janeiro. She denounced the homicides committed by police forces and the army against the young, black population of the shanty towns (*favelas*). Exactly a month later, on the 15 April, the body of Nazildo dos Santos Brito was found in Pará, a constituency of the Amazon area. He was executed by means of a shot in the head and another in the stomach. He was a leader of a *Quilombola* (a term used to describe areas occupied by descendants of slaves) community of Alto Acará. He became very strongly involved in the struggle against palm-oil companies exploiting and illegally expropriating land from black and indigenous communities in the area.

The Pastoral Land Commission, an institution created in 1975 fighting for the rights of rural communities since the dictatorship, has been recording the murder of political activists. The most recent data they have released show that seventy land activists were killed in 2017. Fifty-two of these murders were perpetuated against rural activists, which is the highest level since 2013. Globally, there is a rising number of environmental activists being killed around the world. In 2016, 200 people fighting for environmental rights were executed around the world. Forty-nine came from Brazil alone, followed by Colombia with thirty-seven killings. These two countries together are responsible for almost 50% of global activist murders (Global Witness 2017). These people have been killed because of their power to mobilise collective action to defend core democratic values, such as the equality between human beings and the equal right to access basic natural resources.

In terms of spatial distribution, homicide rates in different regions of South Africa are connected to levels of unemployment among the young population, poverty and the absence of public services. In one of the most unequal countries in the world, which still needs to deal with colonial and apartheid legacies in terms of how 'native' traditions were embedded in the process of formation of South Africa as nation, another important form of violence occurs owing to the status of women. The incidence of violence against women and children has reached one of the highest levels in the world. Ideas such as 'a man has a right to be violent', accompanied by a failure in institutional support for the education of young men, are among the reasons for the high levels of male violence, among themselves and against women and children in particular (Dunkle et al. 2004). According to the South Africa Demographic and Health Survey (2017c), one out of every five women fell victim to male violence in 2016. However, there is no clear information (official data) available about how many women have been murdered by a partner or a close relative in South Africa. In the South African Police Service annual report from the year 2015/2016 (SAPS 2016) it is attested that police did not register at least one out of each three crimes against women (including murder, rape, and so on). There is a strong statistical correlation between being a woman, black, partially educated, not married (above all separated and divorced) and being a victim of sexual violence and other forms of physical violence (STATS SA 2017c). The first sexual relationship in South Africa is often forced, at around 10–28% – even though it is under-reported for reasons of proximity of the victim to the offender, who will be mostly likely to perpetuate a violent sexual relation with the victim (Dunkle et al. 2004). As a consequence, many women who died of HIV became positive as a result of non-consensual (violent) sexual relations.[11]

As in Brazil, crime and violence are part of the quotidian reality of the cities in South Africa. Almost 5% of the houses in South Africa experienced burglary/housebreaking from 2015 to 2016 and only half of the victims reported the crime to the police. With the exception of murder and car theft, with much higher levels of reporting to police, at around 90%, most victims do not report crimes to the police (STATS SA 2017a). The main reason why people do not report crimes is because they believe that the police cannot or will not do anything to help. When it comes to forms of violence against women, as we said before, the difficulty in processing data is much worse. Police and public institutions in general have simply failed in properly assessing what is going on. However, even with the low number of cases reported, it is clear that the integrity of life for black, poor, single women is not respected in the way it should be in a democratic society.

With the end of apartheid, at least, political executions become much less present as a variable that counts for the composition of intentional homicide rates in South Africa. The phenomenon of farm murders,[12] however, has been described in political debates as not part of a 'normal' – not politically motivated – criminal act. The latest data available recognise that, in the 2016–17 period, seventy-four farm murders occurred. In the same period, 638 attacks on small farm holdings were registered. Although the racial profiles of farm attack and murder victims are not systematically recorded, white farmers and their families, along with black workers, are widely understood to be the main victims of these crimes.[13] Along with the police, many non-governmental organisations collect information about this type of crime. They all show that since 2012, there has been a continuous rise in farm attacks. AfriForum, a civil organisation created in 2006 aiming at engaging Afrikaners in democratic South Africa, have been organising campaigns against the farm murders because they see them as a politically motivated crime against the 'white minority'. Ernst Roets, a member of AfriForum, says that white Afrikaners, as members of a minority group in a democratic society, should be enjoying protection from state institutions. But the farm murders show that they are not. He talks about racist, anti-white practices in South Africa.[14] As we might expect, the debate about the victimisation of white South Africans is very controversial. Many black activists say that the black population of farm workers have been suffering from the consequences of farm attacks as much as whites. These crimes are not politically motivated against white Afrikaners. Rather, they are a legacy of the land struggles and land dispossession policies developed under colonialism and apartheid.

Among the world-regions we are looking at, Europe is by far the safest place to live, to enjoy a life of integrity, and also to actively participate in politically contentious fields. Nevertheless, there are still economic areas, groups and categories of persons who are much more vulnerable than others. High-income countries in the European area have a smaller level of interpersonal violence than low- and medium-income countries.[15] Unlike in Brazil and South Africa, adult males (aged 30–59) have been the main victims of intentional homicide. Compared to Brazil and South Africa, the issue of violence in Europe has become much more concerned about the prevalence of hate crimes, racism and gender crimes. There is a growing 'resentment' against the 'outsider' who comes to Europe, which has been expressed in forms of symbolic violence against undocumented and illegal immigrants. As we will see in the next section, violence happens more in the 'borderlands' and along the 'borderlines' (for more on that see Chapter 6) where the encounter with the 'other' occurs. Goodey (2007) shows the difficulty of even collecting data about racist and other forms of violence against the immigrant because of the void where it happens. As in Brazil and South Africa, domestic and female violence constitutes another big issue when it comes to the democratic guarantee of personal well-being. Again, however, the level of violence that happens in private and public spaces against women is much higher in Brazil and South Africa.

Sociologically, the high number of homicides in Brazil and South Africa has been explained by appeal to endemic causes that attributes to these world-regions some sort of 'violent sociability' (Silva 2004) or a 'culture of violence' (Simpson 1993) developed in urban areas. These approaches try to move away from legalist explanations about violence which would focus, for instance, on the impunity of the judicial system as an explanation for the high number of criminal acts. They try to find in the differential patterns of sociability an explanation for why in some contexts violence became more prevalent than in others. Nonetheless, these explanations ended up somewhat 'normalising' violence as something that is part of an urban-peripheral self-understanding. As a consequence, first, they obscure the fact that the nature of this violence reproduces historically contingent patterns of injustice in each context, and, second, that the excluded groups suffering from this violence wish to escape from it. If they cannot, it is because in a life course there are not many other options available.

VIOLENCE AND DEMOCRACY

As we said before, perceptions about violence are formed by the degree to which people possess confidence in the information shared about criminal acts. It is the case that people in Brazil and South Africa feel much more vulnerable to violence than in Europe. Even knowing that a perception is always true in the sense that it manifests how someone feels, we would like to claim that violence does not affect all categories of persons in the same degree. In the present context, the issue of violence will be discussed more directly in terms of how democracy works in the different world-regions by more directly posing the questions of 'who counts as human?', 'whose lives count as lives?' and 'what makes for a *grievable* life?' – to follow the apt questions Butler (2004) has put. Still connected to what we have discussed about inequality and inclusion – in Chapters 6 and 7 – those who have suffered the consequences of historical injustices more directly are the ones who experience the consequences of violence in Brazil, Europe and South Africa more dramatically.

With the imposition of strong boundaries, policies and requirements to legally enter and leave European territory, Europe has followed the historical pattern of displacing to the outside (Chapter 6) conflicts that have been internally solved. This is the way it was with the process of the abolition of serfdom in European states while leading the international commerce of human slaves in the nineteenth century; or with the process of 'pacification' between the states in Europe while taking part in colonial and new Imperial disputes in the rest of the world (of which the 'scramble for Africa' is a good example). So, in the case of the member states of the European Union, it is more difficult to make the general point that we are making just because the main victims of violent actions are not formally in Europe. People whose integrity of life is not regarded to be as worthy of preservation as that of democratic subjects are mostly living in the limbo of European border places. The many lives lost in the Mediterranean Sea through attempts at entry into European Union territory reveals the violent side of the immigration process and of the closing of European borders. It is, however, important to say that we are referring to an exclusionary action with consequences for the general understanding of violence, which is perpetuated because of the action of states and of the European Union border policies and not because European civil society excludes these people.[16]

There are certainly political agendas being developed by conservative groups and reinforced by collective actions taken by, for instance, groups working under the head of nationalist demands, a topic to be further discussed in Chapter 10. However, they have so far shown limited power when it comes to gaining victories in the general democratic process, as is the case with Marine Le Pen and the Front National in France; UKIP in England; or the Party for Freedom in the Netherlands.[17] What they have achieved so far is the increase of racism and violent hate crime in public space. Legislation against hate crimes developed in Europe in the course of the twentieth century has not prevented the rise in hate crime, especially against Islamic communities and illegal immigrants (Bleich 2007, 2011; Goodey 2007). The answer to the question about *what makes for a grievable life* in Europe should be much more nuanced than in the other two world-regions we are putting into this frame. Still, as difficult as it is, taken all together, the violation of the integrity of life of economic immigrants and members of religious communities who want to exist as such is not as generally grievable as it is for European citizens themselves.

The answer to these questions in Brazil is much more straight-forward. A person who combines the characteristics of being black, young, not well educated, poor and living in the *favelas* is much more exposed to the web of violence than anyone else. The affirmation of democracy and democratic institutions in the thirty years since the end of dictatorship did not change the fact that the black population is still much less *grievable* for than the white one, above all when we add to it the economic/class factor. In only one weekend, Saturday/Sunday of 24 and 25 March 2018, thirteen young black men were killed in a *favela* of Rio de Janeiro. These murders were committed by police officers and military forces that were part of interventions to stop the increase of criminal actions in the city. The numbers are so alarming that there are civil organisations calling it a 'genocide' of the black young who live in the peripheral areas of the big Brazilian urban centres such as Rio de Janeiro and São Paulo.[18] Anyone who is minimally acquainted with Brazilian newspapers would notice that a white middle class life mat-ters much more than a black one. Black life generally appears under statistical heads about homicide rates in the country. When a white life is lost, it becomes a matter of substantive and qualitative discussion about the state of violence and the inefficiency of the state in solving the country's security problems.

The situation has deteriorated since 2016, with the politics of repression perpetrated by the federal government. However, it must be said that it is not this very recent political change that is making the situation of this *ungrievable* group worse. One of the reasons why the Dilma government lost its popular support was the case of the 'disappearance' of Amarildo Dias de Souza on 14 July 2013. Amarildo was a black man living in Rocinha (one of the big *favelas* in Rio de Janeiro), forty-seven years old at the time of his disappearance, who worked as bricklayer. Police officers who were part of an action taken in Rocinha under a 'pacification' programme[19] took Amarildo from his home and brought him to the Pacification Police Unit of the area. This was the last time that Amarildo was seen. His body was never found. By 'coincidence' the police unit's CCTV cameras were said to be malfunctioning exactly during the time Amarildo was supposed to be in there. The 'disappearance' of Amarildo happened while one of the main programmes of social intervention to fight violence by the social development of poor areas was being implemented in Rocinha. The case became well known, probably because Amarildo deviated from the usual statistical patterns in terms of his age and employment condition (he was a 'worker'). The event impacted the government, which was itself already facing a legitimation crisis. If it were not for this, he would have gone down in history only as part of the homicide or disappeared persons statistics.

In terms of a life whose integrity is regarded as worthy of preservation, in South Africa probably more than the young males living in what are still spatially segregated areas, the lives of black women also are less grievable than those of others. Officially, more than 40,000 cases of rape were reported to the police in 2017, a significant part of them being reported by women under eighteen years old. As we saw, this number is clearly just the tip of the iceberg because any form of sexual assault is much less reported to the police than any other form of violent crime against women, above all because violence against women is mostly committed by a known partner or relative. This problem affects not only adult women. Rape is also a commonly experienced crime against among children and young women (between fourteen and eighteen years). According to Jinda and colleagues (2008), 40% of the survivors of rape and other forms of gender violence are children and young women under eighteen years old.

High rates of male homicides due to involvement in drug trafficking and robberies, for instance, is an intra-gender issue (men killing men); the intentional homicide of women, on the contrary, is an inter-gender concern (men killing women) and in the South African case is very much connected to the status of women as possessing lives not considered worthy of preservation. And the statistics are proportionally much worse for the black than the white, coloured and Asian populations (MRC 2004). As we said in the previous section, women are particularly vulnerable in South Africa, probably due to the violent forms that patriarchal practices have conventionally taken there.

CONCLUSION

Democratic societies cannot compromise the lives of some for the sake or security of others. What we have seen in this chapter shows the limits that violence imposes on the claim of contemporary societies to be democratic. Violence does appear as a global problem; however, as we have seen, what makes it a problem concerning collective action is that there are specific categories of persons that consistently have to bear the burden of violence more than others. In democratic societies historical injustices against groups have been perpetuated through violent actions both by the members of society among themselves and also by the action of publically organised forces. The closure of borders in Europe has as one of its consequences that many lives have been lost in the borderlands of the European Union; and the harmful consequences of violence are even clearer when it comes to women in South Africa and the black youth in Brazil. The absence of public policies to change the patterns of historical injustices against these groups in these countries combined, in the case of Brazil, with explicit repressive policies that reinforce these injustices, reveals the fragility of democracy in these states and at the same time shows how urgent it has become to address this problem from within state institutions.

Part IV

Rethinking the Possibilities of Political Agency

Chapter 10

DEMOCRACY IN TRANSFORMATION

Democracy is a form of political life that is based on a constant process of interpretation and is continually shaped by movements generated by human action. Under modern conditions, there is no evidence of a historical circumstance in which democracy has been positively transformed solely because of an individual action or because of the simple aggregation of individual preferences. It is rather the case that democracy and the defence of political rights have been reflexively shaped by collective action. This chapter starts out from this interpretation as a way of addressing the question of how to understand collectivities and the role of individuals in the shaping and transformation of contemporary democracies. By discussing the issue of collective action and political formation and transformation, we will deal with a difficult aspect of modern democracy: it needs to be understood as a mode of political life that can never offer an easy and predictable condition for those who form part of a polity. This is so because democracies have always been open to the possibility of contestation of power and also because the idea of a society as the unity of a collective body and mind, often enough proposed, is untenable. Rather, modern democracies are best understood when we work with the power of communication between human beings as constituting specific societal self-understandings. This chapter is thus concerned with the dynamic relation between citizens/persons within a political community, which gives life to democracies. The short history of modern democracy is understood as a history of the contestation (by those on the bottom and also those on the top) of a given situation and of the reshaping of political institutions. In this way, forms of collective action, such as social movements, protests and platforms as well as the role of specific persons, will be analysed as privileged manifestations of how the political is dynamically understood and transformed in different times and contexts. The argument focuses on experiences characterised by a high intensity of democratisation as well as by civic disaffection and dissatisfaction and also provides a general view of processes of the transformation of democracy in light of the role played by collective action.

COLLECTIVE ACTION AND SOCIAL MOVEMENTS

A problem we would like to directly address in this part of the book concerns how the concept of collective action can be used to talk about social movements and other forms of social mobilisation. To avoid confusion, we would like to clarify two important issues. First, by collective action we do not mean a form of rational action taken by a group whose goals are clear to everyone and in which all individuals act in unison to maximise individual interest, sharing the costs of the action.[1] Against this view, we are working with a conception of collective action that is based on the critical-reflexive capacity of human beings as historical agents. However, second, we are also not moving in the direction of treating social movements as the manifestation *par excellence* of collective action. Though an outstanding force of change and manifestation of reflexivity, we would like to suggest that democracies are, in recent years, becoming more transformed by broader forms of collective action than those of social movements themselves. This is not to say that social movements have become redundant. On the contrary. Social movements have changed democracies all around the world and still exert a progressive political force. However, to understand major transformations that are happening in contemporary Brazil, South Africa and Europe we need to open the scope of our analysis to take into account forms of collective action that do not share some of the traditional characteristics of social movements.

The contributions of Alain Touraine (1973) to the study of social movements were an attempt to bring the reflexivity and interpretation of subjects back into the study of social movements. His proposal was to analyse social movements as both (re)producers and critical collective agents of social life. Breaking with the disputes between structuralist approaches to social movements, Touraine wanted to refocus scholarly attention onto the action of collectively organised subjects. Habermas (1984–7) saw social movements as a reaction to attempts of modern market and state rational structures to colonise the lifeworld.

A revised version of this idea was offered by Scott (1991), who saw the ineffectiveness of interest groups in pushing forward civil society demands as generating social movements. Both perspectives share the idea of social movements as a reactive societal response to failures in the working of the political and economic systems. In a critical dialogue with these previous approaches, historical conditions, collective identity formation, network organisation, alliances and contextual solidarities all became central aspects of the study of social movements by the 1990s (Tilly 1984; Tarrow 1991; Foweraker 1995).

Tarrow (1994) developed his idea of 'political opportunities' as a response to the growing incorporation of rational choice theory approaches to the study of social movements that become known as 'resource mobilisation theories'. Against the approach to social movements as a form of collective action whose success is based on the mobilisation of resources for achieving (or not) a goal, Tarrow proposes that social movements should be recognised as products of a historical moment. A social movement is based on collective interpretation of a given situation and the possibility of bringing pressure to bear on political institutions for demands to be met. Thus, social movements need to be understood beside the issue of cost-benefit-goal-achievement analysis (for example, Olson 1965). Understanding social movements demands an analysis of how specific forms of organised collective action became possible in specific contexts (Tilly and Tarrow 2006). In the same line, but coming back to Habermas for a framework to understand collective action, Cohen (1985) challenged rational choice readings of social movements by offering an interpretation in which social action is seen as both a form of generating new experiences and of mobilising for different resources to be made publically available.

This can be taken as a very schematic synthesis of what was going on in terms of the study of social movements as *the* privileged form of collective action in the second half of the twentieth century. Though empirically based on experiences from diverse parts of the globe – especially of Northern societies and also Latin America – these debates were very much dominated by European and US scholars.[2] For a quite long while, Southern societies have been brought into the picture, but they needed to be situated within a Northern frame to become understandable. To illustrate how this happened, we can see how Mann's (2006) approach to Latin American social movements is in terms of what they lack when compared to similar Northern initiatives – for instance, social movements in this part of the globe emerged despite the absence of a separation between state and society, and the research also departed from the absence of something like class consciousness as that which gives more specificity to emerged social movements. This picture has changed, and has become more concerned about global issues and different global forms of mobilisation, as the work of Bringel and Pleyers (2017) shows. However, our argument still does not share the view of social movements as the main form of collective action directing politics in the contemporary global world.

To understand this claim, we need to recognise some of the following basic differences between what we understand as forms of collective action and of social movements. This difference relies basically on how the *common ground* that shapes the action of a group of people (or peoples) is interpreted and constructed. Despite opening up to consider processes of communication and shared interpretation, much research still presupposes a form of collective identity when it comes to the recognition of what a social movement is and is not. Besides, both old and new social movements are still understood as (1) a form of collective action that defines from its beginning what the focus of the collective demand is and (2) which possesses a political life that is constituted and exists outside the state but has the state as a target or a mediator. From an analytical point of view, the focus on collective action does not demand a previous definition of who is included in the action, who is the adversary or the target and how the action will move forward.[3] Collective action is based on a temporary definition of a common ground in which a political self-understanding is constructed and moved forward. It is an interpretative tool that helps us to analyse 'problem-solving' collective action that moves beyond what has been offered by existing work on social movements. The focus on collective action makes it possible to understand democracy fully as a political practice of taking collective decisions in specific circumstances and of bringing collectivities into being in the first place.

Another advantage of working with the concept of collective action is that it becomes possible to expand one's conceptual framework so as to accommodate forms of social mobilisation that are 'conservative' or whose demands do not necessarily endorse inclusiveness and equality among human beings. Social movements have always been analysed as progressive sources of political change. In recent years, however, the motors of important political transformations were fuelled, not from progressive social movements, but from conservative collective action that happened both inside and outside state institutions. In both North and South, side by side with progressive collective action taken by groups demanding agendas such as gender equality and inclusion of immigrants, there is a growing public appearance and mobilisation of nationalistic, religious and racist groups – and they have achieved important outcomes, such as the victory of Donald Trump in US, the Brexit process in the UK, the rise of anti-democratic popular support in countries such as Brazil and South Africa, and in the case of Brazil, the growing societal backing of a dictator-like solution for the societal problems of the country. Though hard to deal with, we do need to find a comprehensive analytical tool that makes it possible to understand how public spaces have been occupied by collective actors that are trying to push political agendas in highly problematic directions if seen from the comprehensive perspective of democracy and human rights. Some authors have been working with the hypothesis of the 'normalisation' of protest by both right and left groups as a characteristic of a new street politics (Torcal et al. 2016). We would say that we probably need to let history move on a little more before talking about something like the *normalisation* of conservative collective action and occupation of public spaces by forces that are at odds with the history of human progress and struggles for democratic rights. It is useful to open up this discussion and to understand the roots of this thought.

During the 1970s, the idea that democracy was entering a crisis became widespread in the global North (for example, Hall et al. 1978). The feeling of a mistrust in governments and the difficulty of accommodating social demands inside state institutions were taken as manifestations of this crisis. Still with this diagnosis of what happened at the end of the twentieth century, Colin Crouch (2004) advanced the proposition that we are living in a 'post-democratic age'. By that, he meant to designate the process of political and economic elites bypassing democratic institutions as a way of preserving their interests and maintaining their privileged position. However, this idea was coined in the North exactly when important democratic innovations were in the process of consolidation in the South. Experiences of high intensity democracy and successful experiences of the inclusion of previously excluded collectivities into the political system were giving new life to Southern democracies and they were mostly accompanied by the rise to power of left-wing political parties previously strongly identified with social movements. So it seems like both ideas – that of the crisis of democracy and of a post-democratic age – were not able to fully address what was going on globally with democracy at the beginning of the twenty-first century. Modernisation theories were embracing something like democratically consolidated regimes. In the absence of anything like that in the real world, theories about the crises of democracy and of political apathy became widespread.

Reflecting on the topic of political action at this moment of history in Brazil, Europe and South Africa requires us to face the fact that the democratic dependence on individual and collective autonomy produces a feeling of constantly approaching a moment in which everything can change. Not because democracy is unstable, but because it is formed and transformed by collective actions that come to exist without pre-established ends. For good and bad, societies are always subject to the revision of what it means to be part of an autonomous collectivity. This makes it necessary to perpetually confront questions about such things as what constitutes the boundaries of the political community in each context, and what the agenda for a shared political project should consist in; it also leads to the ongoing questioning of the legitimacy of established moral and political order. There exist no convincing examples of a stable democracy – either a political regime is democratic (open to contestation and to change), or it is predictable. There is an intrinsic tension in the idea of democratic consolidation. The history of modern democracies, as the examples that we discuss in this chapter show, is the history of moving back and forth. There is no such thing as an example that would make us endorse the argument that we have arrived in a post-democratic age, but there are indeed political transformations going on that seem to remind us of how dangerous it is to believe that democratic achievements will last forever.

COLLECTIVE ACTION AND POLITICAL TRANSFORMATION IN CONTEMPORARY DEMOCRACIES

With this general background in mind, we will deal with the issue of how collective action has been transforming democracies in contemporary Brazil, Europe and South Africa. The image of a lively political life in Brazil and South Africa has been opposed to the idea of a Europe in which new political horizons have not emerged out of collective actions. In the North, Europe witnessed strong social movements in the late nineteenth and early twentieth centuries. These movements led to high-intensity political participation, with the onset of egalitarian-inclusive democracy from 1919 onwards. But these were forms of democracy that often collapsed soon thereafter, giving rise to authoritarian or totalitarian regimes. Not least in the light of these experiences, post-Second World War European democracy is built rather consciously on 'civic apathy', low-intensity political participation and highly routinised political participation in a setting marked by the technocratic exercise of political power.

Following from Di Palma's definition (1969, 1970), political dissatisfaction has been characterised as a state of rejection leading to low levels of political involvement. Unlike this state of *dissatisfaction*, which is still dependent on a low level of engagement, political *disaffection* means that the members of a polity feel detached and distant from the political world: 'Thus, withdrawal, rather than political involvement, often acts to preserve the economy of a person's belief system' (Di Palma 1969: 986). In this scenario, political participation is completely mitigated, meaningless and can happen only sporadically and in very pragmatic ways. This approach was used first in functional political science of the 1950s and 1960s to explain the state of political mobilisation and participation in the US. It was also used to analyse the low level of political participation in Europe and the development of post-Second World War European civil society. Northern democracies have thus been interpreted in terms of the degree of satisfaction (dissatisfaction) and engagement (disengagement/disaffection) that characterise these societies in this specific context. These ideas have been used to express *feelings* that are somehow opposed to trust, support and voluntary participation, and to designate a possible 'state of political apathy' due to the practical development of liberalism in the economic, social and political spheres. This idea of 'civic or political disaffection' in contemporary Europe and the optimistic view about the appearance of a 'high-intensity democracy' in Brazil and, to a lesser extent, South Africa have been explanations widely used to describe how citizens and polities have been interpreted in the light of new democratic developments. Nevertheless, none of these views can fully address the complex phenomenon of political transformations in contemporary societies.

It is true that in Europe, due to some processes such as the affirmation of liberal and neo-liberal policies along with the apparently decreasing presence of social movements, the belief has arisen that a successful democratic system is one in which individual liberty is fully achieved and undisturbed by state interferences – an argument based on the idea that each unit of a political body can realise itself without the constraints collectivities always impose. This comes along with the widespread idea of representative democracy as the aggregation of individual preferences, and also with the affirmation of *homo economicus* who does not have much to gain through his or her political participation, as variables that explain the transformation of European civil society. Following this suggestion, it is not surprising that European societies have been analysed as key cases of *dissatisfied* and *disaffected* democracies (Montero et al. 1997; Magalhães 2005; Torcal and Montero 2006). However, even if one accepts this explanation, one still needs to deal with the fact that *dissatisfied* and *disaffected* European individuals continue to support democracy and accept the legitimacy of this political system. It is a trend in Europe to regard democracy as a much better political regime when compared to any form of authoritarian government.

Since the 1980s, on average around 70% of the European population would prefer democracy to an authoritarian regime – only around 10% say that they are all the same. In Northern countries such as Denmark the legitimacy of democracy reached the level of 92% in 1992 (Montero et al. 1997). Recent data from the *European Value Survey* shows that democracy is still highly valued in Europe. More than 90% of Western European citizens agree with the idea that democracy may have its problems but remains better than any other political system. In contemporary Brazil people are deeply dissatisfied with democracy – more than 70% of the population believe that democracy is not working well in the country. Given specific scenarios – like when corruption is very high and violence grows – more than 50% of the population view a military intervention into politics as a good replacement for democratic institutions (Avritzer 2018). The situation in Brazil does not deviate strongly from the one in South Africa. According to an Afrobarometer survey of 2016, though democracy is still supported by 62% of the South African population, a majority of the interviewed citizens would surrender the vote if it enabled them to have a non-elected government that provides basic services. What is unique and astonishing about this survey is that it shows that 30% of the white population support a hypothetical scenario of returning to apartheid; only 44% of the white population clearly reject a return to this system (Afrobarometer 2016).

We would like to argue that recent developments in European countries robustly challenge the diagnosis of democratic disaffection

Democracy in Transformation   185

and dissatisfaction as a strong mark of European societies. From the uprising of suburban protest in countries regarded as examples of social equality such as Sweden, ongoing anti-Brexit protests, the formation of Irish platforms fighting against the Eighth Amendment of the Constitution Act, 1983 that led to the 'abortion' referendum of May 2018, to the anti-Troika movements in the south of Europe, collective action is still playing an important role and showing that people can be disaffected and disenchanted with traditional politics, but not with politics as a force of social change in itself. The analysis of collective action in Portugal since the fall of the dictatorship, with the Carnation Revolution of 1974–5, to the recent democratic innovations experienced in the country, confirms this argument.

It took almost forty years from the Carnation Revolution for Portugal to witness mass mobilisation with major political consequences. On 12 March 2011 many Portuguese cities saw their streets occupied by almost 500,000 people demonstrating to overcome precariousness and corruption, which had become a feature of post-dictatorship Portugal. However, compared to other European countries, Portugal since 1975 is a country with a very low level of political participation (Baumgarten 2013). Social mobilisation was mostly organised around trade unions, and civil participation in associations was very low in democratic Portugal. After the (re)establishment of democracy, Portugal held its first two referendums in 1998, one about the decriminalisation of abortion and the other on the topic of the power attributed to the regional administrations. As Magalhães (2005) shows, the results of both referendums had to be rejected because they did not attain the minimum threshold of 50% of participation. Based on this data and also on recent surveys about electoral turnout in Portugal, Magalhães describes the country as marked by what we have referred to earlier as a state of disaffection with democracy. In his view, this society is living in a high moment of popular indifference with politics accompanied by a widespread disengagement of citizens from political life. However, this interpretation of Portugal as an example of a disaffected democracy does not explain why the country is at the moment operating under a high intensity, participatory democratic system. The rise of António Costa as the leader of the Socialist Party (*Partido Socialista*, PS) was the result of high participation of both members and non-members of the party. As Santos (2017) shows, the disaffection is probably not related to political life as such, but is a disaffection that relates only to the usual liberal representative politics.

The revival of political participation and democratic innovation in Portugal is better explained by the many forms of collective action in response to the deterioration of living conditions due to neo-liberal austerity politics implemented from 1990. The beginning of the twenty-first century in Portugal was marked by issues that concerned the 'always postponing' generation. This is a generation of young, educated citizens who do not have enough job opportunities and are living in the gap between unemployment and precariousness, while living with their parents for much longer than in any other European country.[4] The rise of the *Geração à Rasca* (the Desperate Generation) as a form of collective actor led to many protests, demonstrations and occupying strategies that have strongly impacted Portuguese politics. On 12 March 2011, for the first time, major political protests were organised in the country independently of the involvement of traditional political actors such as trade unions. The calls that mobilised the protesters were launched on a social network platform by a small group of young people inspired by the song *Parva que Sou* (How Stupid I Am).[5] It took only a short time and very little for the 'Desperate Generation' to take to the streets, thereby demonstrating the limitation of the apathetic diagnosis. Collective mobilisations in Portugal and elsewhere in Europe occur, not because of political apathy in general, but due to the discrediting of traditional forms of liberal representative democracy and the widespread sense of a declining quality of life.[6] The Portuguese example shows how time and contexts (re)shape societal self-understandings and by doing so create new kinds of political actions that are nor pre-organised. As seen in the emergence and the impact of a movement-party such as Podemos in Spain and Syriza in Greece, representative democracies are under pressure from social and political movements. The idea of a stable democracy based on the ideal functioning of liberal representative institutions was supposed to be the culmination of modern democracy. However, this is not the case. In both North and South, contemporary democracies are under transformation as a result of the action of collectivities that are challenging the status quo.

Until very recently, Brazilian democracy was recognised as a successful experience in implementing a constitutionally grounded combination of forms of traditional representation and new forms of participatory institutions as mechanisms of public management and policy making. Since the end of the dictatorship, participatory institutions were created at all levels of government (local, regional and federal) and have been working for almost thirty years. As a response to the closing of previous channels of political participation, the Brazilian project of participatory democracy emerged during the years of dictatorship, above all along the path created by a social movement called *Movimento Sanitarista* (the Sanitary Movement). The 'Sanitarians' were a collective movement composed of doctors, clandestine political organisations, academics, medical students and community associations. They came together through a shared project of building a health system that would be universal, free and organised under participatory democratic principles in which those who used the health system would have a say on policy making and management. With the end of dictatorship and the formation of the Constitutive National Assembly, this proposal for the participatory organisation of some public services became incorporated as a constitutional democratic project. It was only possible to build up a political agenda around participation because this project was embraced by other collective actors, such as the Landless Workers' Movement (*Movimento dos Trabalhadores Sem Terra*, MST), the Unified Workers' Central (*Central Única dos Trabalhadores*, CUT), and other urban social organisations. And even more importantly, because health came to be regarded by a wide range of political actors as indicative of an improved quality of life in all spheres. This went much beyond the understanding of health as care and intervention to develop a project based on the establishment of public health as a problem of political participation. Conservative political parties tried to stop the institutionalisation of participatory political institutions in Brazil in all spheres. However, they did not manage to stop the implementation of participatory institutions as a constitutional principle. This appears in the 1988 constitution as a norm that needs to be regulated by complementary laws. It was in the course of the 1990s and 2000s that those laws were implemented.

During the 1990s the Brazilian experience with participatory democracy entered a period of expansion. Many local participatory councils were created, above all in the municipalities where the PT was elected. The fields of urban planning, social assistance and public health were where most participatory institutions were developed during those years. As a party project, during these years, participatory budgeting (OP, from the Portuguese abbreviation for *Orçamento Participativo*) was also established and became an important part of the movement of democratic innovation in Brazil. OP was first put into practice by Olívio Dutra (PT), elected as the mayor of Porto Alegre (in Rio Grande do Sul) in 1989, and it has been implemented in many localities where the PT were elected. Unlike the institutionalised public policy councils, participatory budgeting is a PT programme that has no constitutional determination. In the transition from the twentieth to the twenty-first century, the general development of Brazilian participatory democracy became really significant and the level of involvement of the population became very high (Avritzer 2009). People that took part in these participatory institutions came from a variety of social organisations – social movements, neighbourhood associations, professional groups, religious associations and, in many cases, just as users of the public services in consideration. Over the years, the participatory political project was strongly adopted by the PT, which used the different mechanisms established through it to create innovative policies. It might be said that the PT privileged participatory institutions as a way of canalising social demands that previously would have been expressed through, for instance, collective action outside the state – as is the case with social movements.[7]

The other side of this story is that some actors ended up completely under-represented in the institutionalised participatory mechanisms created in Brazil. Foremost among the excluded were the youth.[8] This meant that they made no use of the main mechanisms through which state and society were entangled. There were also other areas of public policy that became under-represented in the mechanisms of democratic participation – such as infrastructure, urban mobility and transportation, which are clearly areas of conflict between the population, the private sector and the government. It is not by chance that the protests of June 2013 were basically organised by youth challenging the rise in the price of public transportation in the main cities of Brazil. There are some aspects of the June 2013 protests that are important for our argument about collective action and political transformation. Initially convened by the predominantly youthful Free Fare Movement (*Movimento Passe Livre*), which was part of the aforementioned field of urban transportation, the demonstrations quickly over-spilled the limits of the movement and reached public opinion in general by pluralising and completely extending the agenda of social movements to issues such as public security and quality of public services. It also soon incorporated agendas such as political reform and the need to create stronger mechanisms to fight against corruption. At the same time that this demonstration represented in a strong sense the need to push forward progressive agendas, it has opened the door to the return of conservative sectors to the streets for the first time since 1964.

The first characterising element of the June 2013 demonstrations was the re-establishment of a dynamic of separation between non-institutional mobilisations and institutional mobilisations; a separation between groups that felt pleased with the democratic innovations going on in Brazil and those who did not share this feeling. A second important element was that, for the first time after the re-democratisation process, left-wing groups were not leading the protest. During President Lula's second term, the PT twice faced strong social mobilisation; once against a diversion of the water-course of one of the main rivers in the country (Rio São Francisco), and once against the construction of hydro-electric power plants in the lower Amazon. Environmental groups organised marches and protests in Brasilia and in the cities most affected by these controversial policies. When Dilma Rousseff came to power, succeeding Lula, these fissures first encountered in the environmental domain expanded to other areas, such as urban policies. Thus, the June 2013 demonstrations express both the occupation of public spaces by many actors who were not organised before as social movements and the opening of public spaces for the discussion of agendas that were not determined by left-wing groups. The impeachment of Dilma Rousseff in August 2016 was followed by massive protest on the streets. Many right-wing political parties and groups[9] organised most of the protest that legitimated the constitutional process against the former president. In May 2018, Brazil saw another major social mobilisation that was first presented as a truck drivers' strike against the rise in the price of fuel. However, it was soon found that actually it was a lockout organised by transportation businessmen taking advantage of the rise in fuel prices to put pressure on the government. Many other groups took advantage of the lockout to occupy the streets, making very controversial demands. Among the many banners displayed by the truck drivers and the social actors that were protesting, it was common to see support for a return to military rule.

In South Africa the picture changes, but it has important similarities with Brazil and Europe. As we have seen earlier in this book, resistance and social mobilisation happened throughout the whole apartheid era. Anti-apartheid struggles were also composed of working-class activists who later, with the dismantling of the system of racial oppression, became important actors in institutional politics, such as former president Zuma.[10] With the unbanning of anti-apartheid social movements in 1990 and the liberation of political prisoners such as Nelson Mandela, the democratic transition in South Africa was marked by the intensification of social struggles and the formation of collective action in many fields. The 1994 electoral victory of the ANC, with the support of the SACP and COSATU, opened the door for the creation and incorporation of social demands that come from many social movements created with democracy.[11] To offer a full picture of the beginning of the South African multi-racial democracy, it is important to talk about an action taken by the Afrikaners that culminated in the 1994 *Accord on Afrikaner Self-Determination*. Just before the first general election of post-apartheid South Africa, Afrikaners wanted to have their rights based on an idea of 'power sharing' granted in the new democratic era. They wanted to be sure that the establishment of a proportional political system would not leave the 12% of white Afrikaners completely dominated by the black population that made up 74% of the population at the time.[12]

There are two aspects that we regard as unique about South African collective action and social mobilisation in the post-apartheid era. The first is the engagement in rights battles inside the framework of the new constitution as a tool for seeking social justice.[13] This mode of engagement becomes evident when it comes, for instance, to land restitution and to the exposure of human rights violations during apartheid. The fight against asbestos-related diseases that started in 1995 also became a battle in the field of jurisdiction and internal law because it targeted a multi-national company in the field of asbestos extraction and production: 'working together with international lawyers, activists defined their movement as fitting within the legal framework . . . [T]he demand that an injury or pollution be legally addressed became an integral part of the social demands of the movement' (Simpson and Waldman 2010: 92). Another aspect that is unique concerns the association between social mobilisation groups and NGOs. Robins (2008: 21) argues that the most important forms of political pressure in the post-apartheid era are based on 'NGO–social movement partnerships'. These associations have been responsible for improvements in many areas, such as public health. As Gotlib (2015) contends, in some cases, these aspects come together. The Bhangazi land restitution claim in South Africa was a legal battle supported by NGOs who saw in the restitution of the land to traditional communities a way of preserving the environmental richness of the area. Legal reports have also been used as a source of social mobilisation in seeking historical reparation in South Africa.

Recently, these above-mentioned features of South African collective action in the democratic period have been undergoing transformation.

Since 2009 there has been an increase in the number of protests related to public service delivery, such as sewerage, water supply, sanitation, drainage, public lighting and electricity provision. Mainly organised and led by poor youth, these protests have put South African levels of urban protest far above anywhere else in the world (Alexander and Pfaffe 2014). By 2014, public service delivery protests reached such a high level that it was reported in the press that more than thirty demonstrations were going on every day in South Africa.[14] This process, which has been referred to as a 'rebellion of the poor', shows that South Africa's experience with democracy – one could say a black democracy – solved the problem of racial exclusion by, among other things, creating the legal framework that is necessary for policies to move forward in the direction of social equality by coming back to problems created in an unsettled past.

As in Brazil with the canalisation of social demands happening through the participatory channels created in the democratic period, in South Africa the legal field and NGOs for a long while have refined the way social demands can be incorporated and dealt with. In both countries, it seems today like these respective channels no longer support the flux of demands and the form in which they have been appearing. In Europe, more clearly, collective action as it is happening in the present reveals the limitations of liberal representative democracy as a privileged way to solve political conflicts. In the three world-regions that we are working with it does seem to be the case that collective action has been marked by a connection between the internal configuration of societies in which the youth do clearly see which place they are occupying (and should occupy) with the political opportunities opened to them. These opportunities are not limited to national developments, and have become more globally entangled than ever before (Koopmans 2004; Bringuel and Players 2017). We should be clear in saying that it is not only youth who are very well connected to the Internet but living in precarious conditions that are driving the formation of new collective actions and the transformation of democracies. The act of bringing a collectivity into being leads to an endless process of political reinterpretation and this is potentially the concern of all political subjects. In all of those areas, because of the demands for new ways of embedding political, economic and social life, democracies become reconstituted with the further promise of catching up with what social democratic regimes have offered in terms of equality, inclusion and quality of life. Europe, Brazil and South Africa, when viewed through the prism of how citizens have sought to reshape the polity in recent decades, show very clearly that procedures, institutions and organisations can be points of departure for democratic transformations, but they do not constrain the possibility of change and reinterpretation.

PERSONS, LEADERSHIP AND CONTEXTS

There is another issue that also deserves our attention in this debate about collective action and political transformation. Some people would argue that an 'individualistic' approach better suits the study of how contemporary democracies work and how they are transformed. This is so because we are supposedly living in the era of individual thinking and acting. At this time, holistic perspectives focusing on collectivities are seen as misplaced and, because of that, they are losing ground. Against this view, as Mauss (1938) and also Taylor (1989) show, we would see both the process of the formation of the self and the constitution of a person – both individual and collective – as achieved in specific socio-historical contexts and as an always ongoing processes, never to be completed and ended. From this perspective, it is never the case that, once a self or an individual is formed, they hold enough autonomy to exist and to exercise their will and freedom in a completely independent way. In our approach, even more significant is the fact that, in the history of democracies, the liberal and neo-liberal understandings of political life as an aggregation of individuals in the process of majority will-formation is a defensive reaction of elites against the achievements of bottom-up mobilisations. Gilbert, for instance, argues that neo-liberalism is a political project based on the idea of a society of individuals that aims 'to restore and increase the class power of capital, by extending its own reach and by weakening the power of organised labour' (2014: 47). Without getting into the wider debate on neo-liberalism, what we would like to emphasise at this moment is that when we talk about individual autonomy we are alluding to the possibility of human beings realising themselves in specific times and contexts.

The constitution of social movements around formal organisations was responsible for the construction of key political leadership in the Southern countries that we are analysing, and, we can add now, for the configuration of new forms of political community after the re-establishment of democracies. In this way, political majorities in Brazil and South Africa that won important electoral processes and reshaped the democratic horizon in the last decades of the twentieth century emerged from outright resistance movements: the former president Luiz Inácio Lula da Silva was a trade union leader and Nelson Mandela took part in the black resistance during apartheid as a member of the ANC. Mandela and Lula as leaders of the ANC and the PT, respectively, were able to achieve something approaching hegemony in political debate for a quite long while. Opposition to the ANC and PT not only failed to win elections after Mandela and Lula were first elected president; one can also see that the political positions of the opposition have come to adopt major parts of the hegemonic programme espoused by the ANC and PT. Taking an individualistic view to analyse the role of these political leaders, it could be argued that the successful experiences of democratic transformation in Brazil and South Africa were due to the role played in representative democracy by charismatic and popular leaders such as Lula and Mandela. Nevertheless, the agency of these individuals, who have become key international figures when it comes to the discussion of contemporary politics, cannot be insightfully understood if we look at these figures in isolation. Lula and Mandela became what they are in the first place because they represent an idea that goes far beyond themselves: they represent democracy as a political project based on the fight against exclusion and injustices and the possibility of social transformation from within democratic state institutions, without having regarded themselves as special personalities holding a status that could be understood apart from their context.

In Europe, there are no similar figures after the 1980s.[15] Tony Blair and Silvio Berlusconi are in some ways the two 'exceptional' European politicians of the era. However, neither of them had any inclination towards either problem-oriented reflexivity or transformation-oriented political action. Their 'achievements' have resided in their ability to manage the relation between media and politics while destroying the form of the organised political party within which political debate used to take place. Thus, they were riding the trend towards an individual-aggregative understanding of democracy rather than actively transforming political debate. More recently, the rise of the main leaders of party-movements such as Podemos and Syriza happened together with the rise of the demands they represented inside different collective platforms. Alexis Tsipras and Pablo Iglesias were involved in student movements and the latter became well known for his involvement in global resistance protests such as the Spanish '15M'. At the moment, both leaders are building up their existing place and legacy in the European context. They represent the possibility of experiencing democracy in substantive terms by asking constantly for the involvement of collectivities in their everyday political actions. However, beyond the affirmation of democracy as something that goes beyond the process of representative will-formation and the fact that in their national contexts they try to advance an agenda based on inclusion and equality, it is not clear whether they are advancing the possibility of political agency in the strong sense we advocate here.

The sense of political agency that we emphasise by using the examples of Lula and Mandela requires that political leadership be understood within its context. Contemporary democracies should not be seen either as an aggregation of individual preferences or as the work of an individual leader whose influence is reducible to their ability as a charismatic figure to manage a polity. Lula and Mandela both knew that the project they helped to move forward was bigger than their role as leaders. They cannot be understood as the traditional figure of the 'strong man', as the dictator or the manager of an authoritarian regime; neither do they fit the image of the 'big man', as political leaders who embody a project and make themselves part of a cult of personality, as if the project could not be moved forward without them. Contemporary examples of leaders who regard themselves as embodying the project, as Hugo Cháves was in Venezuela and Evo Morales is still trying to be in Bolivia, are far from resembling what Lula and Mandela represented. It has become clear that the assumption of problem-oriented reflexivity and transformation-oriented political action is not as common in contemporary politics as we would expect.

CONCLUSION

As we have seen, though representing experiences of democratic innovation, both the PT and the ANC governments in Brazil and South Africa have been challenged by other forms of collective action, such as protest movements – service delivery protests in South Africa, and the June 2013 protest movements that were one of the crucial actors that led to the process of impeachment of Dilma Rousseff in 2016. As for Europe with the diagnosis of *disaffected* and *dissatisfied* democracies, both in Brazil and in South Africa it has become usual to refer to the idea of 'disenchantment' or 'disappointment' as an explanation for the rise of protest against progressive governments. From this perspective, the accusations of corruption and the judicial processes initiated against political leaders in both countries are seen as representing the idea that at the end of the day all representative political parties are the same – they all only want to take advantage of the political system. In our argument, recent transformations show something different. For us, under a democratic regime, movements back and forth are part of what we have called the unstable character of democracies. Some of the examples that we worked with show how contemporary democracies have been changed by a variety of collective actions which, in some cases, proceed under the leadership of a specific person who embodies collective demands. They all confirm our historical interpretation that democracies have always been positively transformed by reflexive collective action.

Chapter 11

ENTANGLED HISTORIES, POSSIBLE
FUTURES – SOUTH AND NORTH

In the classical liberal-democratic conception, the agent of political change is the state that stands apart from the market and from civil society. The notion of sovereignty was meant to signal both the authority over a territory and a population and the demarcation from other polities. This double separation was the precondition for effective political agency. True, the insight is not new that this conception was far from any observable reality. From the nineteenth century onwards, state institutions have been denounced as being nothing but the instruments of the elites in society to assert their power. In turn, social movements have been regarded as the means to make claims on state institutions and to undermine the power of the elites. Even this view, however, remains under the influence of the notion that there is a political entity rather clearly separated from society. As a consequence, it tended to dichotomise two views of political agency, a hierarchical one centred on the state and an emancipatory one emanating from social movements. This dichotomy collapsed in recent years, starting out from Northern experiences, when it seemed that states became incapable of effecting political change and social movements were running into a political void. This perception has been our point of departure for this book, aiming to broaden the picture and including other experiences with attempted political change, notably from the South.

By exploring recent experiences with collective action and political transformation in different regions of the globe, the question of the boundaries of states, both internal and external, became central. The account we provide is set into the historical context of the notions of clear territorial delimitations as instituted by the Treaty of Tordesillas and of state sovereignty after the Treaty of Westphalia on the one side, and, on the other, the revolutionary notion of creating polities through social contracts. But the political institutions in Brazil and South Africa were initially instruments of colonial domination by European states, thus sovereign not even in a formal sense. And neither them, not even after independence, nor the European states have been created from any kind of social contract agreed between the residents of their territories. Obvious as this is, during the nineteenth and the twentieth centuries political imagination continued to be guided by those notions. And this not without good reason: if in Brazil, South Africa and Europe there are now formally independent democratic states based on political equality, this is the outcome of struggles inspired by this political imagination.

Nevertheless, our analysis has shown that in both the global North and the global South contemporary states are much less bounded, internally as well as externally, than prevailing conceptions can accept. Both market forces and societal action keep conditioning that which democratic states can do. Endemic corruption in state institutions aiming at granting private benefits represents a strong barrier for the consolidation of democracy. Similarly, the use of state institutions by some groups in society with a view to imposing their interests on other groups undermines the meaning of those institutions. However, we do not see a compelling reason to interpret our findings as leading to the conclusion of a general decline of state capacity, or even more strongly, to the impossibility of bringing positive political change about at all. In conceptual terms, rather, we see the need for developing a notion of collective action that does not oppose states and social movements but instead focuses on the connections and tensions between them (as proposed in Chapter 10). Furthermore, we hold that general conceptual reflections have their limits when assessing possibilities of political change given the variety of situations that one encounters in different settings. When developing our argument, we started out from positive examples that show how the substantive presence of progressive forces inside the states on which our analysis has focused has created, or at least embarked on a search for, democratic solutions to historically persistent problems. Thus, the coming to power of the PT in Brazil enabled the incorporation of the 'social question' into the core agenda of public intervention. Similarly, racial constraints have been removed from the exercise of political autonomy by the population of South Africa. Maybe more moderately, the recent intensification of democratic participation in Europe revives projections of progressive political change while overcoming the visions of traditional leftist parties centrally built upon the idea of class struggles. To a considerable degree, politics has been reinvented in the three world-regions because state borders have been perceived in a different manner – from strong, exclusive and clearly delimitated to more porous and open to conflict. It is from this angle that we will now review our findings with a view to discerning possibilities for future political change.

HOW WE ARRIVED AT WHERE WE ARE: RETHINKING PATH DEPENDENCY

We started our analysis by both rethinking and elaborating the notion of trajectories of modernity through a review of Brazilian, South African and European history (Part I). This has entailed two major consequences: first, modernity is no longer seen as a stable form of socio-political organisation, nor even as a *telos* towards which human history inescapably moves. Rather, modernity refers to a societal self-understanding that undergoes changes in the light of experiences made. Second, trajectories are not pre-existing paths on which societies embark at one point, for some reason or other, and that subsequently determine their ways of going through historical time. Rather, they are the routes that are themselves created by actions taken on the basis of prior experiences. Furthermore, they are not separate, more or less parallel paths, each one of which is specific to one given society. Rather, they intersect and are intertwined in a great variety of ways.

This re-elaboration led us to take distance from two common views of global socio-political history. On the one hand, we do not see a linear process of 'modernisation' on which some societies have embarked earlier and others have followed, and will still follow, at later points. It is not fruitful to see Brazil and South Africa today as 'modernising' or 'emerging' societies that follow the European example with a time lag. Rather, Brazil and South Africa have 'emerged' together with Europe in processes of major socio-political transformation under conditions of global interconnectedness and entanglement. On the other hand, we also do not share the view of global history that postulates the emergence of a 'world-system' at one historical moment, the structure of which then shapes all future interactions and interrelations. World-systems theory and its more recent offsprings rightly underline entanglement; and in contrast to modernisation theory, they focus on the asymmetries and hierarchies that such entanglement entails. Like modernisation theory, though, they assume to a great degree the determination of world-historical developments by a combination of key determining moments – be it the onset of European colonisation or the revolutions of the late eighteenth century – and an imposing logic of historical change – be it the logic of capital or the functional superiority of modernity.

We have tried to develop a view that is more open to historical contingency as well as to transformative political action. But doing so, we stop far short of denying the significance of key historical moments and the constraints to action that asymmetrical and hierarchical constellations entail. Thus, the 'colonial encounter' on the southern Atlantic shores soon transformed into situations of domination and exploitation of the North over the South. And there is now sufficient economic-historical evidence to suppose that colonialism and mercantilism have been responsible for the 'take-off' of north-western European societies, for the 'great divergence' between Europe and the rest of the globe that was to mark global history across the nineteenth and twentieth centuries. Across the nineteenth century, furthermore, economic and military domination came together with the gradual formation of a global 'modern' self-understanding which tended to privilege a specific form of being-in-the-world. While far from becoming globally hegemonic, the self-understanding that was explicitly formulated in Europe became the main point of reference for other world-regional cosmologies and a means, often seen as unavoidable, to re-evaluate themselves. Then, the view was widespread that non-Western ways of world-making were inferior in epistemic terms. What we briefly tried to show above is that what is often called European modernity, even in terms of its cosmology, is less European than is usually assumed but emerged from the experience of the encounter with non-European others (for more detail, see Dussel 2007; Delanty 2013; Wagner 2015; Stråth and Wagner 2017).

The decolonisation of America and later the formation of rather autonomous statehood in the south of Africa went in parallel with new imperial practices around the globe, as world-systems theory rightly underlines. While the three world-regions that we have analysed here remained entangled in asymmetric ways, though, they started to develop parallel practices and institutions that each carried specific features. More room for regional answers to modern questions was opened. A key formative moment, broadly localisable at the turn from the nineteenth to the twentieth century, is the creation of a collective actor in the form of a unified state that forms a 'container' of a territory and a population and endows itself with the capacity for action. By saying that the three world-regions experienced a kind of parallel development, we do not mean that the degrees of global connectedness were low. Even though means of communication and transportation were very different from today, entanglement was intense and significantly shaped socio-political conditions through the movements of goods and people. What we want to assert is that responses to the problems of modern social and political life came to be found increasingly internally, responding to regional conditions and experiences while taking into account changes that happened outside. However, no single 'society' embarked on a 'path' on its own, in isolation from others. The relations of interdependence created enablements and constraints for action. Thus, they conditioned action, but they did not determine it. Paraphrasing Kenneth Pomeranz, we might say that they created a space of 'limited divergence' within an entangled Atlantic modernity.

In substance, much of political action up to the First World War had the democratic political imaginary in its background, but this was not its main inspiring force. Rather, the key issue was the administration of the population by elite groups, old elites in Europe and settler elites in the South, with a view to securing economic efficiency in production for world markets in agriculture and mining (in the South) and in manufacturing industry (in Europe) as well as structures of privilege in everyday life. Given this objective, politico-institutional action was constitutively un- or even anti-democratic, not an early step along a long path of democratisation. As a consequence, constellations of historical injustice were deepened and entrenched rather than alleviated.

Such injustice became increasingly subject to contestation and resistance, which in turn were increasingly directed at and against the state. In particular in Europe, the state came to embody the domination of the elite over the majority of the population, whereas in Brazil the domination by owners of land and mines was more immediate. For this reason, recourse to the democratic political imaginary as an interpretative tool for political transformation became more widespread in Europe, in particular by the workers' and women's movements. The outcome was the extension of suffrage, a formal way to express commitment to democracy.

THE TWENTIETH CENTURY: SEQUENCES OF
REINTERPRETATIONS OF MODERNITY

Looking across all three world-regions, though, inclusion is a more appropriate term than democratisation to capture the course of political transformation during the early twentieth century. Elites became aware of the fact that they had to rely on the consent and co-operation of at least parts of the population. In Brazil and South Africa, this insight led to the selective inclusion of a part of the population: in Brazil, the formally employed, mostly urban workers; in South Africa, the pale-skinned descendants of the European settlers. In both cases, this selective inclusion led to a more pronounced exclusion of the majority of the population, by intention and design through racial laws in South Africa, while in Brazil it was more as an indirect consequence of the fact that few descendants of slaves and native Americans had formal work status. In Europe, the perceived dependence of the elites on the population was more radical. Due to the strength of the workers' movement and the need for soldiers in the First World War, elites saw little prospect of resisting formally equal inclusion of all members of society into socio-political institutions (always bearing inequality of women in the civil law codes in mind), even though they remained largely unconvinced of the viability of such socio-political organisation.

Thus, the early twentieth century provides a historical moment in which one can recognise both the parallelism of globally entangled political transformations and the specificities of the trajectory of each society. Brazil, South Africa and Europe all created some form of organised modernity, based on the ordered inclusion and exclusion of groups with regard to socio-political institutions. In each case, this was a way of coping with the claim of the 'masses' to enter history while at the same time maintaining elite privilege and economic efficiency. But the degree of inclusion and the criteria for inclusion and exclusion varied greatly between the Brazilian Vargas regime, the South African pre-apartheid racialised society and the Europe in which societies with some liberal-democratic elements such as Scandinavia and France coexisted with Italian fascism and German Nazism. Most importantly, the line of exclusion was drawn in the South within the territory and resident population, whereas in Europe the excluded other either remained outside, beyond well-protected borders, or was defined as outside and was expelled and persecuted, such as Jews, Roma and Sinti. Looking in particular at the extreme cases of apartheid and Nazism, extensive historical research has certainly identified causal 'elements' for the emergence of these regimes in prior South African colonial and German/European history, but none of these elements provides the key cause that made the later developments inescapable (see Arendt 1951 for such reasoning on historical transformations).

The limited diversity created during the early twentieth century was significant enough to persist in the post-Second World War trajectories. With Nazism defeated, much of Western Europe could build on the existing inclusion to develop the liberal-democratic Keynesian welfare state that came to be seen as a model form of modernity. In turn, the forms of exclusion and oppression persisted and to some extent became even more pronounced in Brazil and South Africa, even though there were also moments of opening in Brazil until the mid-1960s and increasing resistance in South Africa from the 1960s onwards. While it is possible to consider the liberal-democratic welfare state as a form of organised modernity, it thus differed considerably from the interpretations provided by apartheid South Africa and by Brazil under military dictatorship. For this reason, the major socio-political transformation that started during the 1980s can be seen as another case of the combination of parallel developments with elements that are highly specific to particular societies.

Broadly, we can define this transformation as the exit from organised modernity (Wagner 1994; Larrain Ibañez 1996; Kaya 2004; Domingues 2008). As such, one can identify common features that show parallel developments in a situation of high interconnectedness. The 'post-authoritarian transitions' of Brazil and South Africa happened more or less at the same time as the fall of the Berlin Wall and the dismantling of the Soviet Union; and they also coincided with the move to democratic institutions in other societies of East Asia and Latin America. In all these regions, the transformations can be placed in the larger context of protest movements from the late 1960s onwards. Thus, the varieties of organised modernity appear to give way to a global regime of 'human rights and democracy'. We will return below to the question of whether this is truly such a normatively superior constellation to the one that preceded it, as is often suggested, but now want to underline the fact that, rather than leading to great convergence in 'post-transition' societies, the exit from organised modernity is strongly conditioned by the variety of modernity from which a society exits. Thus, the critique of institutions that are basically inclusive and formally democratic necessarily takes a different form and develops another perspective for the future than the critique of institutions that are based on exclusions and restrictions to participation. In other words, it is highly likely that there will be varieties of interpretations of modernity even after the end of organised modernity.

POLITICAL TRANSFORMATIONS IN A SUPPOSED AGE OF 'HUMAN RIGHTS AND DEMOCRACY'

In Northern societies during the 1990s, the view was widespread that further political transformations were neither necessary nor possible. Going beyond Margaret Thatcher's dictum that there are no alternatives because of the superiority of liberal-market capitalism, referred to in the introduction, this view was also based on the observation that political institutions in more and more countries were founded on the principles of human rights and democracy. Once this stage was reached, so went the argument, no further progressive political change was possible. The best one could achieve politically was to avoid regress (Offe 2009). In the book, though, we have shown that at this same moment new interpretations about democracy and state organisation were created in Southern societies such as Brazil and South Africa.

Despite being widespread, this claim to fully achieved progress remained a predominantly Northern view. In those Southern countries where the creation or recreation of institutions based on human rights and democracy was a dominant political objective of protest and resistance movements, including Brazil and South Africa, the struggle to achieve this objective unleashed enormous political energy. From a Northern point of view, these were struggles of a 'catching-up revolution', to paraphrase Habermas, who used this term for the East European exit from existing socialism. Those Southern societies wanted to arrive where the Northern ones already were. However, this was not at all how many Southern political activists saw their struggle. Based on the experience of institutionally entrenched injustice, the aimed-at political transformation needed not only to establish formal equality but also to create the basis for a society in which the present consequences of past injustice could effectively be overcome. In terms of the political imaginary that emerged in the late eighteenth century, one can say that this political transformation envisaged going beyond establishing personal freedom and legal equality and aimed at reducing social inequality and enhancing solidarity.

The chapters in Part II analysed the fate of the principles of freedom, equality and solidarity in the course of the processes of political transformation that followed the end of organised modernity, giving particular attention to the difference between Northern and Southern situations. We have shown how collective action pressured political institutions as well as markets to address the historical injustice specific to each world-region by creating a new understanding of social freedom, equality and solidarity. The common global context was constituted by an unprecedented degree of interconnectedness, often called 'globalisation'. Furthermore, two elements entered into the global constellation that emerged from the North but were imposed globally. First, economic stagnation in the then so-called 'advanced industrial societies' had led to a critique of the institutions and policies of organised, Keynesian capitalism, suggesting the dismantling of barriers to trade and of institutions of social protection, together known as 'neoliberalism'. Governments in many Southern societies were reluctant to embrace the new guiding principles for their domestic economic and social policies, but they adapted to the rules of global trade as set by global financial institutions. Second, the critique of existing liberal-democratic institutions that was part of the dismantling of Northern organised modernity included a component that tended to see all collective arrangements as possible infringements of personal freedom. As has often been pointed out (see, as an example, Wagner 2002), the Northern '1968' was initially a combination of a political revolution aiming for a new collective project and a cultural revolution desiring greater spaces for personal self-realisation. Whereas the former largely failed, the latter had a lasting impact on Northern societies, often referred to as 'individualisation'. In the South, this component remained comparatively weak for a long time, but has emerged more strongly in the wake of the experiences with the 'post-authoritarian transitions', not least the rise of the 'new middle classes'.

THE FORCE OF COLLECTIVE POLITICAL PROJECTS AND THE WEIGHT OF ENTRENCHED HISTORICAL INJUSTICE

Taking these elements together, the ambivalence within the global constellation becomes clear. In Part II, we showed how the moment when apartheid and dictatorship crumbled in South Africa and Brazil unleashed an enormous amount of political energy that aimed at rather radical political transformation. At the time of writing, true, much of that energy has subsided. In Brazil, the opponents of radical transformation were able to use the partial exhaustion of this transformative energy to oust the PT from institutional power. In South Africa, the initially relatively concise political project of the ANC dissipated due to the heterogeneity of the governing alliance. Nevertheless, the last three decades mark a period of enormous progressive political transformation in both countries. Maybe it is necessary to first describe this success conservatively: both societies have experienced an unprecedented long period of inclusive democratic institutions and practices, characterised by competing political parties, freedom of often highly government-critical media, and stability of the framework of state institutions, including those of government oversight. The ongoing movements of protest as well as investigations into corruption and 'state capture', as instrumental as they probably are in the Brazilian case, provide evidence of political struggle under conditions of a plurality of interests and world-views.

Mainstream political science may see the record of those last decades as an indication of the consolidation of democracy in Brazil and South Africa, but we think this is an erroneous interpretation. Both societies witnessed a considerable change in their political elites, a radical one in South Africa and a more moderate one in Brazil. People who were excluded from political power on formal or socio-cultural grounds for a century and more entered institutional politics at the highest level. Within a very short period, the 'masses' entered political life as enfranchised and participating citizens, and they did so with the demand to overcome the present effects of past exclusion. As this project has not achieved its objectives to a satisfactory degree, it goes on, even though it has encountered obstacles of its own making as well as resistance. Thus, there is no consolidation at all, but an ongoing movement of self-transformation of Brazilian and South African democracy.

We have shown above how considerable achievements were reached in terms of the extension of social protection and the reduction of poverty. These achievements are remarkable in global comparison, because they were made at a time when Northern views assumed an unavoidable decline of the welfare state. We have also shown that there is now a commitment to equal inclusion of all residents in Brazil and South Africa, a principle that was rejected as unviable by the prior elites in both societies until the end of the twentieth century. However, we have also demonstrated the limits of these transformative projects. Social inequality remains among the highest on the globe. Social policies have been extended through redistributing revenues from economic growth, but little or nothing has been done to change the entrenched structures of inequality, due to an existing distribution of wealth and property based on past privileges.

There is political wisdom in not confronting the existing elites too directly, but the side-effects are enormous. On the one hand, such a strategy entails a limitation of the resources available for transformative purposes. On the other hand, and possibly more importantly, it constrains avenues of transformative action. Thus, the creation of a 'black middle class' in South Africa and a 'new middle class' in Brazil is due to increased monetary income, through better employment and social policy. But this monetary income is largely spent for private consumption patterned on the Northern image of affluence, exacerbating well-known problems of resource depletion and environmental damage and leading to a neglect of improving public infrastructures of health, education and transport. Beyond facing resistance, these transformative projects have also created obstacles that now stand in their way. In both countries, this has become visible in declining electoral support for the transformation-oriented political forces. What had once been an almost hegemonic project now faces more critical debate and opposition.

In contrast to the enormous political energy unleashed in Brazil and South Africa, Europe witnessed an extended period of citizen disaffection from the 1990s onwards. This needs to be understood against the background of the fact that, on the one hand, equal political and social inclusion had largely been reached and, on the other, these accomplishments appeared increasingly threatened. Thus, the defence of what there is seemed more important than the striving for new political objectives. In electoral-political terms, the decline of European social democracy is most telling in this respect. Even though not always in power, social democracy had expressed the commitments of the democratic welfare state most clearly, but under the new circumstances of 'globalisation' and 'individualisation' it lacked any compelling perspective to defend or transform egalitarian welfare provision.

In many respects, the process of European integration, making a big leap with the Maastricht Treaty in 1992, was the most promising part of the European response to the new circumstances. Europe as a political entity with agential capacity would possess considerable advantage over the individual European nation states. It would break up the narrowness of (presumed) cultural homogeneity within the nations and provide greater spaces for diversity of self-realisation. It would create an economic space large enough to deal with the impossibility of 'Keynesianism within one country' due to global economic interconnectedness. Supported by its own currency, it would weather global economic fluctuations more easily. And for both of those reasons it would make the organised solidarity of the welfare state more sustainable. Overall, Europe could well be understood as a regional model of close co-operation between states to address problems that go beyond the boundaries of individual states. As such, Europe came to exert the 'force of the example', as it was sometimes seen in other world-regions, such as Latin America and East Asia, as well as in political philosophy (Ferrara 2008).

Despite these apparently obvious advantages, Europe as a political project never entirely took off and at best moved slowly ahead, from one crisis to another. But the reason for this lacking appeal does not reside in the much-discussed 'democratic deficit', referring to the large distance and alienation of European citizens from the decision-makers. Rather, this citizen disaffection is the result of two other causes. First, European integration was never clearly defined as a political project with certain transformative objectives, beyond the initial notion of creating an area of peace and security in a war-torn region of the world. After the onset of the global transformation of the 1980s, therefore, it was not clear in which direction the process should proceed. There was a rather clear distinction between two views, even though it was not always easily perceivable in political debate and policy proposals. On the one hand, integration should make European societies ready for the new circumstances of global economic openness, often called 'neo-liberal globalisation'. Thus, the point was to weaken national rules and replace them with European rules that were rather similar to rules of global exchange (Schulz-Forberg and Stråth 2010). On the other hand, integration was conceived as a defence against neo-liberal globalisation. Building state structures at a larger level would make it possible to maintain many of the beneficial features of European national societies despite the changed global context. These two interpretations remained co-present in European politics, and the dispute between them has never entirely been resolved. It last surfaced during the so-called Euro-crisis in which the imposition of austerity measures on debtor countries prevailed over a commitment to European solidarity.

Second, even when conceived as a political project of the latter kind, European integration has largely remained in denial of many of the changed global circumstances. From our angle, which emphasises entanglement and connectedness, an objective of Europe as a political project is the maintenance of the economic, political and social differential between Europe and large parts of the globe. As we emphasised throughout this volume, this differential was created in the wake of colonial domination through the asymmetric movements of people and goods. It was initially sustained by sheer power, more often than not of a military kind. Such interventions have been less common after decolonisation, though far from absent. They have been replaced by more 'defensive' measures, aimed at maintaining the existing differential rather than expanding it. The core of these measures is border control. Aiming at complete freedom of movement of capital, goods and people inside the European Union, Europe applies highly selective and targeted measures for those movements across European borders. It has opened up considerably to movements of capital, in the wake of financial globalisation, but European policy-makers have started regretting this openness. The movement of goods is to be enhanced through free-trade treaties with other 'Northern' countries, which increasingly encounter opposition, but remains highly regulated towards the South. The movement of people is most strongly regulated, and the ground rule is the denial of permanent residence within the European Union to non-European citizens, with a number of specified exceptions.

Political philosophy has tended to justify, with good reasons, the right of a polity to grant, or not, membership in the polity to outsiders (Walzer 1983). But it mainly proceeds in abstraction and on the basis of equality between polities. Thus, it tends to ignore the history of asymmetrical relations between polities, which lead to historical injustice between people (now increasingly addressed in concerns about global social justice; see Ypi 2012). As we have argued, the past movements of goods and people had a decisive impact on the ways in which polities were formed historically, most importantly with regard to criteria and practices of inclusion and exclusion. From this perspective, the current movement of people from Africa and the Middle East to Europe, often risking and losing their lives when crossing the Mediterranean Sea, is a reversal of historical movements of people. It is a humanitarian crisis of enormous proportions, no doubt. But it is more than that. To put it in short-term policy terms, it puts to the test the European capacity to maintain its economic, political and social differential with large parts of the globe. In broader terms, it shows the need for a rather radical rupture in European political consciousness, accepting injustice inflicted in the past as an urgent political problem of the present. On a highly interconnected globe, freedom, equality and solidarity are not political concepts that lose their significance at a border-control post.

EXTERNALISATION AS A POLITICAL DEVICE

The historical entanglement of Europe with Brazil and South Africa has taken a trajectory on which Europe was able to externalise its problems by shifting the burden southwards (see now Lessenich 2016). Above, we have argued that this is the case for key elements of socio-political organisation such as inclusion and equality. Europe has received praise for its achievements in these respects, and the ways of achieving them have remained rather invisible. Something similar is the case for the questions of ecology and violence that we dealt with in Part III.

It is more and more common to argue that the ecological crisis is the most pressing political issue of the contemporary world (see, for example, Gilbert 2014). In this area, 'externalisation' is a widely applied concept, initially referring to the ways in which an enterprise can use an environmental resource at no cost, such as clean air, while imposing the cost for renewal of the resource on others. Since at least the second half of the twentieth century, collective actions in many parts of the globe have been trying to show the consequences of human action as a geological force of transformation of the earth. The growing acknowledgement of this problem has originated global discussions about who is paying the high price when it comes to the consequences of climate change and who should be recognised as responsible for the damage caused. While this debate is open and of considerable complexity in its details, it is nevertheless clear that the early-industrialising countries of Europe and North America have historically built their living standards on the exploitation of natural resources that now has become a global problem. Furthermore, they have in recent decades improved their own environmental situation and their ecological balance-sheet by 'exporting' highly polluting industries to other world-regions. Thus, we have here another form of current inequality and historical injustice with consequences for the present that is in need of an appropriate redress, made difficult by the urgency of the planetary situation.

Less easily recognisable are the consequences of past and present entanglements for the difference residents of Brazil, South Africa and Europe face in their exposure to violence. Often, it is merely assumed that Southern societies have higher levels of violence, and possibly less efficient police forces and judicial institutions to deal with violence. More nuanced study recognises that poverty, inequality and exclusion lead to violence. Cross-national comparisons, at least at the level of statistics and indicators, exist but there is little reflection on societal co-creation of the conditions for violence. As we have shown, this question opens up when one addresses the further question of which categories of persons are more likely to be victims of violence than others. In everyday conversations in South Africa and Brazil, it is often observed that a human life counts for little in these societies, especially compared to Europe. But the exposure to life risks is highly uneven, and the difference with Europe in everyday exposure to violence is much less pronounced for the upper classes. It is not far-fetched, therefore, to relate the higher levels of violence in the South to the 'surplus population' of descendants of native Americans, Africans and slaves created by the encouraged immigration of Europeans to Brazil and South Africa. This finds its current mirror-image in the unwanted migrants to Europe who drown in the Mediterranean Sea, a particular form of deadly institutional violence since the means are available to rescue all refugees.

Under current conditions of inclusive-egalitarian institutions, the connection of violence to categories of persons is increasingly placed at the core of the discussion about democracy. For a society to be called democratic, the integrity of all lives should be equally preserved. This is far from being the case in Brazil and South Africa, but it is not in Europe either, in particular with regard to those persons who in widely held opinion do not qualify as full Europeans. The two issues, the ecological crisis and the rise of violence against specific groups, connect sadly in those cases when environmental activists are killed in acts of politically motivated violence. With regard to both issues and to both the Northern and the Southern contexts, the problems are recognised and collective action has been undertaken to bring about political change. But neither of the issues is as central to the political agenda as it should be, and they are far too often considered to be marginal compared to the time-honoured issues of inclusion and equality. What our analysis suggests is that this relative neglect is precisely due to the fact that, if recognised in their full importance, it would become clear that they touch the prevailing societal self-understandings at their core and that radical change would be required to deal adequately with them. Furthermore, addressing these problems effectively might require upsetting some of the compromises that have been made when dealing with freedom, equality and solidarity. They are the problems that have not been politically domesticated, the problems that these societies – South and North, in different ways – would prefer not to see.

COLLECTIVE ACTION AND THE PROSPECT OF POLITICAL TRANSFORMATION TODAY

After the exit from organised modernity, as mentioned above, we seem to have arrived at an almost global commitment to 'human rights and democracy', expressed through the institutions of liberal democracy. By looking at Brazil, South Africa and Europe in an interconnected way, though, we can recognise both the sense in which this assertion is true and the sense in which such institutional expression will always remain insufficient. The new global circumstances have thrown into doubt the sustainability of the solutions it was believed had been found in Europe for the question of freedom, equality and solidarity. Furthermore, it has become clear that simply following the European path is not only difficult, but almost impossible, for Brazil and South Africa given their political conditions created across a long, entangled history with Europe. Doing so would also entail persisting in the long-lasting North-driven neglect of ecological sustainability and require the closing of borders on the European 'model' to keep out those whose inclusion would upset socio-economic arrangements. For these reasons, more or less consciously, the political energy unleashed in Brazil and South Africa has always pointed beyond the mere creation of liberal-democratic institutions. Europe, in turn, gradually recovers from its period of citizen disaffection and witnesses signs of an opening to new interpretations of democracy and of collective action.

In conclusion, we want to highlight what we see as possibly the two most important insights from our investigation. First, adequate solutions for the present challenges and those inherited from the past can only be found in democratic collective action, but such action also needs to be based on problem-oriented reflexivity and it needs to aim at turning contestation into effective policy measures. Second, given the current degree of global interconnectedness, those solutions have to be searched for in global communication and co-ordination. Hardly any issue is purely 'domestic' any longer, and to treat them as domestic may precisely entail misrecognition of the problem and/or an attempt at externalising the solution. We will briefly discuss both of these insights in turn.

(1) Across all of our analyses of the political history of the three world-regions, the examples of positive political transformations emerge from democratic collective action, or at least from the mobilisation of the democratic political imaginary. In this continuity, democratising social movements still play an important role in the transformation of society and in the constitution of progressive agendas. But the political changes that have been observed in Europe, Brazil and South Africa show that a broader understanding of collective action as a politically transformative force needs to be developed. In recent years, forms of conservative collective action have gained greater presence in public debate and are sometimes surprisingly capable of garnering wide electoral support. Nationalism, racial supremacism, religious intolerance and even authoritarianism have become an integral part of political agendas pushed forward by collective actors that up to very recently would not have found much space in the public arenas to make their claims. The rise of these phenomena reminds us, above all, that democracy is not as stable and predictable as many theoretical approaches and politicians would like it to be. The locus of democratic power relies on a sovereign people; as such, democracies are always in the process of reinterpretation. Political actors interpret the world they are inserted in, and based on these interpretations they construct their political imaginary in terms of what needs to change in the present to achieve what they regard as valuable in the future.

Sometimes, these interpretations move us back and reinforce dilemmas that we thought were solved by democratic means in the past; sometimes, they do represent a step forward and create conditions for the real exercise of autonomy. Therefore, what is crucial is the capacity to make this distinction. Based on our analysis, we want to suggest that regressive political reinterpretations perform a closure, and progressive ones an opening, and this in two senses of the term. On the one hand, regressive proposals aim to limit the exercise of political reflexivity. They want to address problems with solutions that are already at hand, often derived from some past situation or political project. Nationalism, supremacism and intolerance are all of this kind. They claim that problems cease to exist when societies are – supposedly: again – culturally homogeneous and dissent and diversity are limited. On the other hand, regressive proposals insist on implementing these supposed solutions without further ado. That is why they lean toward authoritarianism, though often accompanied by a kind of plebiscitarian democracy. Thus, the cognitive closure is accompanied by a political closure. In turn, progressive political proposals recognise that no past solution is likely to be fully applicable to a present problem. Thus, they open up to the search for an adequate understanding of the problematic situation as the basis for concrete policy proposals. Furthermore, they would not see such policy proposal as a blueprint that only needs to be implemented by an efficient administration. Rather, they would count on intense political participation not only being compatible with efficacious policy action, but even being conducive to increased efficacy over the medium and longer term.

(2) This latter conviction is based in no small part on the insight that policy adequacy is highly situation-dependent. This applies locally, but also with regard to the diversity of regional situations in an entangled global setting. That is why what is today required, possibly more than ever, is the combination of the nuanced elaboration of local problem analyses with an increase of the capacity for co-operation across local settings, sometimes, and increasingly so, necessarily reaching global extension. Let us illustrate what we want to convey by briefly returning to our observations on the relation between democracy and capitalism.

After the Second World War, the European experience showed that democratic action can change capitalism. But the power of democracy can in one socio-historical context lead to the embedding of capitalism within a nation- and welfare-state, yet in another lead to its disembedding and to the dismantling of the welfare state. The social sciences have often assumed that Europe can supply generally applicable concepts and models (Comaroff and Comaroff 2012). Today we know that these European developments occurred in circumstances that were highly specific and that are unlikely to ever be repeated. To a considerable degree, the temporary success of the European connection between democracy and capitalism after the Second World War was based on European (Western) global dominance. The newness of the current situation may consist in large measure in the fact that the era of such dominance is over. For some time, in the absence of viable democratic answers to the issue, European elites were 'buying time', to use Streeck's expression, by increasing public and private debt. This strategy may have reached its limits today, and if time can no longer be bought, this is because others in this world are claiming equality of rights and of power in this time, in the present. The observable elements of regression of European democracy, not least the return of nationalism, intolerance and even supremacism, are attributable to these changed global circumstances. But at the same time, there is in Europe still a very limited awareness of global change. A leap of the European imagination will be required for a renewed and improved understanding of the place of European societies in the world.

What, though, can one do if, on the one hand, that which was acceptable and desirable in the European 'model' was due to European global domination and, on the other, it is highly probable that the current global restructuring is to the disadvantage of Europe, that it marks the end of a two-centuries-long dominance? This does not necessarily mean that one has to accept greater social inequality and less democracy in Europe as an unavoidable part of global transformations. But certainly one cannot hope that the mechanism for connecting economic strategies with democratic demands will once more be found by virtue of inhabiting a privileged position vis-à-vis the rest of the world. In contrast, not to accept increasing inequality and a democratic deficit may be made easier by the observation that inequality is being reduced and democracy strengthened in other regions of the world, such as Brazil and South Africa, often under the most difficult circumstances. It is still an article of faith in Europe that the combination of a liberal-democratic nation and welfare state and a market economy is the solution to all socio-political problems. Solutions to new challenges are then sought only in incremental changes. The Brazilian and South African experiences make it clear that more radical reorientations must be, but also can be, found. Brazil and South Africa are not so much competitors in a world-capitalist race that Europe is finding more and more difficult as rather pioneers in the search for sustainable social and democratic solutions. To be successful, these new orientations must embrace an understanding of democratic politics that aims, not at maximising the satisfaction of one's own interest in a perceived zero-sum game, but at the definition of the kind of world in which one wants to live. This question is posed constantly in Brazil, South Africa and elsewhere in the global South, not least because it is by no means obvious that former oppressors and oppressed wish to or can live together well and in peace. It is a question that would need to be posed globally as well.

NOTES

INTRODUCTION

1. There are two main reasons why we have chosen Brazil, Europe and South Africa to discuss the conditions for collective action and political change in the present time. Seeking to expand the interpretative framework of the 'multiple modernities' debate, first, we wanted to go beyond the notion of an encounter of crystallised cultures and civilisations with supposedly 'Western' modernity (Wagner 2011 – so as not to overload the text we have provided minimal reference; see also our own works cited, where further references can be found). This intention inspired the research project on the Brazilian, European and South African trajectories of modernity (TRAMOD), on which this book builds. Such an emphasis could have included the US, itself emerging from European colonisation. However, for reasons that we cannot explore here in detail (but see Mota 2015), the experience of the US has been integrated into the history of 'Western' modernity, within which it has been the hegemonic power for a long time. And even though the conditions for political action in the US differ considerably from those in Europe, second, we wanted to confront a 'Northern' experience with a 'Southern' one, which has not only received less attention but has also mostly been interpreted from a 'Northern' angle. As our account could not proceed by fully ignoring the US, we will bring its role and impact in at several points.

2. Given historical changes, we need to specify what socio-political configurations we are speaking about. Brazil refers to what is today the Federal Republic of Brazil, founded in 1889 but with territorial continuity from the Portuguese colony, established in the sixteenth century based on the Treaty of Tordesillas, and Imperial Brazil (1822–9). South Africa refers to the state on the territory of the former Union of South Africa, founded in 1910, which is today the Republic of South Africa. Before 1910 this territory was divided between several polities, in changing constellations, including several African kingdoms, most importantly the Zulu and

215

Xhosa kingdoms, the 'British' Cape Colony, and the 'Dutch' Transvaal Republic and Orange Free State. Even after state unity was introduced, the territory remained partitioned between what came to be called 'population groups', again to be formalised with the creation of 'homelands' by the apartheid regime. Europe has historically no political unity at all, the current European Union possibly coming as close to such a situation as Europe ever got. What we refer to as Europe here is, thus, less precisely defined than Brazil and South Africa, and the capacity for political action is often concentrated in individual states. Most of the time we will be referring to continental Western Europe. When we deviate from this understanding in significant ways, this will be signalled.

CHAPTER 1

1. In contrast, the revolutionary actions that aimed to overcome colonial domination in parts of South America that happened before the consolidation of the revolutions of the late eighteenth century were not interpreted as such because of the absence of an emancipatory framework in which they could have been placed. The most telling case is the revolt of Túpac Amaru II (1780–1) in the area of contemporary Bolivia. This revolt was not perceived as a form of emancipatory action, not even by anti-colonial groups, because such an interpretative horizon was not available at this time. Similarly, African societies defended themselves against settler encroachment on their territory, but they were not fighting for freedom in the sense that was only established later. The modern discourse of autonomy and sovereignty, as we know it today, fully emerged only after the storming of the Bastille had become interpreted as an historical event with consequences far beyond its initial local meaning (Sewell 2005). Even the Declaration of Independence that led to the creation of the United States of America has only later been integrated, in problematic ways, into a linear historical narrative starting with a supposed 'democratic revolution'.
2. For a discussion of what this talk meant for the growth of 'illiberal democracy' see Zakaria (1997).
3. We need to add, though, that the main reason why Brazil did not participate in the Congress was because it was still governed by a European monarchy. Even though independent from Portugal, Brazil was ruled by the Portuguese Braganza dynasty. Besides that, Brazil was still a society based on slavery, and one of the aims of the Panama Congress was to prohibit slavery in the whole region. Simón Bolívar himself was not very enthusiastic about the participation of Brazil in the diplomatic meeting that aimed to create the basis for an American confederal state.

CHAPTER 2

1. A double linguistic matrix has been used to name and identify Brazilian indigenous people. The Tupi-Guarani groups that lived on the coasts used to call Tapuia the ones who lived in the interiors and who did not speak their language. The word Tapuia comes from the Tupi and designates barbarians, foreigners and fugitives.

2. Common Eurocentric accounts used to see in this period the beginning of 'early modernity' on the arduous, three-century-long path to the onset of true modernity at around 1800. In this view, two important features are often overlooked: rather than being a triumphant moment of European man conquering the earth, first, this was a moment of crisis in European history triggered by the fall of the Byzantine Empire and the concomitant endangering of the terrestrial trade routes to Asia. The Portuguese, Spaniards and Dutch set out to sea out of necessity rather than a will to mastery (Darwin 2007). Long-distance maritime trade, second, was not an invention of this period. It had been practised across the Indian Ocean between Asia and East Africa for a long time. The effect of the European voyages rather was to open the Atlantic to create a similar maritime trade area with particular features, most importantly the slave trade and an emerging new division of economic tasks, that would bear full consequences only three centuries after the first voyages.

3. The hypothesis is today mostly seen as based on a fictitious assumption. Arguably, however, for authors such as John Locke this assumption was based on an 'empirical', semi-ethnographical observation of the life of the New World natives (see Mota 2015).

4. Thus, our approach does not entirely share the view that modernity started in the sixteenth century with the discovery of America and the formation of the Atlantic slavery system, as is argued by important authors such as Walter Mignolo (2011) and Enrique Dussel (1994). To place the 'rise' of modernity at this moment is to downplay the significance of the composition of new imaginaries concerning the possibility of autonomy of human beings, connected to the possibility of diverse societal orders and their transformation in different spaces.

5. It is important to note that, unlike in Spanish-American colonies (and also in African colonial history), Brazil became for more than ten years the capital of the Portuguese colonial empire. In 1808, owing to the French invasion, the Portuguese court transferred itself from Portugal to Brazil. Portugal saw itself forced to agree with the Napoleonic *Blocus Continental* and was asked to close down its ports for transactions with the British. From 1808 to 1821 the capital of the kingdom of Portugal was Rio de Janeiro.

6. For a recent representation see Edgar Reitz's film *Die andere Heimat* (2013), featuring an imagined Brazil as both desire and necessity in a German village in the mid-nineteenth century.

7. A subtle reflection of this socio-cultural phenomenon is provided for southern Africa by Hannah Arendt in the first part of *The Origins of Totalitarianism* (1951).

8. In France, the annexation of Alsace-Lorraine by Germany was the most important one of these. And in Brazil the relevant territorial change happened in 1903 with the incorporation of Acre (Amazon) from Bolivia into the national territory.

9. The Mokrani revolt of 1871–2 is telling. It was an uprising of Algerian groups, from Kabylia, whose rights to self-government were encroached upon by the French colonial administration. It occurred at the beginning of the French Third Republic, when France appeared weakened by its military defeat against Germany. After the suppression of the revolt, Kabylian land was confiscated and given to settlers migrating from Alsace and Lorraine, annexed by Germany, thus further increasing colonial pressure on the local society.

10. The difference between the spatial proximity of the shanty towns (*favelas*) and the upper-class areas in Rio de Janeiro, on the one hand, and, on the other, the spatial segregation of townships, such as Soweto, and 'white' residential areas in Johannesburg is a key element in Sergio Rocha Franco's comparative analysis of urban spaces in Southern societies (Franco 2018).

11. 10% of the Brazilian population was eligible for the vote in 1870. Among the countries that counted with elections, only Spain with 26%, France with 20%, and the US with 16% of the population eligible to take part in the electoral process were 'more democratic' than Brazil.

12. It should be added that there was no particular effort made to school the freed slaves after abolition in 1888.

13. The Cape Colony raised property requirements several times during the nineteenth century, clearly fearing that otherwise too many 'non-whites' would qualify. Thus, the non-racialism was more formal than real.

CHAPTER 3

1. These terms are Alain Touraine's, looking back at 'industrial society' from its presumed end-point and forward to the beginning of 'post-industrial society' (Touraine 1971).

2. Shortly after the defeat of the rebellion, the party changed its policy and aimed at recruiting more black miners. As a consequence, many white workers left the party.

3. The recent British television series *Downton Abbey* shows these shifting relations between social groups during the period from 1912 to 1926.

4. The word'masses' acquired a negative meaning in the course of the twentieth century. This is so because it has accompanied a process of intellectual and practical disregard of categories used to describe groups with some kind of passive homogeneity – such as the mob and the crowd – in democratic and individualistic industrial societies (Gilbert 2014). Hardt and Negri (2004) brought the theme back into mainstream intellectual debate by showing how creativity and communicative exchange is part of the very existence of what they call multitudes.

5. In earlier work, one of us characterised this socio-political constellation and its dynamics as 'organised modernity' (Wagner 1994), but based only on analyses of West European societies with some glimpses at the US and the Soviet Union. Due to the 'Northern' focus, the emphasis could there be placed on inclusion and organisation. While we still consider 'organised modernity' a useful term, a widening of the analysis needs to emphasise the combination of organisation and exclusion at work everywhere, but more easily visible in 'Southern' societies. Inclusion and exclusion will be discussed in more detail as a general theme of socio-political organisation in Chapter 6.

6. This account needs to be read in the context of the concomitant rise of the USA and the Soviet Union as two further interpretations of modernity, each with specific features but often seen as embodying two extremes.

7. The concept was coined in the 1930s. It was used by Dutch Reformed Church missionaries, and it started showing up in Afrikaner intellectual and policy discussions in the 1940s.

8. The recent movie *Abschied von Europa* (2016) portrays the Austrian-born writer Stefan Zweig, in exile in Brazil, praising the multi-ethnic country in front of President Vargas's wife as the 'country of the future' (thus, the title of a subsequent book of his) in contrast with Europe, while later showing him in his house in Petrópolis surrounded by dark-skinned servants.

9. Getúlio Vargas was president of Brazil in two different periods: first, from 1930 to 1945, and later from 1951 to 1954. He quit as president in 1945 to avoid a coup that aimed to overthrow his government. He did not leave political life and returned as a president elected by popular vote in 1950. He remained in power until his suicide in 1954.

10. The term 'internal colonisation' was used for projects to develop a national territory more systematically, and often also more equitably. But it also often included a distinction between the included and the excluded, such as in the case of settling German peasants where Polish peasants would otherwise have moved. Importantly, the term is used in these cases positively as part of a project, not critically, as came to be the case after the Second World War.

11. The National Party obtained more seats than its main opponent, the United Party, only because fewer voters were needed to obtain a seat

in rural areas, the party's stronghold, than in urban areas. This pattern repeats itself in recent votes over highly divisive political projects such as the exit of the United Kingdom from the European Union, the election of Donald Trump as president of the US, or the independence of Catalonia from Spain.

12. In 1965, the British sociologist T. H. Marshall went as far as saying that 'it is generally agreed that, whoever provides [the services], the overall responsibility for the welfare of the citizens must remain with the state' (Marshall [1950] (1965): 97).

13. Socialist Eastern Europe showed some similarities, but would need to be discussed on different terms nevertheless.

CHAPTER 4

1. In mainstream economic and political sciences, 'stabilisation' is mostly used for economic processes, meaning a steady and controlled path of economic growth, whereas 'consolidation' is used for political processes, referring to election outcomes with little alteration over time and large majorities for competing moderate parties and the absence of 'unconventional political participation' outside of elections.

2. It is important to notice other developments in terms of the formulation of anti-racism and anti-racism-speech laws that affected the core liberal principle of 'freedom of speech'. After the Second World War, European states entered into a process of critical assessment of the freedom of expression based on other democratic values such as psychological harm, human dignity and conviviality (Bleich 2011).

3. The military coup in Brazil needs to be understood as part of a wider process of political transformation that was happening in America during the Cold War period. Other countries of South America also went through a *coup d'état* during the same period – Argentina and Chile were the most well-known cases. These coups received direct support from the US, which was very worried about the growing number of progressive demands and achievements in the area. Their worry was that the affirmation of democracy and inclusive polices put forward by presidents such as Salvador Allende and João Goulart, side by side with the victory of a communist armed revolution in Cuba (1953–9), would dislodge a key area from the US sphere of influence.

4. This was for a Western public only; on other occasions he would explicitly warn 'the native in South Africa' to renounce any expectations to 'live his adult life under a policy of equal rights. [. . .] There is no place for him in the European community above the level of certain forms of labour' (cited in Thompson 2001: 196).

5. For a contemporary critique see Habermas (1968), and for recent elaborations of the approach see Majone (1996) and Scharpf (1999).

6. Connell (2007: 153–5) suggests that rather similar developments took place in Latin America with the acceptance of the neo-liberal turn in economic policy. She seems, however, to overlook or underestimate the emergence of 'high-intensity' democracy in some countries, most pronouncedly Brazil, and the rethinking of citizen–polity relations in general, introducing notions of 'pluri-national' polities and indigenous rights that are transformative of a standard liberal understanding of the polity (for observations on the long tradition of 'attenuated liberalism' in Latin America, see Mota 2013).

CHAPTER 5

1. Critical analysis in South Africa suggested for some time that South African capitalism required the particular form of exploitation that apartheid provided so that anti-apartheid struggle was necessarily anti-capitalist struggle, following the Marxian tradition of seeing economic phenomena as the most fundamental aspect of the social world. 'Liberal' theorists, in turn, suggested that apartheid constituted a fetter to the fuller development of capitalism because it made reaping the full potential of the 'human resources' of the country impossible. In general, it seems more appropriate to say that capitalism can flourish under different socio-political conditions, and take different forms according to those conditions (see Lipton 2007 for a recent discussion of this debate).

2. A comprehensive social analysis with similar motivations operates with the concept of 'alternative modernities'; see among others Gaonkar (2001).

3. Streeck and Schaefer (2013) develop this perspective further. At the end of the 1990s, as briefly mentioned earlier, these developments were often justified and seen positively as a new understanding of democracy, for instance by Majone (1996) and Scharpf (1999), in a new way linking to the debate about technocracy from the 1960s (see also Mair 2013).

4. Depending on circumstances, the exit option is not only available to the business elites. In other societies workers use it: like the flexibilisation of capital, labour migration can jeopardise a society's ability to create a stable political and economic order. The countries of the South (and today, once again, of Southern Europe) have been far more affected by this, while in the North this question is hardly posed any more.

5. For an impressive account of the finance-capitalist transformation of India, see Dasgupta (2014).

6. As we will see later (Chapter 6), this constitutional innovation opened the door for civil society to take part in the processes of public policy-making. It can be seen clearly in the Brazilian health system, called SUS (*Sistema*

Único de Saúde). SUS was created in accordance with the constitutional principle of making health a universal right that should be provided by the state. Constitutional article 198 determines the three fundamental guidelines that the SUS should have: decentralisation, integral care and popular participation.

CHAPTER 6

1. It has been a procedure exhaustively adopted by modernisation approaches to compare societies through the use of general 'social' indicators, neglecting the specificity of different forms of modern solidarity. At best, these indicators can give us a general picture but they are in most cases driven by biases that do not apply equally to all societies. A good example of this is the use of quantitative data about the proportion of formal workers in a society to infer the level of well-being. There are societies that have job conditions that invalidate such data. In India, 73% of the employed population do not have a job contract (of those, 69% are part of the informal economy). Comparative research based on quantitative tools in such societies will need to use different indicators. In this book, when quantitative data are used, doing so is not meant to express anything of a very general nature. The significance of an aggregated statistical number is very limited when it comes to the interpretation of social injustices and the struggle against them.

2. Just to illustrate the point, from 1880 to 1959 more than 3 million Europeans emigrated to Brazil (Lesser 2013). This number started to fall drastically by 1960 due to both the politics of employment developed in Europe and the change in the political scenario (from democracy to dictatorship) in Brazil.

3. Through the Nationality Act, in 1948 all Commonwealth citizens automatically became British citizens. The arrival of the so-called 'Windrush Generation' in Britain exemplifies how immigrants were initially received and how they have been treated since. Immigrants from the West Indies (ex-Caribbean colonies) were brought to England in an effort to 'rebuild' the country after the Second World War. They have continued to live there but were never given the 'paperwork' that would grant them rights. Under the policy of creating a 'hostile environment', since 2012 many of these immigrants and their families have been living in a condition of complete uncertainty and face deprivation of public services and the threat of deportation.

4. A different form of social life had emerged in Europe in border spaces due to the lack any explicit and justifiable politics of immigration. These spaces (border zones) are geographical areas in which a political limbo determines the existence of individuals in them, such as, for instance, areas of arrival of 'illegal immigrants' in Spain, Greece and France. In

many cases, the borderlands became ends in themselves because they ended up being the end of an immigration route – somewhere in-between a place of origin and a desired place of destiny.

5. It is important to highlight that the good other also included skilled 'Asians'/'Orientals'. Brazil very strongly encouraged Japanese and South Korean immigration at specific moments of the twentieth century and South Africa did the same with 'Asians' – a category that was used then as now to designate very different people such as Indians and Chinese.

6. For a good comprehensive overview on the topic of inequality in Europe see Heidenreich (2016).

7. For Brazil see Lesser (2013) and for South Africa see Crush and MacDonald (2001) and Peberdy (1999).

8. To understand how processes of building up a state were carried out in the absence of an idea of the nation see, for South Africa, Chipkin (2003, 2007) and, for Brazil, Carvalho (2005).

9. For Constant the liberty of the ancients was based on strong moral obliga-tions that a small number of citizens acquired through participation in the state; the liberty of the moderns, on the contrary, became based on the rule of law and the guarantee of civil liberties.

10. José Murilo de Carvalho, one of the most respectable voices when it comes to Brazilian history and politics, shows how a big part of the population was completely excluded from any channel of communication between them and the state. It was like that because most of them lacked the basic conditions for being regarded as members of the polity, such as: not being a slave or ex-slave, being literate or living in the remote interior zones (Carvalho 2005: 237).

11. In relation to this period, it is important to note that even the ex-slaves who became free would not be able to acquire political, economic or social rights because they were not regarded as Brazilian citizens (Mota 2013).

12. See Carvalho (2005) for more information about what those rebellions mean.

13. Sometimes referred to as the Second Boer War or the Anglo–Boer War.

14. Colonial categories and the idea of superiority of some civilisations over others were part of Gandhi's vision of history: 'When Gandhi in 1896 had protested the persistence of two entrances to the Durban Post Office – one for "natives" and Indians, the other for Europeans – his successful petition sought to "do away with the invidious distinction" of being put in the same entrance as "natives", and the new entrance was marked, as Gandhi stated, the "Asiatic" entrance' (Bose 2014: 6).

15. See Thompson and Nicholls (1993) for this.

16. It is important to note that race became connected to skin colour – (black) African, white and coloured – in the course of the three first decades of the twentieth century in the creation of the 'native' policies in South Africa (Bose 2014).

17. 'Segregation was therefore regarded by some as an acceptable and humane means by which to encourage the development of different "cultures"along the lines of their "natural advance"' (Dubow 1989: 8).
18. It is important to note, however, that liberals broke with segregationist discourse in the course of the 1920s to 1930s.
19. Beinart shows that apartheid was based not only on a shared ideology but on seven pillars: 'starker definition of races; exclusive white participation and control in central political institutions (and repression of those who challenged this); separate institutions or territories for blacks; spatial segregation in town and countryside; control of African movement to cities; tighter division in the labor market; and segregation of amenities and facilities of all kinds from universities to park benches' (2001: 148).
20. At the beginning of the twentieth century a third of the world population were still under colonial rule – mostly under European colonial rule (Hobsbawm 1994: 110–11).
21. As Delanty (2013: 188) argues, the development of new technologies of communication and transportation – such as the steamship and the telegraph – were both a product of this time when international competition and national development topped the agenda of European social nationalism.
22. 'The passing and enforcement of immigration restrictions, the introduction of passport obligations, the linkage of social and professional opportunities to citizenship, the emphasis on national attributes in conflicts of all sorts are all phenomena that were introduced or strengthened during the late nineteenth and the early twentieth centuries [. . .] [T]he increased acceptance of the people's right to self-determination at the beginning of the twentieth century, and especially after the First World War, exacerbated the process of imposing nationalized rules on individuals and, furthermore, of excluding groups of other human beings from this right' (Wagner 1994: 90).
23. The conflict regarding the situation of Catalonia should be historically nuanced and carefully approached at this time. However, there is no doubt that much of the problematic situation that we observe in contemporary Spain is due to the inability of the People's Party (a party whose roots extend into the right-wing constituency that once supported the Franco regime) to manage a political conflict with democratic tools. Catalan nationalists also have learned a lot about how to hold on undemocratically to a political conflict. The deadlocked political scenario observed in Spain is, on both sides, an example of undemocratic actions used to uphold elite interests over a shared political agenda of inclusion.
24. Regulation became stronger even when it came to the creation of new labour rights, such as unemployment insurance and compulsory saving

schemes for the workers financed by new income taxes. Those policies were implemented along with very restrictive and violent actions against the 'not included'. The state tried to strengthen the solidarity between that part of the working class that was formally accepted in the labour market at the same time that it excluded a population that was far larger still.

25. The other here is, for instance, poor Afro-Brazilians, indigenous groups and women, all part of what Souza (2009) calls the Brazilian structural 'rabble' (*Ralé*).

26. Gelb (1991) calls South Africa's politico-economic regime under apartheid 'racial Fordism'.

27. These programmes aimed to put an end to economic apartheid and create a system of social and economic security to fight historical injustices.

28. In October 2016 around 6,400 immigrants were evicted from the migrant camp in Calais. A Human Rights Watch Report released in July 2017, called *Like Living in Hell,* showed the abuse of power and violence by police against both children and adults during the evictions (Human Rights Watch 2017). The episode in Spain happened a year later (November 2017). The Minister of Internal Affairs used a prison building in Malaga as a detention centre for foreigners (*Centro de Internamiento de Extranjeros*, or CIE, in Spanish) where more than 500 illegal immigrants recently arrived from sub-Saharan Africa were 'provisionally and exceptionally' incarcerated.

CHAPTER 7

1. The clear example here would be the discussion about the humanity of indigenous people during the colonisation of America. Or more recently, we see these concerns arising in debates about which humans should or should not have the right to vote and to take part in the electoral process – as it was with women, and as can still be seen with those considered too young to vote and convicted criminals who are locked up and as such suffer a 'civil death'. An example of the importance of this issue comes from Brazil. According to data released by the National Penitentiary Department in October 2016, Brazil has the third largest prison population in the world – the current number is around 726,712 – and only the US and China surpass this figure. What is unique about the Brazilian prison population is that 40% of them are in prison without having been tried. They are actually long-term provisional prisoners awaiting trial. More than half of this population are young men between eighteen and twenty-nine years old, and 64% are black.

2. We hope this idea is not misunderstood as yet another argument for what Marshall [1965] (1950) has proposed as the evolution of the system of modern citizenship rights in England – conceived as the affirmation of

civil rights in the eighteenth century, political rights in the nineteenth century and social rights in the twentieth century. In this account, which proved to be very persuasive for England and other parts of Europe, civil, political and social rights are all marked by an attempt to achieve equality and justice.

3. In Brazil the judiciary is still completely controlled by a white intellectual and economic elite. With the exception of a former minister of justice, Joaquim Barbosa, the Supreme Court only has white members, most of them from families that became important during the Empire and First Republic. This has created a situation of non-independence of the judiciary in relation to the other structures of democratic power (Oliveira et al. 2017).

4. Brazil is not an exception to this history. And the very recent developments in the country help us to illustrate the point. The absence of a full democratisation of state institutions is one of the causes that explain the blockage of the progressive policies that were initiated by the PT in the first decade of this century. We will return to this point later in this chapter.

5. The idea of equalising and disequalising factors has been used to explain global income inequalities. Mainly, these factors refer to global forces and movements, such as the industrialisation of poor areas of the globe. The equalising factors that have played a significant role in the improvement of global inequalities are connected to faster economic growth of some areas of the globe, general income growth, and differences in population size. Disequalising factors refer to the slow development, in both economic and societal terms, of parts of sub-Saharan Africa (Firebaugh and Goesling 2004: 297–8).

6. The Democracy Index has been released every year since 2010 by a private UK company. It measures the development of democratic conditions in more than 150 countries around the world. They classify all of the analysed countries into four types of regime: full democracy, flawed democracy, hybrid regime and authoritarian. Only nineteen countries of the world are full democracies according to this index. Among the Northern countries that have also been characterised as flawed democracies are: the US, France, Italy, Portugal, Greece and Belgium.

7. Among specialists there is a major dispute in relation to which indexes better represent social inequalities. Traditionally, those indexes are very much based on financial standards such as income and income and consumption expenditure – like the Gini index itself. The Palma index has been used by the United Nations because it is more sensitive to what happens in the middle stratum than the Gini index is. However, in both the Gini and Palma indexes South Africa and Brazil appear among the most unequal countries in the world; Central European countries would appear among the least unequal countries in the world.

8. In more detail: in 2006 Germany had a Gini index of 31.8; France 29.7; the United Kingdom 34.6; and Spain 32.5.

9. On 8 October 2008 the then Brazilian president Lula made a famous speech in which he said Brazilians should not worry about the crisis. He said that in the US and Europe the crisis was experienced as a tsunami and in Brazil, if the crisis were to reach the country at all, it would be 'no stronger than little sea waves on a very calm day'. In the EU-CELAC Brussels meeting of 2015, former president Dilma Rousseff returned to the metaphor used by Lula in 2008 and said that in 2008 the crisis did not hit Brazil. But the successive growth of the 'little economic crisis' made the little sea wave swell to enormous size. Over this same period, Northern economies recovered very quickly and Southern economies proved to be much less prepared to deal with global financial speculation and other cumulative economic and political variables directly associated with it.

10. Cardoso (2010) analyses the persistence of inequalities in Brazil through the constitution and transformation of working labour and compares it with other Northern countries. The data he uses about the perception of inequalities come from the International Social Survey Program – an institutional voluntary consortium that aims to compare countries in relation to perceptions and values.

11. In Germany, for instance, the share of the wage tax for total tax revenue dropped from 33.8% to 24.8% between 1992 and 2012, whereas the share of VAT rose from 27% to 32.4%.

12. In Brazil, the rich tend to indulge in consumption trips to the US. It is a common topic among the elites to discuss how often they go to Miami for shopping.

13. According to Silveira (2012: 78), Brazil did not in fact redress the regressive tributary system that it relies on. But during the years of the PT government there was at least some observable progress in terms of state expenditure on public services.

14. There are two main conclusions that Morgan presents based on his research about income and inequality in Brazil from 2001 to 2015. The first is that 'the richest 10% in the population receive over half of all national income, while the bottom half in the population, a group five times larger, receives five time less. The middle 40% in the distribution receives just less than one third of total income, less than its proportional share. This reveals that inequality in Brazil is about the large division between the top and the bottom of the income hierarchy.' The second conclusion is that inequality has indeed increased. 'Despite the slight gains made by the Bottom 50%, which increased its share of national income from 11% to 12%, the Top 10% income share also evolved positively, from 54% to 55%, both at the expense of a continuously squeezed Middle 40%' (Morgan 2017: 15). This evidence becomes even more substantial when compared

to other countries. The bottom 50% has improved their condition while the elites belonging to the top 1% have gained much more when compared to their counterparts in places such as the US, China, Colombia and South Africa (Morgan 2017: 18).

15. When Dilma Rousseff first attempted to push a programme of fiscal reform she was impeached in a very controversial judicial process, as we will see in the next section.

16. Morgan (2017) offers this conclusion in a research based on three different data sources: the Continuous National Household Sample Survey (*Pesquisa Nacional por Amostra de Domicílios*), official fiscal data from Brazil's Federal Tax Office (*Receita Federal Brasileira*), and the Integrated National Accounts (*Contas Econômicas Integradas*). A combination of these data offers a much more nuanced and systematic account of income inequalities than the use of the Gini index alone.

17. For instance, it is still a big challenge to South Africa to provide flush toilets to houses. In 1996, 49.1% of houses had a flush toilet; in 2016 the service is estimated at 60.6% of houses, a growth of only 10% in the space of 10 years.

18. In Brazil, racial forms of stratification did not acquire the same formal status as those of South Africa. However, through a different political and legal system established after the proclamation of the republic in 1889, the colonial elites managed to keep their power by controlling both the economic and the political systems. The absence of a transformative democratic moment in Brazil in which the poorest, ex-slaves and other minority ethnic groups could have made their underprivileged condition be seen not as a matter of deservedness but of the absence of opportunity and of equal conditions is one of the historical factors that explains the emergence of the very misleading image of the country as a 'racial democracy' (Freyre 1933; for an empirical critique of this idea see Telles 2006). In fact, what has happened in Brazil is the establishment of a racist politico-economic system in which, until very recently, public discussion about racial difference and social and political inequality was not present. By keeping the discussion focused on the recent past, both under apartheid in South Africa and the dictatorship in Brazil, we can observe economic growth accompanied by a strengthening of the mechanisms that undermine attempts to really challenge patterns of reproduction of social and political inequality.

19. In 2003, 8.0% of the population were living in extreme poverty. This proportion has dropped to 3.4% in 2011. People living in poverty were 15.9% of the population in 2003 and have dropped to 6.3% in 2011.

20. The Lava-Jato anti-corruption operation started in 2014 and has basically targeted leaders of the PT who were supposed to be connected to (or maybe leading) corrupt schemes linking constructors and Petrobrás (the

main Brazilian oil company). This operation is at the centre of the ongoing Brazilian political crisis. Oliveira and colleagues, in a prosopographic study published in 2017, showed that the judges leading this operation were all part of elitist families that have long operated inside state institutions. All of these individuals are part of the same family and social groups that are inside state institutions in similar positions since, at least, the dictatorship – in some cases this so-called 'dynasty' can be traced back to colonial times. The authors characterise this group as part of a 'juridical dynasty' (Oliveira et al. 2017) that cannot be fully separated from the other constituted powers of the executive and the legislature. It is clear that this anti-corruption operation should have had a wider scope and targeted a corrupt scheme rather than a political group. In the context of Brazil, we believe that there is clear evidence that the limitations of this operation came from the socially highly uneven composition of the judiciary.

21. When president Dilma Rousseff was impeached, Brazil had 22.1% of its population living under the poverty line (less than 5.5 US dollars per day). From 2016 to 2017 this number grew to 25.4% of the population, which indicates that there are up to 52.5 million people living under the poverty line. These statistics alone show how dangerous the situation in the country is becoming. But the picture becomes even bleaker when we face the reality that race, gender and the structure of the family count a lot for the composition of these statistics. An unmarried, single, black mother is much more likely to be living under the poverty line. According to the Brazilian Institute of Statistics and Geography (IBGE), 64% of women with these characteristics were living under the poverty line in 2017.

22. In practical terms, the conditionalities have been dropped, such that at present caregivers for all children up to 18 years old are entitled to the grant.

23. Brazil was undergoing an economic and political crisis when the slogan 'More changes, more future' was launched during the re-election campaign of President Dilma Rousseff. Exactly one month before the presidential election, we held a joint workshop with the Participatory Democracy Project (PRODEP/UFMG) in Belo Horizonte (Brazil). Southern African intellectuals were invited to the workshop and they were all amazed by the fact that even in a time of crisis the idea of a 'future' was still in use as a political representation of Brazilian societal self-understanding. Professor Ivor Chipkin was especially surprised by that. On more than one occasion he said that, compared to Brazil, in South Africa it seems like there is no future. Or, at least, that a better future is not something that represents a political project worth pursuing. However, based on the analysis that we present in this part of the book, it does seem to be the case that, in the absence of strong rupture, South Africa is showing more commitment in accepting the challenge of building a better place to be in the future than is Brazil.

24. This Ministry was created by Lula and became a central actor for the growth of inclusion in contemporary Brazil.

CHAPTER 8

1. It was not the first event to cause major health effects. Air and water had increasingly been used to dilute pollutants, but in many cases the pollutants only become less easily perceived, not necessarily less poisonous, especially over the long- and medium-term. Furthermore, when the people whose health was affected were from the lower classes, such as mine workers or agricultural workers, their situation tended to cause little concern and even less action. Thus, the reason why the London event stood out in terms of its publicness and the extent of remedial action was that it took place in a capital city of metropolitan Europe.
2. The Social Democrats lost this election, but Brandt remained their candidate and was successful in 1969. During his period in office, the government adopted a comprehensive environmental programme, passed several laws for the protection of the environment, and created a Federal Agency for the Environment.
3. In some way, they may be proven wrong at some point: human hubris has started entertaining the idea of 'de-extinction', that is, reproducing extinct animal species based on retrievable DNA information.
4. R. Bale (2018), 'More than 1,000 rhinos killed by poachers in South Africa last year', *National Geographic*, 25 January 2018.
5. A. J. Barca (2016), 'La presidenta Rousseff: "Quieren que renuncie para evitar echarme ilegalmente"', *El País*, 25 March 2016.
6. For the general shift in discourse within European development policy, see Karagiannis 2004.
7. IWW Water Centre (2017), 'It is possible again to swim in the Ruhr', 24 May 2017. Available at <www.iww-online.de> (accessed 18 July 2018). This was after forty-six years of bathing prohibition.
8. See, for instance, the European Commission on the Paris Agreement to combat climate change: 'The EU has been at the forefront of international efforts towards a global climate deal'. Available at <https://ec.europa.eu/clima/policies/international/negotiations/paris_en> (accessed 23 July 2018).
9. The 'post-industrial society' theorem already arose during the 1960s, but it was then seen as a relative shift from employment in the industrial sector towards the third, or service sector. Under assumptions of high general growth rates, typical of the 1960s, the advent of 'post-industrial society' did not necessarily mean less industrial employment in absolute terms. By contrast, 'de-industrialisation' is at least partly a crisis discourse, as it requires adaptive measures often not welcomed by those concerned.

10. South Africa had high growth of industrial production until a drop in 2009, but considerably lower growth rates since then. Brazil had moderate growth rates before 2009, recovered quickly from the drop in 2009, but faced a second decline in 2016.

11. Stephan Lessenich (2016) coined the term 'externalisation society' for a constellation in which one type of society systematically shifts the negative consequences of its production and lifestyle onto other societies.

12. The wording is 'common but differentiated responsibilities'; United Nations (2015), 'Paris Agreement', preamble and article 4, 3. Available at <https://unfccc.int/process-and-meetings/the-paris-agreement/the-paris-agreement> (accessed 11 August 2018).

13. Germany, which prided itself on being 'at the forefront' even within Europe, is falling behind in reaching its self-set target objectives for 2030, and there are calls by politicians to be more 'realistic'. But this falling behind has triggered a wide critical debate with reference to the Paris Agreement. The fact that the commitment for 2050 has been explicitly made within a formal international agreement makes it discursively difficult to just renounce fulfilling it.

14. M. McManus (2015), 'Why countries need to count their "outsourced" emissions', *World Economic Forum*, 5 June 2015. Available at <https://www.weforum.org/agenda/2015/06/why-countries-need-to-count-outsourced-emissions/> (accessed 23 July 2018).

15. M. R. Murmis and C. Lorrea (2015), 'We can start leaving the oil in the ground right now – here's how', *The Guardian*, 9 February 2015. Available at <https://www.theguardian.com/environment/andes-to-the-amazon/2015/feb/09/we-can-start-leaving-the-oil-in-the-ground-right-now-heres-how>; see also 'Amazon rainforest', *Encyclopaedia Britannica*. Available at <https://www.britannica.com/place/Amazon-Rainforest> (both accessed 23 July 2018).

16. J. Watts (2018), 'Almost four environmental defenders killed each week in 2017', *The Guardian*, 2 February 2018. Available at <https://www.theguardian.com/environment/2018/feb/02/almost-four-environmental-defenders-a-week-killed-in-2017> (accessed 23 July 2018).

17. Here and throughout this book, we use the terms 'South' and 'North' for want of better ones, not because they neatly describe a current global divide. Considering Brazil and South Africa, one needs to add, first, that these countries are the base of companies in the areas of agriculture and mining that operate in the same way as those with a base in the North and, second, that these relatively powerful members of the BRICS association have themselves acquired some capacity to displace conflicts elsewhere in the South.

18. Such methodological nationalism, it needs to be underlined, is not a conceptual assumption in this approach, but an effect of data and methodology.

19. The average per capita use of resources and impact on the environment remains considerably higher in Europe than in most other parts of the world, with the main exception of the US.

CHAPTER 9

1. For Malešević (2013), however, in historical-empirical terms, it would be problematic to assume that the concern with self-preservation has made the modern age less violent than other forms of organisation of life. Developing a historical-sociological approach, he argues that levels of violence remain more or less similar throughout human history. From a cognitive-psychological point of view, Pinker (2011) develops a different argument, showing that modern developments in terms of the monopoly of use of force, of human communication and reflexivity, and commerce were all responsible for the decline in the use of violence as a problem-solving tool. The debate itself about how best to approach violence from a long historical perspective is not settled yet.
2. This argument bears some similarities to Norbert Elias's discussion of the connection between violence and the civilising process.
3. This observation is similar to Jürgen Habermas's understanding of modernity as marked by the constitutionalisation of violence rather than violence as a means to solve problems.
4. In 2015, taken together, blacks and Hispanics represented no more than 32% of the US population. But when it comes to the US's incarcerated population they constitute up to 56% of the total.
5. For Arendt (1970: 52), violence is the 'hope of those who have no power'. However, there is still much to be said about it, above all when paying attention to forms of resistance against illegitimate states in Southern societies. Many struggles and wars that erupted in the second half of the twentieth century in Africa and America against different forms of dictatorship pursued their political objectives with violent means – as was the case, as we will see in Chapter 10, for Dilma Rousseff and Nelson Mandela. Other more specific forms of communitarian resistance have used violence against property (not against people) to pursue their demands, such as the actions of a Mapuche community in Chile when they 'destroyed' part of a Spanish company that constructed a dam close to the area where they were living, causing their water supply to vanish and destroying the richness of the soil that they used to produce their food.
6. Centeno (2002) connects violence and the existence of 'parallel' states in Latin America to the absence of consolidated states through war, as was the case in Europe. For Africa, Schmidt (2013) argues that foreign intervention from both the colonial and post-colonial periods was responsible

for the de-structuration of Africans' original forms of cohesion. Besides, in both world-regions, the explanation can be found also in the very patterns of inequality.

7. There are, however, many problems involved in data collection and comparison. As Goodey (2007) argues for Europe, there is no common way of tackling violence in all its aspects. When it comes to very sensitive topics such as racism and gender violence, it is even worse. This is because, beside the fact that there is no shared definition of what kind of crimes count as racism and gender violence, the victims of these violent actions tend to under-report such incidents because of proximity with the aggressor and/or because of the shame that accompanies them.

8. Countries in Central America, the Caribbean and South America have the highest homicide rates in the world. The United Nations Office on Drugs and Crimes, from the beginning of 2018, put El Salvador at the top of the list with a rate of 82.84. The most recent data about Brazil shows a rate of 29.53, quite similar to the year 2016.

9. However, if we take the European region as a whole we will observe that the rate varies quite a lot. The Russian Federation has the highest rate in the region with 13.1 intentional homicides to every 100,000; in the safest/richest places in the region, such as Norway and Switzerland, the rate is about 0.6.

10. In Brazil, it should be noted that a combination of being transsexual, poor and black is lethal. The life expectancy of someone who fits this demographic is around thirty-five years.

11. According to the data, young women between fifteen and twenty-four years of age are much more likely to become HIV-positive than young males in the same age group (STATS SA 2017c).

12. The reference to this type of violence as murder could distract from the general attention that has been given to attacks, including rape, that happen in farming areas of the country. Awareness of this broader issue has, on occasion, filtered into contemporary South African literature. For instance, J. M. Coetzee's *Disgrace*, a novel published in 1999, narrates many conflicts involving violence in contemporary South Africa and their apartheid roots. The plot explores the rape of a white homosexual woman living in the Eastern Cape province.

13. The last statistical measure that shows the race of the victims is from 2001: 61.6% were white, 33.3% black and 5.1% Asian/other. It should be noted that the great majority of farms in South Africa are still owned by whites and staffed by black labourers.

14. Talk available at: <http://www.politicsweb.co.za/opinion/antiwhite-racism-in-south-africa>.

15. Interpersonal violence, especially against women, is still a challenge in Europe.

16. On the contrary, there are many collective actions being taken in Europe asking for the opening of the borders for refugees and people who have been rescued in the Mediterranean area, and to have their situation as immigrants legalised.
17. These examples could be explored a bit more to show how, despite the fact that these parties did not win general elections, in many cases they attained impressive victories when it comes to the election of members to the parliaments. The point we want to make, however, is that they do express the feelings of conservative actors but are not able to democratically build up an agenda that would encompass demands that go beyond those compatible with nationalist feelings.
18. Human rights activists such as Marielle Franco have been threatened and in some cases executed after initiating judicial processes against the police and the military, who are mostly responsible for the death of the young black population.
19. Interventions referred to as 'pacification' were taken as part of the Growth Acceleration Programme (*Programa de Aceleração do Crescimento*, PAC) developed by the PT government since 2006.

CHAPTER 10

1. A perspective established in the US, especially with the contribution of Olson (1965).
2. There are exceptions to this rule. Some Southern scholars came together under a United Nations programme inaugurated at the end of the 1980s aiming at co-ordinating research about the challenges for development in the 'Third World'. Some of these scholars focused on the capacity of social movements to empower the people. Contributions from this group can be found in Wignaraja (1993).
3. Borch (2012) develops a similar conception of crowds and their politics that can be even used for the formation of a new history of sociology.
4. Data from Eurostat (2010) shows that 60% of the young population live with their parents. A percentage much higher than the 20% that is found in Northern countries such as Denmark, Sweden or Finland.
5. This song was sung by Deolinda, a Portuguese music group, in a concert in January 2011. It expresses the feelings of the young Portuguese generation. In one of its verses, it says: 'How stupid I am / and I am thinking / What a stupid world / In which to be slave one needs to study'.
6. The appearance of such collective action is not only dependent on the concrete determination of life conditions; it is also becoming increasingly dependent on the 'emotional mobilisation' that offers a mechanism by which 'anguish' can be transformed into political action (Estanque et al. 2013: 4). Another clear example of this emotional mobilisation is found

in the speech the Labour leader Jeremy Corbyn gave at a music festival in 2017 at Glastonbury (UK). He took advantage of this event attended by thousands of youth to transform the anxieties of the 'desperate generation' into a call for unity and action to bring about a new world.

7. Even though nobody would have said that the birth of a new 'high intensity' democracy in Brazil was taking place when the constitution of 1988 was proclaimed, there was nonetheless a feeling that the beast was finally waking up to the advantages of inclusive democracy. The conditions for the creation of new channels of participation in political life were put in place. It resignified the meaning of democracy in the country and abroad thanks to the action of key social movements and political bodies. To understand this transformation and how the idea of 'hope for a better future' became materialised in the new era of democracy in Brazil, see Unger (1998) and Ireland (1994).

8. The average age of participants in participatory institutions is over forty years.

9. One of the most important organisations is the Free Brazil Movement (*Movimento Brasil Livre*, MBL) which remains strongly opposed to any agenda encompassed by left-wing political parties. The MBL fight became associated with conservative parties and agendas such as those pushing for a reform in the education system to remove history as a mandatory subject in secondary education. The MBL is composed of very young activists that use the Internet as their main tool to call for popular support and to organise themselves.

10. Robin (2008) shows how Zuma, who received minimal formal schooling, obtained his political education by being involved for many years in liberation struggles.

11. Among the most important social movements we find in post-apartheid South Africa are: the South African Homeless People's Federation (created in 1994); the Treatment Action Campaign, concerned with people who are HIV-positive (created in 1998); the community-based and anti-privatisation organisations that came to constitute the Concerned Citizens Forum (created in 1999); the Anti-Eviction Campaign, founded to fight evictions and for the improvement of public services (created in 2000); the Anti-Privatisation Forum (created in 2000); the Landless People's Movement (created in 2001); the Coalition of South Africans for the Basic Income Grant (created in 2001); and *Abahlali base Mjondolo* (also known as the Durban Shack Dwellers' Movement, created in 2005), which fights for the improvement of the living conditions of marginalised people.

12. The Freedom Front (a party created by moderate Afrikaner political leaders), the ANC and the National Party signed the accord. The *Afrikaner Volksfront* became a central organisation representing many right-wing Afrikaner organisations that were not completely satisfied with the

accord; however, while such Afrikaner demands live on, this organisation was dismantled in 1996.

13. It would be possible to argue that Brazil's 1988 constitution has also been mobilised as a source of social organisation. However, this has not been done in the same systematic way as in South Africa. At present, indeed, it could be the case that there is decreasing popular support for the rights that the constitution has guaranteed.

14. On 9 February 2014, the Sunday *City Press* newspaper, based in Johannesburg, had on its front page an article claiming that 2,947 protests happened in South Africa in the previous three months; the number of protests between January 2009 and August 2012 was 3,258; thirty-two protests per day happened in South Africa in the previous three months (source: https://africacheck.org/reports/are-there-30-service-delivery-protests-a-day-in-south-africa-2/). These numbers could be inflated because they refer to police records, not to a systematic database. All the same, they still offer a picture of how collective action has been evolving in recent years in South Africa.

15. There could be one possible European exception: Vaclav Havel, in post-socialist Europe. Despite becoming president of the Czech Republic, Havel seems to have been a reluctant politician *par excellence*. In fact, he can hardly be called a successful politician. His reflections about the political condition of the time make him an example of problem-oriented reflexivity, however limited that was by his moralising. But his moralising also prevented him from being able to represent in his person the collective will and from helping to promote transformative interventions through the state.

REFERENCES

Afrobarometer (2016), 'Support for democracy in South Africa declines amid rising discontent with implementation', <http://afrobarometer.org/sites/default/files/publications/Dispatches/ab_r6_dispatchno71_south_africa_perceptions_of_democracy.pdf> (accessed 3 July 2018).

Agier, M. (2016), *Borderlands: Towards an Anthropology of the Cosmopolitan Condition*, Cambridge: Polity.

Aglietta, M. [1976] (1979), *A Theory of Capitalist Regulation: the US Experience*, London: New Left Books.

Albert, M. (1998), *Capitalisme Contre Capitalisme*, Paris: Seuil.

Alexander, P. and P. Pfaffe (2014), 'Social relations to the means and ends of protest in South Africa's ongoing rebellion of the poor: the Balfour insurrections', *Social Movements Studies*, 13: 2, pp. 214–21.

Almond, G. A. and S. Verba (1963), *The Civic Culture: Political Attitudes and Democracy in Five Nations*, Princeton, NJ: Princeton University Press.

Amable, B. (2005), *Les Cinq Capitalismes: Diversité des Systèmes Économiques et Sociaux dans la Mondialisation*, Paris: Seuil.

Anzaldúa, G. (1987) *Borderlands/La Frontera: The New Mestiza*, San Francisco: Aunt Lute Books.

Arendt, H. (1951), *The Origins of Totalitarianism*, Chicago: Harcourt, Brace, Jovanovich.

Arendt, H. (1970), *On Violence*, New York: Harcourt Brace & Company.

Avritzer, L. (2007), 'Modes of democratic deliberation', in B. S. Santos (ed.), *Democratizing Democracy*, London: Verso, pp. 377–404.

Avritzer, L. (2009), *Participatory Institutions in Democratic Brazil*, Baltimore: Johns Hopkins University Press.

Avritzer, L. (2016), *Impasses da Democracia no Brasil*, Rio de Janeiro: Civilização Brasileira.

Avritzer, L. (2018), 'A Cara da Democracia' (Research Report of a Survey), <https://www.institutodademocracia.org/single-post/A-Cara-da-Democracia-brasileiros-mostram-situcoes-que-seria-justificavel-golpe-militar> (accessed 3 July 2018).

Baker, K. M. (1990), *Inventing the French Revolution*, Cambridge: Cambridge University Press.

Baumgarten, B. (2013), 'Geração à Rasca and beyond: mobilizations in Portugal after 12 March 2012', *Current Sociology*, 61: 4, pp. 457–73.

Bayly, C. A. (2004), *The Birth of the Modern World, 1780–1914*, Oxford: Blackwell.

Bayly, C. A. (2012), *Recovering Liberties: Indian thought in the age of Liberalism and Empire*, Cambridge: Cambridge University Press.

Beck, U. (1986), *Risk Society*, London: Sage.

Beinart, W. (2001), *Twentieth Century South Africa*, Oxford: Oxford University Press.

Belich, J. (2009), *Replenishing the Earth: The Settler Revolution and the Rise of the Anglo-world*, 1783–1939, Oxford: Oxford University Press.

Berlin, I. [1958] (1971), 'Two concepts of liberty', in I. Berlin, *Four Essays on Liberty*, Oxford: Oxford University Press.

Bernstein, H., C. Leys and L. Panitch (2008), 'Reflections on violence today', *Socialist Register 2009*, Pontypool: Merlin Press.

Bettio, F. and J. Plantenga (2008), 'Comparing care regimes in Europe', *Feminist Economics*, 10: 1, pp. 85–113.

Bleich, E. (2007), 'Hate crime policy in Western Europe: responding to racist violence in Britain, Germany, and France', *American Behavioral Scientist*, 51: 2, pp. 149–65.

Bleich, E. (2011), 'The rise of hate speech and hate crime laws in liberal democracies', *Journal of Ethnic and Migration Studies*, 37: 6, pp. 917–34.

Boltanski, L. (2009), *De la critique: précis de la sociologie de l'émancipation*, Paris: Gallimard.

Boltanski, L. and E. Chiapello (1999), *Le Nouvel Esprit du Capitalisme*, Paris: Gallimard.

Borch, C. (2012), *The Politics of Crowds: An Alternative History of Sociology*, Cambridge: Cambridge University Press.

Bose, N. (2014), 'New settler colonial histories at the edges of empire: "Asiatics", settlers, and law in colonial South Africa', *Journal of Colonialism and Colonial History*, 15: 1.

Breckenridge, K. (2007), 'Fighting for a white South Africa: white working-class racism and the 1922 Rand revolt', *South African Historical Journal*, 57, pp. 228–43.

Bringel, B. and G. Pleyers (eds) (2017), *Protesta e Indignación Global: los movimientos sociales en el nuevo orden mundial*, Buenos Aires: CLACSO; Rio de Janeiro: FAPERJ.

Brockerhoff, S. (2010), 'Monitoring the Progressive Realisation of Socio-economic Rights: A Review of the Development of Social Security Policy in South Africa', Johannesburg: Studies in Poverty and Inequality Institute.

Buettner, E. (2014), *Europe after Empire*, Cambridge: Cambridge University Press.

Butler, J. (2004), *Precarious Life: the Power of Mourning and Violence*, London: Verso.

Campello, T. and M. N. Neri (eds) (2013), *Programa Bolsa Família: uma década de inclusão e cidadania*, Brasília: IPEA.

Cardoso, A. M. (2010), *A Construção da Sociedade do Trabalho no Brasil: uma investigação sobre a persistência secular das desigualdades*, Rio de Janeiro: FGV editora.

Cardoso, F. H. and E. Faletto (1979), *Dependency and Development in Latin America*, Berkeley: University of California Press.

Carvalho, J. M. (1990), *A Formação das Almas: o imaginário da república no Brasil*, São Paulo: Companhia das Letras.

Carvalho, J. M. (2005), *Pontos e Bordados: escritos de história e política*, Belo Horizonte: Editora UFMG.

Castel, R. (1995), *Les Métamorphoses de la Question Sociale: une chronique du salariat*, Paris: Fayard.

Castoriadis, C. (1997), 'Fait et à faire', in C. Castoriadis, *Fait et à Faire: les Carrefours du Labyrinthe*, vol. 5, Paris: Seuil.

Centeno, M. A. (2002), *Blood and Debt: War and the Nation-State in Latin America*, University Park: Pennsylvania State University Press.

Chipkin, I. (2003), 'The South African nation', *Transformation: Critical Perspectives on Southern Africa*, 51, pp. 25–47.

Chipkin, I. (2007), *Do South Africans Exist? Nationalism, Democracy, and the Identity of 'the people'*, Johannesburg: Wits University Press.

Chipkin, I. (2016), 'The State, Capture and Revolution in Contemporary South Africa', Working Paper, Public Affairs Research Institute. Johannesburg, <https://47zhcvti0ul2ftip9rxo9fj9-wpengine.netdna-ssl.ccm/wp-content/uploads/2017/05/08-August-2016-State-Capture-and-Revolution-Working-Paper-2-ilovepdf-compressed.pdf> (accessed 10 August 2018).

Chipkin, I. and M. Swilling (eds) (2018), *Shadow State: The politics of state capture*, Johannesburg: Wits University Press.

Cohen, J. (1985), 'Strategy or identity: new theoretical paradigms and contemporary social movements', *Social Research*, 52: 4, pp. 663–716.

Comaroff, J and J. L. Comaroff (2012), 'Theory from the South: or, how Euro-America is evolving toward Africa', *Anthropological Forum*, 22: 2, pp. 113–31.

Connell, R. (2007), *Southern Theory: The Global Dynamics of Knowledge in Social Science*, London: Polity.

Constant, B. [1819] (1988), 'The liberty of the ancients compared with that of the moderns', in B. Fontana (ed.), *Political Writings*, Cambridge: Cambridge University Press, pp. 308–28.

Costa, E. V. (1986), *A Abolição*, São Paulo: Global editora.

Costa, S. (2011), 'Researching Entangled Inequalities in Latin America: The Role of Historical, Social, and Transregional Interdependencies', Working Paper 9, desiguALdades.net, International Research Network on Interdependent Inequalities in Latin America, Berlin.

Crouch, C. (2004), *Post-Democracy*, Cambridge: Polity.

Crouch, C. and W. Streeck (eds) (1997), *Political Economy of Modern Capitalism: Mapping Convergence and Diversity*, London: Sage.

Crozier, M., S. Huntington and J. Watanuki (1975), *The Crisis of Democracy: Report on the Governability of Democracies to the Trilateral Commission*, New York: New York University Press.

Crush, J. and D. A. McDonald (2001), 'Introduction to the special issue: evaluating South African immigration policy after apartheid', *Africa Today*, 48: 3, pp. 1–13.

Darwin, J. (2007), *After Tamerlane: A Global History of Empire*, London: Allen Lane.

Dasgupta, R. (2014), *Capital: The Eruption of Delhi*, New York: Penguin.

Delanty, G. (2013), *Formations of European Modernity: A Historical and Political Sociology of Europe*, London: Palgrave Macmillan.

Delanty, G. (2018), 'What unites Europe and what divides it? Solidarity and the European heritage reconsidered', *Asian Journal of German and European Studies*, 3: 3.

Di Palma, G. (1969), 'Disaffection and participation in Western democracies: the role of political oppositions', *Journal of Politics*, 31: 4, pp. 984–1010.

Di Palma, G. (1970), *Apathy and Participation: Mass Politics in Western Societies*, New York: Free Press.

Didry, C. and P. Wagner (1999), *La Nation comme cadre de l'action économique. La première guerre mondiale et l'émergence d'une économie nationale en France et en Allemagne*, in B. Zimmermann, C. Didry and P. Wagner (eds), *Le travail et la nation. Histoire croisée de la France et l'Allemagne*, Paris: Éditions de la Maison des Sciences de l'Homme.

Dlamini, J. (2015), 'On being in time: modern African elites and the historical challenge to claims for alternative and multiple modernities', in P. Wagner (ed.), *American and European Trajectories of Modernity: Past Oppression, Future Justice? Annual of European and Global Studies*, vol. 2, Edinburgh: Edinburgh University Press.

Domingues, J. M. (2008), *Latin America and Contemporary Modernity: A Sociological Interpretation*, London: Routledge.

Domingues, J. M. (2013), 'Democratic theory and democratization in contemporary Brazil and beyond', *Thesis Eleven*, 114: 1, pp. 15–33.

Dubow, S. (1989), *Racial Segregation and the Origins of Apartheid in South Africa: 1919–1936*, New York: Palgrave MacMillan.

Dunkle, K., R. Jewkes, H. Brown, G. Gray, J. A. McIntyre and S. Harlow (2004), 'Prevalence and patterns of gender-based violence and revictimization among women attending antenatal clinics in Soweto, South Africa', *American Journal of Epidemiology*, 160: 3, pp. 230–9.

Dussel, E. (1994), *El Encubrimiento del Otro: hacia el origen del 'mito de la modernidad'*, La Paz: Plural Editores e Universidade Maior de San Andrés.

Dussel, E. (2007), *Política de la liberación: historia mundial y crítica*, Madrid: Trotta.

Estanque, E., H. A. Costa and J. Soeiro (2013), 'The new global cycle of protest and the Portuguese case', *Journal of Social Science Education*, 1, pp. 1–23.

Eurostat (2010), *Young People on the Labour Market*, <http://ec.europa.eu/eurostat/statistics-explained/index.php/Young_people_on_the_labour_market_-_statistics> (accessed 30 July 2018).

Fabian, J. (1983), *Time and the Other*, New York: Columbia University Press.

Fausto, B. (1999), *A Concise History of Brazil*, Cambridge: Cambridge University Press.

Ferrara, A. (2008), *The Force of the Example: Explorations in the Paradigm of Judgement*, New York: Columbia University Press.

Firebaugh, G. and B. Goesling (2004), 'Accounting for the recent decline in global income inequality', *American Journal of Sociology*, 110: 2, pp. 283–312.

Fleury, S. (2010), '¿Qué protección social para cuál democracia? Dilemas de la inclusión social en América Latina', *Medicina Social*, 5: 1, pp. 41–60.

Fleury, S. (2012), 'Las Reformas Pendientes: desafíos para la gobernabilidad en Brasil', *Revista CIDOB d'Afers Internacionals*, 97/98, pp. 33–54.

Fórum Brasileiro de Segurança Pública (2017), *Anuário Brasileiro de Segurança Pública 2017*, São Paulo: Fórum Brasileiro de Segurança Pública.

Foweraker, J. (1995), *Theorizing Social Movements*, London: Pluto Press.

Franco, S. H. R. (2018), 'Urban trajectories: a comparative study of Rio de Janeiro's favelas and Johannesburg's townships', PhD dissertation, University of Barcelona.

Freyre, G. [1933] (1988), *Casa Grande & Senzala*, Rio de Janeiro: Record.

Froebel, F., J. Heinrichs and O. Kreye (1979), *Die neue Internationale Arbeitsteilung*, Reinbek: Rowohlt.

Gaonkar, D. P. (ed.) (2001), *Alternative Modernities*, Durham, NC: Duke University Press.

Gelb, S. (1991), *South Africa's Economic Crisis*, Cape Town: David Philip.

Giddens, A. (1990), *The Consequences of Modernity*, Cambridge: Polity.

Gilbert, J. (2014), *Common Ground: Democracy and Collectivity in an Age of Individualism*, London: Pluto Press.

GIZ (Deutsche Gesellschaft für Internationale Zusammenarbeit) Inclusive Violence and Crime Prevention Programme (2014), *Toolkit for Participatory Safety Planning*, Pretoria: GIZ.

Global Witness (2017), *Defenders of the Earth: Global Killings of Land and Environmental Defenders in 2016*, London: Global Witness.

Glyn, A. and B. Sutcliffe (1972), *British Capitalism, Workers and the Profit Squeeze*, Harmondsworth: Penguin.

Gonzáles Casanova, P. (1980), *Sociología de la Explotación*, Mexico City: Siglo XXI.

Goodey, J. (2007), 'Racist violence in Europe: challenges for official data collection', *Ethnic and Racial Studies*, 30: 4, pp. 570–89.

Gotlib, J. (2015), 'Land and restitution in comparative perspective: analysing the evidence of right to land for black rural communities in Brazil and South Africa', in Peter Wagner (ed.), *African, America and European Trajectories of Modernity: Past Oppression, Future Justice?*, Edinburgh: Edinburgh University Press, pp. 174–94.

Habermas, J. (1968), *Erkenntnis und Interesse*, Frankfurt am Main: Suhrkamp.

Habermas, J. (1973), *Legitimationsprobleme im Spätkapitalismus*, Frankfurt am Main: Suhrkamp.

Habermas, J. [1981] (1984–7), *The Theory of Communicative Action*, 2 vols, Boston: Beacon.

Hall, P. A. (2013), 'The political origins of our economic discontents', in M. Kahler and D. Lake (eds), *Politics in the New Hard Times*, Ithaca, NY: Cornell University Press, pp. 129–49.

Hall, P. A. and D. Soskice (eds) (2001), *Varieties of Capitalism: The Institutional Foundations of Comparative Advantage*, Oxford: Oxford University Press.

Hall, P. A. and M. Lamont (eds) (2009), *Successful Societies: How Institutions and Culture Affect Health*, Cambridge: Cambridge University Press.

Hall, S., C. Critcher, T. Jefferson, J. Clarke and B. Roberts (1978), *Policing the Crisis: Mugging, the State, and Law and Order*, London: Macmillan.

Halperin, S. (2004), *War and Social Change: The Great Transformation Revisited*, Cambridge: Cambridge University Press.

Hardt, M. and A. Negri (2004), *Multitude: War and Democracy in the Age of Empire*, Cambridge: Harvard University Press.

Hartz, L. (ed.) (1964), *The Founding of New Societies: Studies in the History of the United States, Latin America, South Africa, Canada, and Australia*, Orlando, FL: Harcourt Brace.

Hatton, T. J. and J. G. Williamson (1992), 'What drove the mass migrations from Europe in the late nineteenth century?', NBER Historical Working Papers 41, National Bureau of Economic Research, Cambridge, MA.

Hauff, V. and F. Scharpf (1975), *Modernisierung der Volkswirtschaft*, Frankfurt am Main: EVA.

Heidenreich, M. (ed.) (2016), *Exploring Inequality in Europe: Divergent Income and Employment Opportunities in the Crisis*, Cheltenham: Edward Elgar Publishing.

Henningsen, M. (2009), *Der Mythos Amerika*, Frankfurt am Main: Eichborn.

Hirschman, A. (1970), *Exit, Voice, and Loyalty*, Cambridge, MA: Harvard University Press.

Hirschman, A. (1977), *The Passions and the Interests*, Princeton, NJ: Princeton University Press.

Hobsbawm, E. (1994), *Age of Extremes: The Short Twentieth Century, 1914–1991*, London: Michael Joseph.

Holston, J. (2008), *Insurgent Citizenship: Disjunctions of Democracy and Modernity in Brazil*, Princeton, NJ: Princeton University Press.

Human Rights Watch (2017), '"Like Living in Hell": Police Abuses Against Child and Adult Migrants in Calais', Report, 26 July.

Inglehart, R. (1977), *The Silent Revolution: Changing Values and Political Styles among Western Publics*, Princeton, NJ: Princeton University Press.

Ireland, R. (1994), 'Brazil and a sociology for hope', *Thesis Eleven*, 38: 1, pp. 72–92.

Jinda, R., R. Jewkes, N. Christofides and L. Loots (2008), *Caring for Survivors of Sexual Assault and Rape: A Training Programme for Health Care Providers in South Africa*, Pretoria: Department of Health (of South Africa).

Karagiannis, N. (2004), *Avoiding Responsibility. The Politics and Discourse of EU Development Policy*, London: Pluto.

Karagiannis, N. (2007), *European Solidarity*, Liverpool: Liverpool University Press.

Karagiannis, N. (2016), 'Democratic surplus and democracy-in-failing: on ancient and modern self-cancellation of democracy', in G. Rosich and P. Wagner (eds), *The Trouble with Democracy*, Edinburgh: Edinburgh University Press.

Kaya, A. (2004), 'Political participation strategies of the Circassian diaspora in Turkey, *Mediterranean Politics*, 9: 2, pp. 221–39, <https://www.tandfonline.com/doi/abs/10.1080/1362939042000221286> (accessed 10 August 2018).

Kilby, J. (2013), 'Introduction to special issue: theorizing violence', *European Journal of Social Theory*, 16: 3, pp. 261–72.

Kling, M. (1956), 'Towards a theory of power and political instability in Latin America', *Western Political Quarterly*, 9: 1, pp. 21–35.

Knöbl, W. (2003), 'Theories that won't pass away: the never-ending story of modernization theory', in G. Delanty and E. F. Isin (eds), *Handbook of Historical Sociology*, London: Sage.

Koopmans, R. (2004), 'Political opportunity structure: some splitting to balance the lumping', in J. Goodwin and J. Jasper (eds), *Rethinking Social Movements*, Lanham, MD: Rowman and Littlefield.

Koskenniemi, M. (2001), *The Gentle Civilizer of Nations: The Rise and Fall of International Law, 1870–1960*, Cambridge: Cambridge University Press.

Larrain Ibañez, J. (1996), *Modernidad, Razón e Identidad en América Latina*, Santiago: Andres Bello.

Lessenich, S. (2016), *Neben uns die Sintflut: Die Externalisierungsgesellschaft und ihr Preis*, Berlin: Hanser Berlin.

Lesser, J. (2013), *Immigration, Ethnicity, and National Identity in Brazil: 1808 to the Present*, Cambridge: Cambridge University Press.

Leubolt, B. (2009), 'Correlations of forces and policy outcomes: the political economy of inequality in Brazil and South Africa', Conference Paper, 5th ECPR General Conference, Potsdam.

Leubolt, B. (2015), 'One or two nation projects? Discourse on inequalities and equality-related policies in South Africa and Brazil', *Revista de Sociologia e Política*, 23: 55, pp. 35–51.

Lijphart, A. (1975), *The Politics of Accommodation*, Berkeley: University of California Press.

Lijphart, A. (1999), *Patterns of Democracy: Government Forms and Performance in Thirty-Six Countries*, New Haven, CT: Yale University Press.

Lindert, P. H. (1994), 'The rise in social spending 1880–1930', *Explorations in Economic History*, 31, pp. 1–37.

Lipton, M. (2007), *Liberals, Marxists and Nationalists. Competing Interpretations of South African History*, New York: Palgrave Macmillan.

Magalhães, P. C. (2005), 'Disaffected democrats: political attitudes and political action in Portugal', *West European Politics*, 28: 5, pp. 973–91.

Mair, P. (2013), *Ruling the Void: The Hollowing out of Western Democracy*, London: Verso.

Majone, G. (1996), *Regulating Europe*, London: Routledge.

Malešević, S. (2013), 'Forms of brutality: towards a historical sociology of violence', *European Journal of Social Theory*, 16: 3, pp. 273–91.

Mamdani, M. (1996), *Citizen and Subject: Contemporary Africa and the Legacy of Late Colonialism*, Princeton, NJ: Princeton: University Press.

Mann, M. (1993), *The Sources of Social Power: The Rise of Class and Nation-States (1760–1914)*, vol. 2, Cambridge: Cambridge University Press.

Mann, M. (2006), 'A crise do estado-nação brasileiro', in J. M. Domingues and M. Maneiro (eds), *América Latina Hoje: Conceitos e Interpretações*, Rio de Janeiro: Civilização Brasileira.

Marshall, T. H. [1950] (1965), *Citizenship and Social Class, and Other Essays*, Cambridge: Cambridge University Press.

Marx, K. [1852] (2010), *The Eighteenth Brumaire of Louis Bonaparte*, <https://www.marxists.org/archive/marx/works/download/pdf/18th-Brumaire.pdf> (accessed 13 August 2018).

Mauss, M. [1938] (1985), 'A category of the human mind: the notion of person; the notion of self', in M. Carrithers, S. Collins and S. Lukes (eds), *The Category of the Person: Anthropology, Philosophy, History*, Cambridge: Cambridge University Press.

Mayer, A. J. (1981), *The Persistence of the Old Regime: Europe to the Great War*, New York: Pantheon Books.

Mignolo, W. (2011), *The Darker Side of Western Modernity: Global Futures, Decolonial Options*, Durham, NC: Duke University Press.

Mill, J. S. [1859] (1956), *On Liberty*, Indianapolis, IN: Bobbs-Merrill.

Montero, J. R., R. Gunther and M. Torcal (1997), 'Democracy in Spain: legitimacy, discontent, and disaffection', *Studies in Comparative International Development*, 32: 3, pp. 124–60.

Morgan, M. (2017), 'Extreme and Persistent Inequality: New Evidence for Brazil Combining National Accounts, Surveys and Fiscal Data 2001–2015', Working Paper 2017/12, World Wealth and Income Database.

Mota, A. (2013), *Sobre Metamorfoses e Adaptações: a proposta liberal constituional latino-americano*, Buenos Aires: CLACSO.

Mota, A. (2015), 'The American divergence, the modern western world and the paradigmatisation of history', in P. Wagner (ed.), *American and European*

Trajectories of Modernity: Past oppression, future justice? Annual of European and Global Studies, vol. 2, Edinburgh: Edinburgh University Press.

Mota, A. (2017),'On spaces and experiences: modern displacements, interpretation and universal claims', in P. Wagner (ed.), *Annual of European and Global Studies*, vol. 4, *The Moral Mappings of South and North*, Edinburgh: Edinburgh University Press.

MRC (Medical Research Council) (2004),'Every six hours a woman is killed by her intimate partner: a national study on female homicide in South Africa', *Medical Research Council Policy Brief* 5.

MRC (Medical Research Council) (2010), *The War @ Home – Preliminary Findings of the Gauteng Gender Violence Prevalence*, Gender Links and the Medical Research Council.

Narr, W. and C. Offe (eds) (1975), *Wohlfahrtsstaat und Massenloyalität*, Köln: Kiepenheuer und Witsch.

Noiriel, G. (1991), *La Tyrannie du National*, Paris: Calmann-Lévy.

O'Connor, J. (1973), *The Fiscal Crisis of the State*, New York: St Martin's Press.

OECD (Organisation for Economic Co-operation and Development) (1981), *The Welfare State in Crisis*, Paris: OECD.

OECD (Organisation for Economic Co-operation and Development) (2010), *Tackling Inequalities in Brazil, China, India and South Africa: The Role of Labour Market and Social Policies*, Paris: OECD.

OECD (Organisation for Economic Co-operation and Development) (2017), *OECD Revenue Statistics 2017*, <https://www.oecd.org/tax/tax-policy/revenue-statistics-2016-highlights.pdf> (accessed 9 August 2018)

Offe, C. (1998),'Demokratie und Wohlfahrtsstaat. Eine europäische Regierungsform unter dem Stress der europäischen Integration', in W. Streeck (ed.), *Internationale Wirtschaft, nationale Demokratie*, Frankfurt am Main: Campus, pp. 99–136.

Offe, C. (2009), 'Political disaffection as an outcome of institutional practices? Some post-Tocquevillean speculations', in A. Brodocz, M. Llanque and G. S. Schaal (eds), *Bedrohungen der Demokratie*, Wiesbaden: VS, pp. 42–60.

Oliveira, R. S., J. M. Monteiro, M. H. H. S. Goulart and A. C. Vanali (2017), 'Prosopografia Familiar da Operação Lava-Jato e do Ministério Temer', *Revista Núcelo de Estudos Paranaenses*, Curitiba, 3: 3, pp. 1–28.

Olson, M. (1965), *The Logic of Collective Action: Public Goods and the Theory of Groups*, Cambridge, MA: Harvard University Press.

Osterhammel, J. (2009), *Die Verwandlung der Welt*, Munich: Beck.

Pagden, A. (ed.) (2000), *Facing Each Other: The World's Perception of Europe and Europe's Perception of the World*, London: Ashgate.

Paiva, L. H., T. Falcão and L. Bartholo (2013),'Do Bolsa Família ao Brasil sem Miséria: um resumo do percurso brasileiro recente na busca da superação da pobreza', in T. Campello and M. N. Neri (eds), *Programa Bolsa Família: uma década de inclusão e cidadania*, Brasília: IPEA, pp. 25–43.

Passerini, L. (1996), *Autobiography of a Generation: Italy, 1968*, Middletown, CT: Wesleyan University Press.

Paulani, L. M. (2016), 'Modernity and capitalist progress: the case of Brazil', *European Journal of Social Theory*, 19: 2, pp. 210–27.

Peberdy, S. (1999), 'Selecting immigrants: nationalism and national identity in South Africa's immigration polices, 1910–1998', PhD dissertation, Queen's University, Canada.

Pinker, S. (2011), *The Better Angels of Our Nature: Why Violence Has Declined*, New York: Viking.

Piore, M. J. and C. F. Sabel (1984), *The Second Industrial Divide*, New York: Basic Books.

Plagerson, S. and M. S. Ulriksen (2015), 'Cash Transfer Programmes, Poverty Reduction and Empowerment of Women in South Africa', Working Paper, International Labour Office, Gender, Equality and Diversity Branch, Conditions of Work and Equality Department, Geneva.

Polanyi, K. [1944] (1973), *The Great Transformation: The Political and Economic Origins of Our Time*, Frankfurt am Main: Suhrkamp.

Profeta, P., R. Publisi and S. Scabrosetti (2013), 'Does democracy affect taxation and government spending? Evidence from developing countries', *Journal of Comparative Economics*, 41: 3, pp. 684–718.

Quijano, A. (2005), 'Colonialidad del Poder, eurocentrismo e América Latina', in E. Lander (ed.), *A Colonialidad do saber: eurocentrismo e ciências sociais, Perspectivas latino-americanas*, Collección Sur-Sur, Buenos Aires: CLACSO.

Rabinbach, A. (1996), 'Social knowledge, social risk and the politics of industrial accidents in Germany and France', in D. Rueschemeyer and T. Skocpol (eds), *States, Social Knowledge and the Origins of Modern Social Policies*, Princeton, NJ: Princeton University Press, pp. 48–79.

Randeria, S. (1999), 'Geteilte Geschichte und verwobene Moderne', in J. Rüsen, H. Leitgeb and N. Jegelka (eds), *Zukuntsentwürfe. Ideen für eine Kultur der Veränderung*, Frankfurt am Main: Campus.

Randeria, S. (2006), 'Entangled histories: civil society, caste solidarities, and legal pluralism in post-colonial India', in J. Keane (ed.), *Civil Society: Berlin Perspectives*, New York: Berghahn Books.

Ribeiro, D [1995] (2000), *The Brazilian People: The Formation and Meaning of Brazil*, Gainesville: Florida University Press.

Robins, S. (2008), *From Revolution to Rights in South Africa: Social Movements, NGOs and Popular Politics after Apartheid*, Suffolk: James Currey.

Sadian, S. (2018), 'Consumer studies as critical social theory', *Social Science Information*, 52: 2, pp. 273–303.

Santos, B. S. (2017), 'La ola podemos', in B. Bringel and G. Pleyers (eds), *Protesta e Indignación Global: los movimientos sociales en el nuevo orden mundial*, Buenos Aires: CLACSO; Rio de Janeiro: FAPERJ.

Santos, W. G. (1962), *Quem Dará o Golpe no Brasil?*, Rio de Janeiro: Civilização Brasileira.

Santos, W. G. (1979), *Cidadania e Justiça: a política social na ordem brasileira*, Rio de Janeiro: Campos.

SAPS (South African Police Service) (2016), *Annual Report 2015/16 of the South African Police Service*.

SARS (South Africa Revenue Service) (2017), '2017 Tax Statistics', National Treasury and SARS, <http://www.sars.gov.za/About/SATaxSystem/Pages/Tax-Statistics.aspx> (accessed 9 August 2018).

Scantimburgo, J. (1980), *O Poder Moderador*, São Paulo: Secretaria de Estado da Cultura.

Scharpf, F. (1999), *Governing in Europe: Effective and Democratic?*, Oxford: Oxford University Press.

Schmidt, E. (2013), *Foreign Intervention in Africa: From the Cold War to the War on Terror*, Cambridge: Cambridge University Press.

Schmitt, C. [1950] (1997), *Der Nomos der Erde*, Berlin: Duncker & Humblot.

Schulz-Forberg, H. and B. Stråth (2010), *The Political History of European Integration: The Hypocrisy of Democracy-through-Market*, London: Taylor & Francis.

Schumpeter, J. A. (1991), *The Economics and Sociology of Capitalism*, Princeton, NJ: Princeton University Press, pp. 99–140.

Schwarcz, L. M. (1998), *As Barbas do Imperador: Dom Pedro II, um monarca nos trópicos*, São Paulo: Companhia das Letras.

Scott, J. (1991), *Social Network Analysis*, London: Sage.

Seekings, J. (2014), 'South Africa: Democracy, Poverty, and Inclusive Growth since 1994', Democracy Works Conference Paper, Legatum Institute, London.

Seekings, J. (2016), 'State-building, market regulation and citizenship in South Africa', *European Journal of Social Theory*, 19: 2, pp. 191–209, <http://journals.sagepub.com/doi/10.1177/1368431015600021> (accessed 13 August 2018).

Seekings, J. and N. Nattrass (2006), *Class, Race and Inequality in South Africa*, Durban: University of KwaZulu-Natal Press.

Sewell, W. H., Jr (2005), *Logics of History: Social Theory and Social Transformations*, Chicago: University of Chicago Press.

Shonfield, A. (1966), *Modern Capitalism*, Oxford: Oxford University Press.

Silva, L. A. M. (2004), 'Sociabilidade violenta: por uma interpretação da criminalidade contemporânea no Brasil urbano', *Sociedade e Estado*, 19: 1, pp. 53–84.

Silveira, F. G. (2012), *Equidade Fiscal: Impactos Distributivos da Tributação e do Gasto Social*, Tesouro Nacional.

Simpson, G. (1993), 'Gewalt in Südafrika', *Weltfriedensdienst Quersbrief*, 3, pp. 10–15.

Simpson, N. and L. Waldman (2010), 'Mobilization through litigation: claiming health rights on asbestos issues in South Africa', in L. Thompson and C. Tapscoot (eds), *Citizenship and Social Movements: Perspectives form the Global South*, London: Zeta Books, pp. 87–109.

Slemian, A. and J. P. Pimenta (2003), *O Nascimento Polítido do Brasil: as origens do Estado e da Nação (1808–1825)*, Rio de Janeiro: DP&A.

Sousa, R. G. and P. H. G. F. Osorio (2012), *O Bolsa Família depois do Brasil Carinhoso: uma análise do potencial de redução da pobreza extrema*, Brasília: Nota Ténica IPEA.

South African History Online (2018), 'The Natives Land Act of 1913', <http://www.sahistory.org.za/topic/natives-land-act-1913> (accessed 3 July 2018).

Souza, J. (2009), *A Ralé Brasileira: quem é e como vive*, Belo Horizonte: Editora UFMG.

STATS SA (Statistics South Africa) (2017a), 'Victims of Crime Survey 2015–2016', Pretoria: Statistics South Africa.

STATS SA (Statistics South Africa) (2017b), 'Poverty trends in South Africa: an examination of absolute poverty between 2006 and 2015', Pretoria: Statistics South Africa.

STATS SA (Statistics South Africa) (2017c), 'South Africa Demographic and Health Survey 2016: Key Indicator Report', <http://www.mrc.ac.za/reports/south-africa-demographic-and-health-survey-2016-key-indicators-report> (accessed 10 August 2018).

Stavenhagen, R. (1969), *Las Clases Sociales en las Sociedades Agrarias*, Mexico City: Siglo XXI.

Stråth, B. (2016), *Three Utopias of Peace and the Search for a European Political Economy*, London: Bloomsbury.

Stråth, B. and P. Wagner (2017), *European Modernity: A Global Approach*, London: Bloomsbury.

Streeck, W. (2011a), 'Taking capitalism seriously: towards an institutional approach to contemporary political economy', *Socio-economic Review*, 9, pp. 137–67.

Streeck, W. (2011b), 'The crises of democratic capitalism', *New Left Review*, 71, pp. 5–29.

Streeck, W. (2012), 'How to study contemporary capitalism?', *Archives européennes de sociologie*, 53, pp. 1–28.

Streeck, W. (2013), *Gekaufte Zeit. Die vertagte Krise des demokratischen Kapitalismus, (Adorno-Vorlesungen 2012)*, Frankfurt am Main: Suhrkamp.

Streeck, W. and A. Schaefer (eds) (2013), *Politics in an Age of Austerity*, Cambridge: Polity.

Tarrow, S. (1991), 'Struggle, politics and reform: collective action, social movements and cycles of protest', *Cornell Studies in International Affairs*, Western Societies Paper 21, Center for International Studies, Cornell University.

Tarrow, S. (1994), *Power in Movement: Social Movements and Contentious Politics*, Cambridge: Cambridge University Press.

Taylor, C. (1989), *Sources of the Self: The Making of the Modern Identity*, Cambridge, MA: Harvard University Press.

Telles, E. (2006), *Race in Another America: The Significance of Skin Color in Brazil*, Princeton, NJ: Princeton University Press.

Telò, M. (1988), *Le New Deal Européen: la Pensée et la Politique Sociales-Démocrates à la Crise des Années Trente*, Brussels: Ed. De l'Université de Bruxelles.

Therborn, G. (1989), 'The two-thirds, one-third society', in S. Hall and M. Jacques (eds), *New Times: The Changing Face of Politics in the 1990s*, London: Lawrence & Wishart, pp. 103–15.

Therborn, G. (1995), *European Modernity and Beyond: The Trajectory of European Societies, 1945–2000*, London: Sage.

Thompson, L. (2001), *A History of South Africa*, 3rd edn, New Haven, CT: Yale University Press.

Thompson, R. J. and B. M. Nicholls (1993), 'The Glen Grey Act: forgotten dimensions in an old theme', *South African Journal of Economic History*, 8: 2, pp. 58–70.

Tilly, C. (1984), 'Social movements and national politics', in C. Bright and S. Hardering (eds), *Statemaking and Social Movements: Essays in History and Theory*, Ann Arbor: University of Michigan Press, pp. 297–317.

Tilly, C. (1990), *Coercion, Capital, and European States (A.D. 990–1992)*, Oxford: Blackwell.

Tilly, C. and C. Tarrow (2006), *Contentious Politics*, Oxford: Oxford University Press.

Tocqueville, A. [1840] (2003), *Democracy in America and Two Essays on America*, London: Penguin.

Tomka, B. (2013), *A Social History of Twentieth-Century Europe*, London: Routledge.

Torcal, M. and J. R. Montero (2006), *Political Disaffection in Contemporary Democracies: Social Capital, Institutions and Politics*, London: Routledge.

Torcal, M., T. Rondon and J. M. Hierro (2016), 'Word on the street: the persistence of leftist-dominated protest in Europe', *West European Politics*, 39: 2, pp. 326–50.

Touraine, A. (1971), *The Post-Industrial Society – Tomorrow's Social History: Classes, Conflicts and Culture in the Programmed Society*, New York: Random House.

Touraine, A. (1973), *Production de la Société*, Paris: Seuil.

Touraine, A. (1992), *Critique de la Modernité*, Paris: Fayard.

UNDP (United Nations Development Programme) (2016), 'Human Development Report 2016: Human Development for Everyone', <http://hdr.undp.org/en/2016-report> (accessed 12 August 2018).

Unger, M. (1998), *Democracy Realized: The Progressive Alternative*, London: Verso.

Van Vuuren, H. (2014), 'South Africa: Democracy, Corruption, and Conflict Management', Democracy Works Conference Paper, London: Legatum Institute.

Vianna, L. W. (1978), *Liberalismo e Sindicato no Brasil*, Rio de Janeiro: Paz e Terra.

Vianna, S. T. W. (2000), Tributação sobre Renda e Consumo das Famílias no Brasil: avaliação de sua incidência nas grandes regiões urbanas 1996, Master's dissertation in Economics, Instituto de Economia, Universidade Federal do Rio de Janeiro.

Wagner, P. (1990), *Sozialwissenschaften und Staat: Frankreich, Italien, Deutschland, 1870–1980*, Frankfurt am Main: Campus.

Wagner, P. (1994), *A Sociology of Modernity: Liberty and Discipline*, London: Routledge.

Wagner, P. (2002), 'The project of emancipation and the possibility of politics, or, what's wrong with post-1968 individualism?', *Thesis Eleven*, 68: 1, thematic issue on '1968–2001 – measuring the distance: Continuities and discontinuities in recent history', pp. 31–45.

Wagner, P. (2003), 'Social science and social planning during the twentieth century', in T. Porter and D. Ross (eds), *The Cambridge History of Science*, vol. 7, *The Modern Social Sciences*, Cambridge: Cambridge University Press, 2003, pp. 591–607.

Wagner, P. (2008), *Modernity as Experience and Interpretation: A New Sociology of Modernity*, Cambridge: Polity Press.

Wagner, P. (2011), 'From interpretation to civilization – and back: analyzing the trajectories of non-European modernities', *European Journal of Social Theory*, 14: 1, pp. 89–106.

Wagner, P. (2012), *Modernity: Understanding the Present*, Cambridge: Polity.

Wagner, P. (2013), 'Transformations of democracy', in J. P. Arnason, K. Raaflaub and P. Wagner (eds), *The Greek Polis and the Invention of Democracy*, Oxford: Blackwell.

Wagner, P. (ed.) (2015), *Annual of European and Global Studies*, vol. 2, *American and European Trajectories of Modernity: Past Oppression, Future Justice?*, Edinburgh: Edinburgh University Press.

Wagner, P. (ed.) (2017), *Annual of European and Global Studies*, vol. 4, *The Moral Mappings of South and North*, Edinburgh: Edinburgh University Press.

Wagner, P. (2018; forthcoming), 'Modernity', in P. Kivisto (ed.), *Cambridge Handbook of Social Theory*, Cambridge: Cambridge University Press.

Wagner, P. and B. Zimmermann (2003), 'Nation – Die Konstitution einer politischen Ordnung als Verantwortungsgemeinschaft', in S. Lessenich (ed.), *Wohlfahrtsstaatliche Grundbegriffe*, Frankfurt am Main: Campus, pp. 243–66.

Wagner, P. and B. Zimmermann (2004), 'Citizenship and collective responsibility: on the political philosophy of the nation-based welfare state and beyond', in B. Stråth and L. Magnusson (eds), *A European Social Citizenship?: Preconditions for Future Policies from a Historical Perspective*, Brussels: Peter Lang, pp. 31–53.

Wagner, P., C. Weiss, B. Wittrock and H. Wollmann (eds) (1990), *Social Sciences and Modern States: National Experiences and Theoretical Perspectives*, Cambridge: Cambridge University Press.

Waiselfisz, J. J. (2015), *Mapa da Violência: Morte Matadas por Arma de Fogo*, Brasilia: Governo Federal.

Walzer, M. (1983), *Spheres of Justice: A Defence of Pluralism and Equality*, New York: Basic Books.

WHO (World Health Organization) (2002), 'World Report on Violence and Health: Summary', <www.who.int/violence_injury_prevention/violence/world_report/en/summary_en.pdf> (accessed 10 August 2018).

Wignaraja, P. (ed.) (1993), *New Social Movements in the South: Empowering the People*, London: Zed Books.

Wittrock, B. (1983), 'Governance in crisis and the withering of the welfare state: the legacy of the policy sciences', *Policy Sciences*, 15: 3, pp. 195–203.

Wittrock, B. and S. Lindström (1984), *De Stora Programmens Tid: forskning och energi i svensk politik*, Stockholm: Liter.

Woolard, I. and M. Leibbrandt (2010), 'The evolution and impact of unconditional cash transfers in South Africa', Working Paper 51, Southern Africa Labour and Development Research Unit, Cape Town.

World Bank (2014), 'South Africa Economic Update: Fiscal Policy and Redistribution in an Unequal Society', South Africa economic update, 6, Washington, DC, <openknowledge.worldbank.org/handle/10986/20661> (accessed 3 July 2018).

Ypi, L. (2012), *Global Justice and Avant-Garde Political Agency*, Oxford: Oxford University Press.

Yun-Casalilla, B. and P. K. O'Brien (2012), *The Rise of Fiscal States: A Global History, 1500–1914*, Cambridge: Cambridge University Press.

Zakaria, F. (1997), 'The rise of illiberal democracy', *Foreign Affairs*, 76: 6, pp. 22–43.

INDEX

EU representative:
Easy Access System Europe
Mustamäe tee 50, 10621 Tallinn, Estonia
Gpsr.requests@easproject.com

www.ingramcontent.com/pod-product-compliance
Lightning Source LLC
Chambersburg PA
CBHW051957270326
41929CB00015B/2693